NEHRU ON SOCIAL ISSUES

NEHRU ON SOCIAL ISSUES

Edited by

S.P. Agrawal
J.C. Aggarwal

CONCEPT PUBLISHING COMPANY, NEW DELHI-110059

ISBN 81-7022-207-9

First Published 1989

S. P. AGRAWAL (*b*. 1929-)
J. C. AGGARWAL (*b*. 1928-)

Published by
Ashok Kumar Mittal
Concept Publishing Company
A/15-16, Commercial Block, Mohan Garden
NEW DELHI-110059 (India)

Lasertypeset by
Microtech Advance Printing Systems (P) Ltd.
H-13, Bali Nagar, NEW DELHI-110015

Printed at
New Gian Offset Printers
Shahzada Bagh, DELHI-110035 (India)

Foreword

Jawaharlal Nehru, the architect of modern India, was a man of dynamic vision, intellectual integrity and profound qualities of leadership. His sense of history made him look, not only into the past, but also into the future, altogether placing India in the category of a leading nation in the world. His adoption of the socialist pattern of society for India has resulted in the country's taking massive strides into modernisation and all that the concept has stood for through the centuries. He, however, never forgot that India had a great cultural heritage and he would, therefore, like to combine tradition with modernity. In this book an attempt has been made to collect his thoughts on social issues at one place. Thirteen different aspects discussed by him at different places and points of time have been brought together. The aspects covered are: social philosophy of life; historiography; political and economic systems of State and government; democratic ideals; national reconstruction; national integration; education; women, youth; children; social problems; communication and communications; and peace on the earth with good will for Mankind.

Nehru rightly argues that there should not be any break with the past but past should also not be allowed to dominate the present. Discussing the role of religion, he writes that it has undoubtedly brought comfort to innumerable human beings and has stabilized society by its values, but on the debit side, it has checked the tendency to change and progress which is inherent in human society. Though science has made the world leap forward, but without controls it has created a monster that can run amok. Nehru hoped that new developments in biology, psychology and other sciences, and, more importantly, their interpretations would help human beings to appreciate the danger and the need of control of science by man.

Nehru realised that democracy weakened towards the end of nineteenth century owing to lack of adaptation to the new ethos of society. But in the wake of its revival in the twentieth century, democracy joined hands with science to weaken the hold of theological dogmas. People began to dare examine the Bible, as if it was an ordinary book and not a treatise that must be accepted blindly and without question.

With the growth of capitalist industry in the nineteenth century, the problems of the working class grew. Some people in England, Germany and France considered various alternatives to the capitalist system. Socialism, collectivism and social democracy were thought to be viable alternatives. Initially socialistic ideas were just the preserve of the intellectuals but gradually they gained momentum. However, the path of socialism was different in the three leading industrial countries in Europe–England, France and Germany. Nehru has also discussed the growth of the three major forces of the twentieth century–communism, dictatorship and fascism.

Nehru wanted India to be a welfare state and have a socialist economy. To attain this goal he emphasized that we have to increase production and aim at an economy of plenty. He also gave importance to equitable distribution and desired that no privileged individual and groups should have preferential treatment. Besides developing the public sector, Nehru also wanted to encourage private sector and to give it an opportunity of full play within its allotted sphere provided it was prepared to coordinate with planned development of the country.

India has adopted the democratic process because it promotes free growth of human beings and of society. Nehru wants this creative and adventurous spirit to grow. He regarded democracy as the right and peaceful means to achieve egalitarian ends. It removes pressure on the individual and transforms the discipline which is imposed by authority largely to self-discipline. Democracy also gives an opportunity to the individual to develop his best self. According to Nehru the parliamentary form of government is a peaceful method of dealing with problems. It is a method of argument, discussion, and decision and of accepting that decision, even though one may not agree with it. He also emphasized the role of the minority in a parliamentary form of government. He tried to combine democracy with socialism, through peaceful and legitimate methods. This was Nehru's great contribution to nation-building in India.

In order to achieve the social objectives of an expanding and technologically progressive economy and to establish a social order based on social justice and offering equal opportunity to every citizen, Nehru emphasized the need of planned development. His yardstick to measure the success of a plan was the extent of relief it gave to the millions of our people who live on a bare subsistence level. The fight against poverty and unemployment and the attempt at economic betterment were considered as the major objectives of planned development in India.

For Nehru the cooperative movement was the key to the future growth of peasants in the country. He wanted the cooperative movement to spread all over the country and encompass all the villages and peasants of the vast land. He wished that the cooperative spirit should enter into the life of the peasant in as many ways as possible and together with the panchayat system, it may become the main bulwork of India's social structure. Instead of joint farming as recommended by some, Nehru preferred relatively small cooperatives comprising one, two or three villages.

In Nehru's India, communalism, separatism, isolationism, untouchability, bigotry and exploitation of man by man have no place. Though religious freedom is there, it is not allowed to interfere with the political and economic aspects of the nation's life. As far as our political life is considered, we must behave as Indians first and as Hindus, Muslims, Christians or Sikhs only later. We must all collectively try to build a united but composite nation where both individual and national freedom are secure.

Nehru did not distinguish among Hindu, Muslim and Christian cultures. He recognised only the composite culture of the Indian people, which has been influenced by many civilizations. Indian culture had a remarkable capacity for synthesis and for absorbing new components, which Nehru would always emphasize. He was proud of India's rich and varied cultural heritage. He thus honestly believed in unity in diversity.

Commenting on the social relevance of education, Nehru has written that all education must have a definite social outlook and must train youth for the kind of society we wish to have. The real foundations of a society, according to Nehru, are laid in teaching at our schools and colleges. The real change will have to come in the minds of men, though that change can and will be helped greatly by external changes in the environment. A properly trained student, according to Nehru, is one who can face life and its problems; otherwise his education has been a wasted effort. Politics and economics deal with live issues facing men and society and no person is properly educated unless he understands them. He emphasized that, whether one could offer solution to a problem or not, one must at least know its nature. Nehru wanted thinking individuals, especially senior students, to grapple with problems facing mankind intelligently and constructively.

Nehru wanted every child to be treated as an individual and given every opportunity to grow as an individual. It is also equally important to treat children as social beings capable of living at peace and cooperating with others. It is necessary to develop cooperative habits and traits in children; otherwise they will find it difficult to fit in society. Usually single children, who have been looked after a great deal, have a hard time when they go out into the world and have to fend for themselves.

The position of Indian women, according to Nehru, is very dubious. We can praise them and find many examples in favour of the praise, and at the same time we can also condemn their position in actual life and also find examples to justify the act of denunciation. Nehru had no doubt that, though women in India had played an important part in every branch of national activity, from high learning to valour on the battlefield , it was their unobtrusive work in the household, in the village or in the larger community that has moulded the nation.

Discussing the role of the joint family in India, Nehru writes that it comes in the way of the development of individual life as well as the larger national life. Since it does not fit in with the thought and elemental forces that move the world today, it must fade away, as it is indeed doing. For psychological needs he favoured the smaller family. He, however, recognised that the economic bonds in the joint family often help the individual but he also felt that they suppressed him and prevented his growth.

Nehru has shown concern for scheduled castes and scheduled tribes. Reservation of seats for them is only one step, we must try to advance them rapidly in the economic and educational sphere and then only they will be able to stand on their own legs. Nehru was opposed to the idea of exhibiting tribal people as museum specimens. Neither did he want them to be forcibly absorbed into the normal pattern of social life. He preferred that they should be given protection so that no outsider could take possession of their lands or forests or interfere with them in any way except with their consent and goodwill.

On the language issue, Nehru writes that a language must base itself on its ancient roots and at the same time, vary and expand with growing needs and be essentially the language of the masses and not of a select coterie. As far as possible, language should have common or similar words in regard to scientific or technical terms. They must be receptive, accepting from outside that which fits into their general structure.

Nehru had favoured Gandhi's non-violent technique of action which was not only peaceful but also effective. It showed its effectiveness in the way it brought about freedom and the fact that it led to no ill-will between India and the United Kingdom. It was our own decision to cooperate with England in many ways and we have continued to cooperate with her even today. This is what Nehru honestly believed and worked for.

He saw a close and intimate relationship between the end we aim at and the means adopted to attain it. Even if the end is right but the means are wrong, it will vitiate the end or divert us in a wrong direction. Means and ends are thus intimately and inextricably connected and cannot be separated. This has been the lesson, that we can derive from many great men in the past, particularly, Gandhi. Nehru, however, regretted that people would seldom remember it.

Nehru never believed in the negative meaning of non-alignment. He always asserted its positive connotation which visualises nations as objecting to lining up for war, to military blocs, to military alliances and the like. In this sense alone non-alignment and peace would go together.

Altogether thus Nehru was a vigorous thinker - a man of ideas which should always inspire mankind to a better vision of life. The best way to pay homage to Jawaharlal Nehru on the eve of his birth centenary is to present to the reading world a bouquet of his ideas. This is what the present book precisely does. We are, therefore, thankful to S.P. Agrawal, Director, NASSDOC and his associate for this collection which, in a manner of speaking, can be taken as a tribute to the memory of this great son of India on behalf of the Indian Council of Social Science Research.

Delhi.
December 29, 1987.

IQBAL NARAIN

Contents

SOCIAL PHILOSOPHY OF LIFE

1. Integral Vision of Life.
2. Ethical Approach to Life.
3. Social Code of Conduct.
4. Ends and Means.
5. Curbing the Devil in U S.
6. Life is Affirmation.
7. Facing Ever-Changing Present.

ONE

SOCIAL PHILOSOPHY OF LIFE

Integral Vision of Life

India must break with much of her past and not allow it to dominate the present. Our lives are encumbered with the dead wood of this past; all that is dead and has served its purpose has to go. But that does not mean a break with, or a forgetting of, the vital and life-giving in the past. We can never forget the ideals that have moved our race, the dreams of the Indian people through the ages, the wisdom of the ancients, the buoyant energy and love of life and nature of our forefathers, their spirit of curiosity and mental adventure, the daring of their thought, their splendid achievements in literature, art and culture, their love of truth and beauty and freedom, the basic values that they set up, their understanding of life's mysterious ways,their toleration of other ways than theirs, their capacity to absorb other peoples and their cultural accomplishments, to synthesize them and develop a varied and mixed culture; nor can we forget the myriad experiences which have built up our ancient race and lie embedded in our subconscious minds. We will never forget them or cease to take pride in that noble heritage of ours.If India forgets them she will no longer remain India and much that has made her our joy and pride will cease to be.[1]

It is not this that we have to break with, but all the dust and dirt of ages that have covered her up and hidden her inner beauty and significance, the excrescences and abortions that have twisted and petrified her spirit, set it in rigid frames, and stunted her growth. We have to cut away these excrescences and remember afresh the core of that ancient wisdom and adapt it to our present circumstances. We have to get out of traditional ways of thought and living which,for all the good they may have done in a past age, and there was much good in them, have ceased to have significance today. We have to make our own all the achievements of the human race and join up with others in the exciting adventure of man, more exciting today perhaps than in earlier ages, realizing that this has ceased to be governed by national boundaries or old divisions and is common to the race of man everywhere. We have to revive the passion for truth and beauty and freedom which gives meaning to life, and develop afresh that dynamic outlook and spirit of adventure which distinguished those of our race who, in ages past, built our house on these strong and enduring foundations. Old as we are, with memories stretching back to the early dawns of human history and endeavour, we have to grow young again, in tune with our present time, with the irrepressible spirit and joy of youth in the present and its faith in the future.

Truth as ultimate reality, if such there is, must be eternal, imperishable, unchanging. But that infinite, eternal and unchanging truth cannot be apprehended in its fullness by the finite mind of man which can only grasp, at most, some small aspect of it limited by time and space, and by the state of development of that mind and the prevailing ideology of the period. As the mind develops and enlarges its scope, as ideologies change and new symbols are used to express that truth, new aspects of it come to light, though the core of it may yet be the same. And so, truth has ever to be sought and renewed, reshaped, and developed, so that, as understood by man, it might keep in line with the growth of his thought and the development of human life. Only then does it become a living truth for humanity, supplying the essential need for which it craves, and offering guidance in the present and for the future.

But if some one aspect of the truth has been petrified by dogma in a past age, it ceases to grow and develop and adapt itself to the changing needs of humanity; other aspects of it remain hidden and it fails to answer the urgent questions of a succeeding age. It is no longer dynamic but static, no longer a life-giving impulse but dead thought and ceremonial and a hindrance to the growth of the mind and of humanity. Indeed, it is probably not even understood to the extent it was understood in that past age when it grew up and was clothed in the language and symbols of that age. For its context is different in a later age, the mental climate has changed, new social habits and customs have grown up, and it is often difficult to understand the sense, much less the spirit, of that ancient writing. Moreover, as Aurobindo Ghose has pointed out, every truth, however true in itself, yet taken apart from others which at once limit and complete it, becomes blind the intellect and a misleading dogma; for in reality each is one thread of a complex weft and no thread must be taken apart from the weft.

Religions have helped greatly in the development of humanity. They have laid down values and standards and have pointed out principles for the guidance of human life. But with all the good they have done, they have also tried to imprison truth in set forms and dogmas, and encouraged ceremonials and practices which soon lose all their original meaning and become mere routine. While impressing upon man the awe and mystery of the unknown that surrounds him on all sides, they have discouraged him from trying to understand not only the unknown but what might come in the way of social effort. Instead of encouraging curiosity and thought, they have preached a philosophy of submission to nature, to establish churches, to the prevailing social order, and to everything that is. The belief in a supernatural agency which ordains everything has led to a certain irresponsibility on the social plane, and emotion and sentimentality have taken the place of reasoned thought and inquiry. Religion, though it has undoubtedly brought comfort to innumerable human beings and stabilized society by its values, has checked the tendency to change and progress inherent in human society.

Philosophy has avoided many of these pitfalls and encouraged thought and inquiry. But it has usually lived in its ivory tower cut off from life and its day-to-day problems, concentrating on ultimate purposes and failing to link them with the life of man. Logic and reason were its guides and they took it far in many directions, but that logic was too much the product of the mind and unconcerned with fact.

Science ignored the ultimate purposes and looked at fact alone. It made the world jump forward with a leap, built up a glittering civilization, opened up innumerable avenues for the growth of knowledge, and added to the power of man to such an extent that for the first time it was possible to conceive that man could triumph over and shape his physical environment. Man became almost a geological force, changing the face of the planet earth chemically, physically, and in many other ways. Yet when this sorry scheme of things entirely seemed to be in his grasp, to mould it nearer to the heart's desire, there was some essential lack and some vital element was missing. There was no knowledge of ultimate purposes and not even an understanding of the immediate purpose, for science had told us nothing about any purpose in life. Nor did man, so powerful in his control of nature, have the power to control himself and the monster he had created ran amok. Perhaps new developments in biology, psychology, and similar sciences, and the interpretation of biology and physics, may help man to understand and control himself more than he has done in the past. Or, before any such advances influence human life sufficiently, man may destroy the civilization he has built and have to start a new.

There is no visible limit to the advance of science, if it is given the chance to advance. Yet it may be that the scientific method of observation is not always applicable to all the varieties of human experience and cannot cross the uncharted ocean that surrounds us. With the help of philosophy it may go a little further and venture even on these high seas. And when both science and philosophy fail us, we shall have to rely on such other powers of apprehension as we may possess. For there appears to be a definite stopping place beyond which reason, as the mind is at present constituted, cannot go.

...Science deals with the domain of positive knowledge but the temper which it should produce goes beyond that domain. The ultimate purposes of man may be said to be to gain knowledge, to realize truth, to appreciate goodness and beauty. The scientific method of objective inquiry is not applicable to all these, and much that is vital in life seems to lie beyond its scope - the sensitiveness to art and poetry, the emotion that beauty produces, the inner recognition of goodness. The botanist and zoologist may never experience the charm and beauty of nature; the sociologist may be wholly lacking in love for humanity. But even when we go to the regions beyond the reach of the scientific method and visit the mountain tops where philosophy dwells and high emotions fill us, or gaze at the immensity beyond, that approach and temper are still necessary.

Very different is the method of religion. Concerned as it is principally with the regions beyond the reach of objective inquiry, it relies on emotion and intuition. And then it applies this method to everything in life, even to those things which are capable of intellectual inquiry and observation. Organized religion, allying itself to theology and often more concerned with its vested interests than with things of the spirit, encourages a temper which is the very opposite of that of science. It produces narrowness and intolerance, credulity and superstition, emotionalism and irrationalism. It tends to close and limit the mind of man, and to produce a temper of a dependent, unfree person.

...It is therefore with the temper and approach of science, allied to philosophy, and with reverence for all that lies beyond, that we must face life. Thus we may develop an integral vision of life which embraces in its wide scope the past and the present, with all their heights and depths, and look with serenity towards the future. The depths are there and cannot be ignored, and always by the side of the loveliness that surrounds us is the misery of the world. Man's journey through life is an odd mixture of joy and sorrow; thus only can he learn and advance. The travail of the soul is a tragic and lonely business. External events and their consequences affect us powerfully, and yet the greatest shocks come to our minds through inner fears and conflicts. While we advance on the external plane, as we must if we are to survive, we have also to win peace with ourselves and between ourselves and our environment, a peace which brings satisfaction not only to our physical and material needs but also to those inner imaginative urges and the adventurous spirit that have distinguished man ever since he started on his troubled journey in the realms of thought and action. Whether that journey has any ultimate purpose or not we do not know, but it has its compensations, and it points to many a nearer objective which appears attainable and which may again become the starting point for a fresh advance.

Ethical Approach to Life

What was my philosophy of life? I did not know. Some years earlier I would not have been so hesitant. There was a definiteness about my thinking and objectives then which has faded away since....

This doubt and difficulty about fundamental matters did not come in my way in regard to immediate action, except that it blunted somewhat the sharp edge of that activity. No longer could I function as I did in my younger days, as an arrow flying automatically to the target of my choice ignoring all else but that target. Yet I functioned, for the urge to action was there and a real or imagined co-ordination of that action with the ideals I held. But a growing distaste of politics as I saw it seized me and gradually my whole attitude to life seemed to undergo a transformation.[2]

The ideals and objectives of yesterday were still the ideals of today, but they had lost some of their lustre and, even as one seemed to go towards them, they lost the shining beauty which had warmed the heart and vitalized the body. Evil triumphed often enough, but what was far worse was the coarsening and distortion of what had seemed so right. Was human nature so essentially bad that it would take ages of training, through suffering misfortune, before it could behave reasonably and raise man above that creature of lust and violence and deceit that he now was? And, meanwhile, was every effort to change it radically in the present or the near future doomed to failure?

Ends and means: were they tied up inseparably, acting and reacting on each other, the wrong means distorting and sometimes even destroying the end in view? But the right means might well be beyond the capacity of infirm and selfish human nature.

What then was one to do? Not to act was a complete confession of failure and a submission to evil to act meant often enough a compromise with some form of that evil, with all the untoward consequences that such compromises result in.

My early approach to life's problems had been more or less scientific, with something of the easy optimism of the science of the nineteenth and early twentieth century. A secure and comfortable existence and the energy and self-confidence I possessed increased that feeling of optimism. A kind of vague humanism appealed to me.

Religion, as I saw it practised, and accepted even by thinking minds, whether it was Hinduism or Islam or Buddhism or Christianity, did not attract me. It seemed to be closely associated with superstitious practices and dogmatic beliefs, and behind it lay a method of approach to life's problems which was certainly not that of science. There was an element of magic about it, an uncritical credulousness, a reliance on the supernatural.

Yet it was obvious that religion had supplied some deeply felt inner need of human nature, and that the vast majority of people all over the world could not do without some form of religious belief. It had produced many fine types of men and women, as well as bigoted, narrow-minded, cruel tyrants. It had given a set of values to human life, and though some of these values had no application today, or were even harmful, others were still the foundation of morality and ethics.

In the wider sense of the word, religion dealt with the uncharted regions of human experience, uncharted, that is, by the scientific positive knowledge of the day. In a sense it might be considered an extension of the known and charted region, though the methods of science and religion were utterly unlike each other, and to a large extent they had to deal with different kinds of media. It was obvious that there was a vast unknown region all around us, and science, with its magnificent achievements, knew little enough about it, though it was making tentative approaches in the direction. Probably also, the normal methods of science, its dealings with the visible world and the processes of life, were not wholly adapted to the physical, the artistic, the spiritual, and other elements of the invisible world. Life does not consist entirely of what we see and hear and feel, the visible world which is undergoing change in time and space: it is continually touching an invisible world of other, and possibly more stable or equally changeable, elements, and no thinking person can ignore this invisible world.

Science does not tell us much, or for the matter of that anything about the purpose of life. It is now widening its boundaries and it may invade the so-called invisible world before long and help us to understand this purpose of life in the widest sense, or at least give us some glimpses which illumine the problem of human existence. The old controversy between science and religion takes a new form - the application of the scientific method to emotional and religious experiences.

Religion merges into mysticism and metaphysics and philosophy. There have been great mystics, attractive figures, who cannot easily be disposed of as self-deluded fools. Yet mysticism (in the narrow sense of the word) irritates me; it appears to be vague and soft and flabby, not a rigorous discipline of the mind but a surrender of mental faculties and a living in a sea of emotional experience. The experience may lead occasionally to some insight into inner and less obvious processes, but it is likely to lead to self-delusion.

Metaphysics and philosophy, or a metaphysical philosophy, have a greater appeal to the mind. They require hard thinking and the application of logic and reasoning, though all this is necessarily based on some premises, which are presumed to be self-evident, and yet which may or may not be true. All thinking persons, to a greater or lesser degree, dabble in metaphysics and philosophy, for not to do so is to ignore many of the aspects of this universe of ours. Some may feel more attracted to them than others, and the emphasis on them may vary in different ages. In the ancient world, both in Asia and Europe, all the emphasis was laid on the supremacy of the inward life over things external, and this inevitably led to metaphysics and philosophy. The modern man is wrapped up much more in these things external, and yet even he, in moments of crisis and mental trouble, often turns to philosophy and metaphysical speculations.

Some vague or more precise philosophy of life we all have, though most of us accept unthinkingly the general attitude which is characteristic of our generation and environment. Most of us accept also certain metaphysical conceptions as part of the faith in which we have grown up. I have not been attracted towards metaphysics; in fact, I have had a certain distaste for vague speculation. And yet I have sometimes found a certain intellectual fascination in trying to follow the rigid lines of metaphysical and philosophic thought of the ancients or the moderns. But I have never felt at ease there and have escaped from their spell with a feeling of relief.

Essentially, I am interested in this world, in this life, not in some other world or a future life. Whether there is such a thing as a soul, or whether there is a survival after death or not, I do not know; and, important as these questions are, they do not trouble me in the least. The environment in which I have grown up takes the soul (or rather the *atman*) and a future life, the Karma theory of cause and effect, and reincarnation for granted. I have been affected by this and so, in a sense, I am favourably disposed towards these assumptions. There might be a soul which survives the physical death of the body, and theory of cause and effect governing life's actions seems reasonable, though it leads to obvious difficulties when one thinks of the ultimate cause. Presuming a soul, there appears to be some logic also in the theory of reincarnation.

But I do not believe in any of these or other theories and assumptions as a matter of religious faith. They are just intellectual speculations in an unknown region about which we know next to nothing. They do not affect my life, and whether they were proved right or wrong subsequently, they would make little difference to me.

Spiritualism with its seances and its so-called manifestations of spirits and the like has always seemed to me a rather absurd and impertinent way of investigating psychic phenomena and the mysteries of the after-life. Usually it is something worse, and is an exploitation of the emotions of some over-credulous people who seek relief or escape from mental trouble. I do not deny the possibility of some of these psychic phenomena having a basis of truth, but the approach appears me to be all wrong and the conclusions drawn from scraps and odd bits of evidence to be unjustified.

Often, as I look at this world, I have a sense of mysteries, of unknown depths. The urge to understand it, in so far as I can, comes to me: to be in tune with it and to experience it in its fullness. But the way to that understanding seems to me essentially the way of science, the way of objective approach, though I realize that there can be no such thing as true objectiveness. If the subjective element is unavoidable and inevitable, it should be conditioned as far as possible by the scientific method.

What the mysterious is I do not know. I do not call it God because God has come to mean much that I do not believe in. I find myself incapable of thinking of a deity or of any unknown supreme power in anthropomorphic terms, and the fact that many people think so is continually a source of surprise to me. Any idea of a personal God seems very odd to me. Intellectually, I can appreciate to some extent the conception of monism, and I have been attracted towards the Advaita (non-dualist) philosophy of the Vedanta, though I do not presume to understand it in all its depth and intricacy, and I realize that merely an intellectual appreciation of such matters does not carry one far. At the same time the Vedanta, as well as other similar approaches, rather frighten me with their vague, formless incursions into infinity. The diversity and fullness of nature stir me and produce a harmony of the spirit, and I can imagine myself feeling at home in the old Indian or Greek pagan and pantheistic atmosphere, but minus the conception of God or Gods that was attached to it.

Some kind of ethical approach to life has a strong appeal for me, though it would be difficult for me to justify it logically. I have been attracted by Gandhiji's stress on right means and I think one of his greater contributions to our public life has been this emphasis. The idea is by no means new, but this application of an ethical doctrine to large-scale public activity was certainly novel. It is full of difficulty, and perhaps ends and means are not really separable but form together one organic whole. In a world which thinks almost exclusively of ends and ignores means, this emphasis on means seems odd and remarkable. How far it has succeeded in India I cannot say. But there is no doubt that it has created a deep and abiding impression on the minds of large numbers of people.

A study of Marx and Lenin produced a powerful effect on my mind and helped me to see history and current affairs in a new light. The long chain of history and of social development appeared to have some meaning, some sequence, and the future lost some of its obscurity. The practical achievements of the Soviet Union were also tremendously impressive. Often I disliked or did not understand some development there and it seemed to me to be too closely concerned with the opportunism of the moment or the power politics of the day. But despite all these developments and possible distortions of the original passion for human betterment, I had no doubt that the Soviet revolution had advanced human society by a great leap and had lit a bright flame which could not be smothered, and that it had laid the foundations for that new civilization towards which the world could advance. I am too much of an individualist and believer in personal freedom to like over much regimentation. Yet it seemed to me obvious that in a complex social structure individual freedom had to be limited, and perhaps the only way to real personal freedom was through some such limitation in the social sphere. The lesser liberties may often need limitation in the interest of the larger freedom.

Much in the Marxist philosophical outlook I could accept without difficulty: its monism and non-duality of mind and matter, the dynamics of matter and the dialectic of continuous change by evolution as well as leap, through action and interaction, cause and effect, thesis, antithesis and synthesis. It did not satisfy me completely, nor did it answer all the questions in my mind, and, almost unawares, vague idealist approach would creep into my mind, something rather akin to the Vedanta approach. It was not a difference between mind and matter, but rather of something that lay beyond the mind. Also there was the background of ethics. I realized that the moral approach is a changing one and depends upon the growing mind and an advancing civilization; it is conditioned by the mental climate of the age. Yet there was something more to it than that, certain basic urges which had greater permanence. I did not like the frequent divorce in communist, as in other, practice between action and these basic urges or principles. So there was an odd mixture in my mind which I could not rationally explain or resolve. There was a general tendency not to think too much of those fundamental questions which appear to be beyond reach, but rather to concentrate on the problems of life - to understand in the narrower and more immediate sense what should be done and how. Whatever ultimate reality may be, and whether we can ever grasp it in whole or in part, there certainly appear to be vast possibilities of increasing human knowledge even though this may be partly or largely subjective, and of applying this to the advancement and betterment of human living and social organization.

There has been in the past, and there is to a lesser extent even today among some people, an absorption in finding an answer to the riddle of the universe. This leads them away from the individual and social problems of the day, and when they are unable to solve that riddle they despair and turn to inaction and triviality, or find comfort in some dogmatic creed. Social evils, most of which are certainly capable of removal, are attributed to original sin, to the unalterableness of human nature, or the social structure, or (in India) to the inevitable legacy of previous births. Thus one drifts away from even the attempt to think rationally and scientifically and takes refuge in irrationalism, superstition, and unreasonable and inequitable social prejudices and practices. It is true that even rational and scientific thought does not always take us as far as we would like to go. There is an infinite number of factors and relations all of which influence and determine events in varying degrees. It is impossible to grasp all of them, but we can try to pick out the dominating forces at work and by observing external material reality, and by experiment and practice, trial and error, grope our way to ever-widening knowledge and truth.

How amazing is this spirit of man! In spite of innumerable failings, man, throughout the ages, has sacrificed his life and all he held dear for an ideal, for truth, for faith, for country and honour. That ideal may change, but that capacity for self-sacrifice continues, and, because of that, much may be forgiven to man, and it is impossible to lose hope for him. In the midst of disaster, he has not lost his dignity or his faith in the values he cherished. Plaything of nature's mighty forces, less than a speck of dust in this vast universe, he has hurled defiance at the elemental powers, and with his mind, cradle of revolution, sought to master them. Whatever gods there be, there is something godlike in man, as there is also something of the devil in him.

The future is dark, uncertain. But we can see part of the way leading to it and can tread it with firm steps, remembering that nothing that can happen is likely to overcome the spirit of man which has survived so many perils; remembering also that life, for all its ills, has joy and beauty, and that we can always wander, if we know how to, in the enchanted woods of nature.

What else is wisdom? What of man's endeavour

Or God's high grace, so lovely and so great?
To stand from fear set free, to breathe and wait;
To hold a hand uplifted over Hate;

And shall not Loveliness be loved for ever?

Social Code of Conduct

1. In spite of political differences, everyone should unite for the defence and well-being of the country and co-operate with others to implement programmes for the common good.
2. The unity and good of the nation should be given first importance and people should, therefore, rise above differences of caste, creed, language and province, and think more of the country as a whole.
3. Violence of any kind must be shunned and avoided. Violence creates hatred and is disruptive.
4. Religion is meant to raise an individual and to make him tolerant of others. Narrow prejudices and intolerance do not create respect for one's own religion in the eyes of others. We should honour not only our own religion but the religion of others also.
5. We should aim at equality of treatment and avoid feelings of high and low and touchable and untouchable.
6. We should aim at becoming good citizens, subordinating self-interest and aiming at the common good.
7. Women should be treated with respect and as comrades. They should not be kept in purdah or seclusion, but given opportunities to participate in national activities.
8. Children should be treated with affection and gentleness and not beaten or scolded.
9. Liquor and all other intoxicants should be avoided.
10. Village and cottage industries should be encouraged, and as far as possible khadi should be used.
11. Adulteration of foodstuffs and other articles must be prevented.
12. The giving or accepting of bribes is bad, both for the giver and taker, and must be vigorously dealt with.

13. The house, street and village or town should be kept neat and clean.
14. We should try to understand the great developmental work that is going on in the country, such as the Five-Year Plan, the community development schemes, etc., and co-operate in furthering and implementing it.
15. Manual labour should be respected and everyone should endeavour to engage himself in some form of manual labour for constructive work.

Ends and Means[3]

What is the purpose of life and what is the joy in life? It is a difficult question to answer. But I could tell you this: that the true joy in life is to ally yourself to a great purpose, to throw yourself into it heart and soul, to forget your little self, your little complaints and whimperings and to work your hardest for the realization of that purpose. And when you have exhausted your energy, well, it does not matter if you are thrown on the scrap-heap. You have done your job. I am not just complaining all the time about life's misfortunes, or other misfortunes and leading a whimpering life.

That is the true joy in life. We cannot all or any one of us order results. The world is too complicated, but we can work for great things and I have no doubt that every bit of work rightly done, rightly intentioned, produces some result somewhere, even though we might not see it. And, therefore, I have no doubt that if work has the right intentions, the right means, it must produce good results. But if even in your attempt to reach a right objective, you adopt wrong means, wrong intentions, something with a trace of evil in it, then even your ends become distorted and you might go astray. That is the doctrine of ends and means. We should always adopt right means. We should not justify wrong means by saying that our objective is good. That is finally the distinction between the ways of war and the ways of peace. That is the tremendous distinction between the way of co-operation and the way of conflict; the way of affection and the way of hatred.

Curbing the Devil in US

...I suppose that Indians, by and large, are gentler than almost any people in the world. They dislike violence. Most of them will deliberately avoid treading on an ant or any other insect, and yet they are callous to animals. They may show reverence to the cow, but they ill-treat her, as they ill-treat other animals. Even more so, the picture came before me of the horrible occurrences and inhumanities committed by our own countrymen after the partition....

How was it that these people who are essentially friendly and gentle committed these inhumanities? I have no explanation except to say that all of us, individuals and people have two sides to our nature, the gentle side and the brutish, the divine and the devilish... Civilization has not curbed sufficiently the devil in us. That devil may come out because of various reasons, but above all was fear and hatred. And so it ill becomes us to criticize others because we are all made of the same mixture of good and evil. We are apt to see the evil in others and to ignore the evil in ourselves. Charity and compassion are suppressed by outbursts of passionate fear and hatred. It has been my good fortune to see many peoples in many countries and to find them friendly and full of affection and goodwill. In some other circumstances those very people might become brutish. In war this happens inevitably. In a war of extermination through nuclear[4] weapons there will probably be an extremity of fear and hatred which will reduce humanity to the lowest level of degradation, apart from the destruction it will cause. It is this inner decay and degradation that is more fearful than any outside damage or injury.

Life is Affirmation

Two of your letters..., were full of the burden of sorrow and an emotional upheaval at the suddenness of death and all the questionings that this experience gives rise to. Out of this eternal questioning has arisen philosophy with all its problems, and throughout the ages innumerable people have wondered over this mystery of life and death. Philosophy has come to you early because not only of personal shock but also the larger tragedies that surround us. It depends on each one of us how we face these questions, how we react to them. Adequate answers we may not have but our imaginative self give some kind of an unconscious response which affects our individual lives. We weaken under the stress and lose our sense of poise and equilibrium, or grow stronger and more capable of riding the storm and yet being not too much affected by it. Life is amazingly dynamic and while it lasts, has an extraordinary capacity to adapt itself and to express itself forcibly. We see this daily in the exuberance of nature and we are parts of that nature and have, or should have, the same exuberance and vitality. So we carry on along our appointed course, and, though limited by circumstances, still endeavour to mould that circumstance itself according to the urge that is within us.[5]

Reason and agreement go some way to shape our minds and direct our activities. Yet in the final analysis we act because of that inner urge within us, which has been formed and conditioned by so many factors which have gone to our making – our own experience chiefly, piling up one on top of the other from birth and childhood onwards, the influence of others, our heredity and our racial and cultural inheritance, our education, the sensations we have known and experienced.

So our reactions to events vary. Some, and among them have been wise men, think all this business of life a thing of sound and fury, signifying nothing. Others have discovered or felt a meaning in it all. Yet others, uncertain whether there is any meaning or not, still are compelled by some force within them to adopt objectives and codes of behaviour and follow them with all their might. Perhaps that itself signifies some deep intuitive faith in a meaning. However that may be, most of us, affirm life and it is right that we should do so positively, rather than just carry on negatively.

Twenty-five hundred years ago the Buddha addressing his followers said: '...while ye, O disciples, experienced this sorrow through long ages, more tears have flowed from you and have been shed by you, while ye strayed and wandered on this pilgrimage of life, and sorrowed and wept, because that was your portion which ye abhorred, and that which ye loved was not your portion, than all the waters which are in the four great oceans.'

A sad thought and though a true one, yet perhaps with an overemphasis on the pain and suffering of life. Buddha was frequently emphasizing this and many people therefore call Buddhism a religion of pessimism. Yet the face of Buddha in the statues that his faithful followers have made with loving care, and even more so in the image of him that I have in my mind, is so devoid of pain and sorrow, so full of peace and calm and compassion, that I cannot connect it with suffering. Or, does it represent the conquest over sorrow? I do not think of him as a man of sorrow.

And then going to the lands where Buddhism still flourishes, we do not find the people pessimistic at all. Where could there be more of the joy and affirmation of life than in the Chinese people? Is that a racial characteristic, I wonder, which has overcome and transmuted the pessimistic tendencies of the faith, or is it something else? I do not know. But I do know that I am seldom depressed for long by events, however painful they might be for the moment, and a certain unreasoning faith in life rises up in me and keeps me going. I cannot argue about it, but it fills me, and therefore life is an affirmation to me and not a negation. Even if that subconscious faith were absent, I suppose, I would continue to function in much the same way, but that urge helps and gives me vitality. Experiencing this myself, I want others to share it with me.

What a letter I am writing! A vague and possibly unmeaning attempt at philosophy in its relation to life, or perhaps, just a glimpse of that restless and wandering creature, my mind. I have written as I have done because I want you to have such glimpses and to realize as I do the extraordinary fascination of life's adventure. That pilgrimage would be no adventure if it lay in the ruts of normal experience and cautious conduct, safely first in everything, like the slow-moving river on an almost level plain. The body has its adventures and experiences, and many are wrothhaving, but the real adventures are of the mind. Indeed all feelings and experiences are ultimately of the mind, and the mind itself is part of the body.

There is the adventure of the individual, the adventure of the race, and finally the world adventure - and all tend to get mixed up together - and we can be parties to all these adventures. If the individual's adventure has an ending, the others continue and carry us to an endless future. Our country, tragic as she may appear to us at the present moment, has been carrying on her story and her quest since the dawn of history many thousands of years ago. That quest will surely continue and merge itself in the conditions of the modern world, into the world-quest for life and freedom and adventures of the mind and spirit.

Facing Ever-changing Present

Life is full of untoward happenings and since the world began persons with sensitive minds and those who are called philosophers have tried to understand its complex and baffling texture. Others, dissatisfied with many of its aspects, have sought to alter them. In the course of time it has changed gradually but it still fails to satisfy our minds or our impulses. Everywhere there is what is called the strength of life. In its crude aspects this is evident enough, but it is equally evident in the sphere of the mind. All action is really a challenge to life. Only those minds which are in a rut and fearful of any change, refuse this challenge, and yet even they cannot escape the hard knocks of life. Possibly they get them more, or sense them more, because they fear them more and are often taken unawares. The only real conflict which is oppressive is the conflict of the mind which arises from doubt and indecision--the old question of Hamlet -- to be or not to be, to do or not to do. If one decides one way or the other, it is done with, whatever the consequences. The conflict is over, though other conflicts will no doubt trouble the mind. To look back continually with regret is to lose oneself in the unchangeable past and thus miss both the present and the future. And so more regrets follow and we wallow in a very ocean of regret, never catching up with the living moment. Surely that is not a satisfactory state of affairs. Often enough it is the little things of life that pursue us and trouble us far more than the big things. And yet it is the big things that count.....

To lose our perspective in life is to lose our bearings. To look back is necessarily to look away from the present and the future which count. We must face the ever-changing present and have the power of quick decisions. Decide this way or that after weighing the pros and cons and act up to the decision. Not to decide is to live in a fog of doubt and misgiving. Whether it is a matter relating to the narrow sphere of the family or the larger sphere of life, one must solve and resolve our problems as they arise and go ahead, not regretting over much or pining for what is not, not complaining, not holding others responsible for something that might have been otherwise.[6]

What is happiness? There is the solid content of a fairly prosperous peasant; there are higher grades of intellectual and emotional happiness. There is the happiness of the person who is drunk or who is under influence of some drug. I suppose, if you analyse your mind, you will find that happiness is more often negative than positive an absence of pain & suffering. And yet how is one to be happy if he knows and sees another in pain? A sensitive person will suffer continually on behalf of others. An insensitive person may escape that but at the cost of much that is fine in life. Long ago (probably 140 years ago) Leopardi the Italian poet wrote to his sister on the occasion of her marriage: 'Thou shall have children, either cowards or unhappy; choose thou the latter.' That is perhaps an extreme view but there is some truth in it.[7]

Ultimately we cannot be really happy till the whole world is happy and that is a large order. Mere avoidance of unhappiness, not easily possible, may itself result in isolation and boredom and a malaise which is worse than definite unhappiness. We are so organically' connected with others and with the world that we cannot both live a full life and yet avoid the world's ills. Escapism does not pay in the long run, quite apart from it normal worths.

What then is one to do? That is a big question which has been asked almost since human beings began to think. It seems to me that the only thing to aim at is the power or capacity to extract happiness, or perhaps it is better to call it peace and calm, out of unhappiness itself. Not to escape from anything but to face it and yet be above it in a way; not to be overcome by it and to retain in spite of everything a sense of life and its larger purposes, a feeling of life fulfilment. How to do that is a difficult enough job and each person has to learn for himself and it seems that only life, with all its waywardness and shock, can teach. The most we can do is to prepare the background for it.

REFERENCES

1. Discovery of India, 1946.
2. Discovery of India, 1946.
3. From a speech at Tokyo University, October 8, 1957.
4. A Note on Impression of a Visit to Japan, October 15, 1957.
5. Letter to Indira Gandhi February 1, 1949.
6. A letter to Krishna Hutheesing, 22 March 1914.
7. A Letter to Indira Gandhi, June 1944.

HISTORIOGRAPHY

1. Fascinating Facets
2. Social History
3. The Asian Angle

TWO

HISTORIOGRAPHY

Fascinating Facets

History is not pleasant. Man, in spite of his great and vaunted progress, is still a very unpleasant and selfish animal. And yet perhaps it is possible to see the silver lining of progress right through the long and dismal record of selfishness and quarrelsomeness and in humanity of man. I am a bit of an optimist and am inclined to take a hopeful view of things, but optimism must not blind us to the dark spots around us and to the danger of an unthinking optimism itself being very much misplaced.[1]

...If history interests you, if you feel some of the fascination of history, you will find your way to many books which will help you to unravel the threads of past ages. But reading books alone will not help. If you would know the past you must look upon it with sympathy and with understanding. To understand a person who lived long ago, you will have to understand his environment, the conditions under which he lived, the ideas that filled his mind. It is absurd for us to judge of past people as if they lived now and thought as we do. There is no one to defend slavery to-day, and yet the great Plato held that slavery was essential. Within recent times scores of thousands of lives were given in an effort to retain slavery in the United States. We cannot judge the past from the standards of the present. Every one will willingly admit this. But everyone will not admit the equally absurd habit of judging the present by the standards of the past. The various religions have especially helped in petrifying old beliefs and faiths and customs which may have had some use in the age and country of their birth, but which are singularly unsuitable in our present age.

If, then, you look upon past history with the eye of sympathy, the dry bones will fill up with flesh and blood, and you will see a mighty procession of living men and women and children in every age and every clime, different from us and yet very like us, with much the same human virtues and human failings. History is not a magic show, but there is plenty of magic in it for those who have eyes to see.

...The past brings us many gifts; indeed, all that we have today of culture, civilization, science, or knowledge of some aspects of truth, is a gift of the distant or recent past to us. It is right that we acknowledge our obligation to the past. But the past does not exhaust our duty or obligation. We owe a duty to the future also and perhaps that obligation is even greater than the one we owe to the past. For the past is past and done with, we cannot change it; the future is yet to come and perhaps we may be able to shape it a little. If the past has given us some part of the truth, the future also hides many aspects of the truth and invites us to search for it. But often the past is jealous of the future and holds us in a terrible grip, and we have to struggle with it to get free to face advance towards the future.

History, it is said, has many lessons to teach us; and there is another saying that history never repeats itself. Both are true, for we cannot learn anything from it by slavishly trying to copy it, or by expecting it to repeat itself or remain stagnant; but we can learn something from it by prying behind it and trying to discover the forces that move it. Even so what we get is seldom a straight answer. 'History', says Karl Marx, 'has no other way of answering old questions than by putting new ones.'

Social History

Now, I do not know what many of you feel when you think about a historical subject. For my part I feel tremendously fascinated by and interested in the subject of history and my mind begins to wander a little trying to think of this long sweep and trying to draw not only interest, but inspiration or knowledge or understanding or all of them. I do not know if one always succeeds in getting that inspiration from it as a whole; one does sometimes find other aspects of it which are far from inspiring. In any event, one has to go back to it to understand the present and to try to understand what the future ought to be. They say that history never repeats itself. I suppose that is true. Nevertheless, to understand anything you have to go back to the roots of the forces and the various other happenings that are taking place today and they are the only possible data which you can have; otherwise you have to trust your imagination only.

History, as a famous writer has described it, is a record of the martyrdom of man. Perhaps so. It is also a record of repeated resurrections after every crucifixion. So you see this process of martyrdom and crucifixion and man, and resurrection following it, in interminable succession. You may consider history as the onward march of humanity, of the human spirit, and yet sometimes we are pulled back by seeing how that onward march is suddenly arrested and thrown back.[2]

Now, every age, I suppose, thinks that it is an age of transition. Nevertheless, I suppose there is an element of truth in our thinking that the present age we live in is peculiarly an age of transition and change: at any rate the problems we have to face appear to be far bigger and acuter than any other problems, partly because of the extent of the problems and because every problem now becomes a world problem. It is quite impossible today to think of current events or of history in the making in terms of any one nation or country or patch of territory; you have inevitably to think in terms of the world as a whole. You may, of course, and you should, think of each of the smaller aspects of that larger picture; you may examine them more closely. But the whole conception of the history of a country being the names of a large number of kings and emperors, and our learning them by heart, I suppose, is long dead. I am not quite sure whether in the schools and colleges of India it has ceased to exist or not, but I hope at any rate that it is dead, because anything more futile than children's study of the record of kings' reigns and battles I cannot imagine.

The other aspect of history which has come much more to the forefront--the social aspect of history, the development of the social organism--involves much closer research into the daily lives of the common man. May be in family budgets a hundred or a thousand years ago, there were a hundred and a thousand and one things which make us realise something of what the life of humanity was in the past age. It is only then that we can really clothe the dry bones of history with life, flesh and blood. I must confess that even now, in spite of this acknowledged new approach, most of the books on history and papers on history that appear, interesting though the subject matter may be, appear to me to be quite singularly lifeless and dead. They are just the dry bones; there is no flesh and blood in them. And I suppose the only way really to read, write or understand history is to evoke in the mind a picture of a living society functioning, thinking and having all the virtues and failings which the human being has possessed, and gradually changing whether in the direction of progress or in some other.[3]

The Asian Angle

I never studied history in the formal way but informally I have been greatly interested in history, chiefly because of my seeking to understand the past rather in terms of the present and even of the future to come. I have approached it as an exciting story. I have approached it as a developing drama, leading up to the present and making me wonder where it will lead to in the future. I never got into the habit of trying to learn the names of kings, dates, etc. And I confess I am singularly ignorant of names and dates except those I could not help picking up.

The whole course of history has fascinated me. Being an Indian, facts relating to the past of India interested me more. Being as Asian, facts relating to Asia also interested me more. But on the whole what has interested me really is the story of man developing himself wherever he might be. It is from that point of view I have tried to co-ordinate such little knowledge of history as I possess.

I remember about 40 years or more ago one of the earliest books dealing with world history came out, namely H.G. Wells's *Outline of History*. It is very easy to criticize Wells, but his was a new approach, and it was a great success. He did try to bring in one compass the tremendous story of man. He did also something which was new for most European leaders, that is, he paid some attention to what was happening in Asia; his world was not merely the Mediterranean world in ancient times, as had been imagined in Europe. China came in, and India, the Middle East and the other countries. Since then this type of history has become more common. Other forms of history, social histories and the like, have been written and they attract much more attention than the political histories of the past.

So far as Asia is concerned, we have been grossly maltreated by most historians from other countries. And as a reaction to that, sometimes our own historians have perhaps gone too far. I suppose it is difficult for any person with strongly held ideas to write what might be called in impartial history. Sometimes I have wondered if impartiality was not the quality of a weak mind. There must be a positive quality in a human being. If there is this positive quality, that aspect of the mind impresses itself on the subject which it deals with and perhaps slightly distorts it. I do not know how we can get over this difficulty. On the one side, there is the nationalist history which, starting from a strong nationalist bias, praises everything that is national at the expense of other things and, on the other side, there is the reverse of this. In the case of India, a Western scholar, especially from the United Kingdom, inevitably tended to look at the history of India as if the past few thousand years were a kind of a preparation for the coming British dominion in India. And there was the nationalist reaction to it. It seems to me that our historians burrow too much into details and thereby lose sight of the main theme. Both these approaches were limited and both failed to look at the picture in a broad way. In the main, the nationalist approach and imperialist approach distort history. They sometimes suppress history.

We have had examples of some kind of an organized approach or a philosophy of history, and this has led to curious results. One of the books which I had occasion to read in the leisure moments of my prison life was Spongler's *Decline of the West*. I was rather fascinated by it, as one is fascinated by some evil thing. I dislike intensely its sweeping approach. It seems to me that as soon as we start looking at history with any preconceived approach, it turns us away from some patent facts which do not fit in with our theory. And we select things which agree with our own thinking. It does not do harm provided we can get the main currents of history right and if stress is placed on one aspect in order to draw attention to it. The stress on the social aspect has certainly been very helpful, in balancing one's approach to history.

The old idea of writing a history of any one country has become progressively out of date. It is impossible today to think of the history of a country isolated from the rest of the world. The world is getting integrated. We have really to consider history today in a world perspective.

What is the basic philosophy of history? I try to think of history as a process that leads man to higher and better stages of progress. Then I find, to my surprise, that those higher stages have been represented by great men in the long past. Having been fascinated by the scientific and technological civilization which has been built up in Europe and in America, I gradually come to a state when it seems to me to have stopped. I begin seeking for something deeper than merely the physical aspect of civilization. I find that my mind is more interested in what Plato or the Buddha said, which has a timelessness about it. So I wonder if our present-day history, having fulfilled its destiny in so far as science and technology are concerned, is at all moving on to a higher plane of human existence. I do not presume that the average historian will be able to answer such a question unless he himself becomes a great seer who can pierce the veil of the future. But he can help in putting things in proper perspective.

The immediate object of the History Congress should of course be to straighten out all the twists which Asian history has received at the hands of Europeans. while some of them are very fine historians, their approach has nevertheless been based on Europe being the centre of the world, naturally that affects their appreciation of the histories of Asian countries.

REFERENCES

1. Glimpses of World History, 1939.
2. Inaugural address to the Asian History Congress, New Delhi, December 9, 1961.
3. Address to the Indian Historical Records Commission, New Delhi, December 23, 1948.

POLITICAL AND ECONOMICS SYSTEMS OF STATE AND GOVERNMENT

1. Emergence of Democratic Ideas
2. Socialism and Anarchism
3. Communism, Dictatorship, Facism
4. Nationalism Vs Internationalism
5. Evolution from Capitalism
6. Capitalism in India
7. Welfare State

THREE

POLITICAL AND ECONOMIC SYSTEMS OF STATE AND GOVERNMENT

Emergence of Democratic Ideas

...One notable book, ... came out in England in the second half of the eighteenth century. This was Adam Smith's *Wealth of Nations* [1776].[1] It was not a book on politics as such, but on political economy or economics. The subject, like all other subjects at the time, was mixed up with religion and ethics, and there was thus a great deal of confusion about it. Adam Smith dealt with it in a scientific way and, disregarding all ethical complications, tried to find natural laws which governed economics. Economics deals with the management of the income and expenditure of the people or a country as a whole, of what they produce and what they consume, and their relations with each other and other countries and peoples. Adam Smith believed that all these rather complicated operations took place according to fixed natural laws, which he set down in his book. He also believed that full liberty should be given for the development of industry so that these laws might not be interfered with. This was the beginning of the doctrine of *laissez-faire*... Adam Smith's book had nothing to do with the new democratic ideas which were germinating in France at the time. But his attempt at scientific treatment of one of the most important problems which affected men and nations shows that men were going in a new direction, away from the old theological way of looking at everything....

The new science of economics was confined to professors and a few well-read men. But meanwhile the new ideas of democracy were spreading, and the American and French Revolutions gave them tremendous popularity and advertisement. The fine-sounding words and phrases of the American Declaration of Independence and the French Declaration of Rights stirred people to the depths. To the millions who were oppressed and exploited they brought a thrill and a message of deliverance. Both the declarations spoke of liberty and equality and of the right to happiness which every one has. The proud declaration of these precious rights did not result in the people obtaining them. Even now, more than a century and a half after these declarations, few can be said to enjoy them. But even the declaration of these principles was extraordinary and life-giving.

The old idea in Europe as elsewhere, in Christianity as in other religions, was that sin and unhappiness were the common and inevitable lot of man. Religion seemed to give a permanent and even an honoured place to poverty and misery in this world. The promises and rewards of religion were all for some other world; here we were told to bear our lot with resignation and not to seek any fundamental change. Charity was encouraged, the giving of crumbs to the poor, but there was no idea of doing away with poverty, or with a system which resulted in poverty. The very ideas of liberty and equality were opposed to the authoritarian outlook of the Church and society.

Democracy did not, of course, say that all men were in fact equal. It could not say this, because it is obvious enough that there are inequalities between different men: physical inequalities which result in some being stronger than others, mental inequalities which are seen in some people being abler or wiser than others, and moral inequalities which make some unselfish and others not so. It is quite possible that many of these inequalities are due to different kinds of upbringing and education or want of education. Of two boys or girls who are similar in ability, give one a good education and the other no education, and after some years there will be a vast difference between the two. Or give one of them healthy food and the other bad and insufficient food, and the former will grow properly, while the latter will be weak and ailing and under-developed. So one's upbringing and surroundings and training and education make a vast deal of difference, and it may be that if we could give the same training and opportunities to everybody, there would be far less inequality than there is now. This is indeed very likely. But so far as democracy is concerned, it admitted that men were as a matter of fact unequal, and yet it stated that each one of them should be treated as having an equal political and social value. If we accept this democratic theory in its entirety, we are led to all manner of revolutionary conclusions. We need not go into these at this stage, but one obvious consequence of the theory was that each person should have a vote for the election of a representative to the governing assembly or parliament. The vote was the symbol of political power, and it was assumed that if every one had a vote, each such person would have an equal share in political power. Therefore one of the principal demands of democracy, right through the nineteenth century, was the extension of the franchise – that is, the right to vote. Adult suffrage or franchise meant that every adult or grown-up person should have the vote. For a long time women were not allowed to vote, and there was not very long ago a tremendous agitation by them, especially in Britain. In most advanced countries now there is adult suffrage for both men and women.

But, curiously enough, when most people had got the vote they found that it did not make very much difference to them. In spite of having the vote, they had no power, or very little power, in the State. A vote is of little use to a hungry man. The people with real power were those who could take advantage of his hunger and make him work to do anything else that they wanted to their own advantage. Thus political power, which the vote was supposed to give, was seen to be a shadow with no substance, without economic power, and the brave dreams of the early democrats, that equality would follow from the vote, came to nothing.

This was, however, a much later development. In the early days–the end of the eighteenth and the beginning of the nineteenth centuries there was great enthusiasm among the democrats. Democracy was going to make everybody a free and equal citizen and the government of the State would work for the happiness of everybody. There was a great reaction against the autocracy of kings and governments of the eighteenth century and the way they had abused their absolute power. This led people to proclaim the rights of individuals in their declarations. Probably these statements of the rights of individuals in the American and French declarations erred somewhat on the other side. In a complex society it is not an easy matter to separate individuals and give them perfect freedom. The interests of such an individual and of society may and do clash. However this may be, democracy stood for a great deal of individual freedom.

England, which was backward in political ideas in the eighteenth century, was greatly affected by the American and French Revolutions. The first reaction was one of fear against the new democratic ideas and the possibility of a social revolution at home. The ruling classes became even more conservative and reactionary. But still the new ideas spread among the intellectuals. Thomas Paine was an interesting Englishman of this period. He was in America at the time of the War of Independence and helped the Americans. He seems to have been partly responsible for converting the Americans to the idea of complete independence. On his return to England he wrote a book, *The Right of Man*, in defence of the French Revolution which had just begun. In this book he attacked monarchy and pleaded for democracy. The British Government outlawed him because of this, and he had to fly to France. In Paris he soon became a member of the National Convention, but in 1793 he was put in prison by the Jacobins because he had opposed the execution of Louis XVI. In the Paris gaol he wrote another book called *The Age of Reason*, in which he criticized the religious outlook. Paine being out of reach of the English courts (he was discharged from the Paris prison after the death of Robespierre), his English publisher was sentenced to imprisonment for issuing this book. Such a book was considered dangerous to society, as religion was supposed to be necessary to keep the poor in their place. Several publishers of Paine's book, including women, were sent to prison. It interesting to find that Shelley, the poet, wrote a letter of protest to the judge.

In Europe the French Revolution was the parent of the democratic ideas that spread throughout the first half of the nineteenth century. Indeed, the very ideas of the Revolution persisted, although conditions were rapidly changing. These democratic ideas were the intellectual reaction against kings and autocracy. They were based on condition prior to industrialization. But the new industry – steam and big machinery – were completely upsetting the old order. Yet, strange to say, the radicals and democrats of the early nineteenth century ignored these changes and went on talking in the fine phrases of the Revolution and the Declaration of the Rights of·Man. To them perhaps these changes were purely material and did not affect the high spiritual and moral and political demands of democracy. But material things have a way of refusing to be ignored. It is very interesting to find how extraordinarily difficult it is for people to give up old ideas and accept new ones. They will shut their eyes and their minds and refuse to see; they will fight to hold on to the old even when it harms them. They will do almost anything but accept the new ideas and adapt themselves to new conditions. The power of conservatism is prodigious. Even the radicals, who imagine themselves very advanced, often stick to old and exploded ideas, and shut their eyes to changing conditions. It is no wonder that progress is slow, and often there is a great lag between actual conditions and people's ideas-resulting in revolutionary situations.

Democracy was thus for many decades the carrying on of the traditions and ideas of the French Revolution. This failure to adapt itself to the new conditions led to the weakening of democracy towards the ends of the century, and later, in the twentieth century, to its repudiation by many people.

The early democrats naturally took to rationalism. Their demand for freedom of thought and speech could hardly be reconciled with dogmatic religion and theology. Thus democracy joined with science to weaken the hold of theological dogmas. People began to dare to examine the Bible, as if it was an ordinary book and not something that must be accepted blindly and without questioning. This criticism of the Bible was called the "higher criticism." The critics came to the conclusion that the Bible was a collection of documents written by different persons in different ages. They also were of the opinion that Jesus had no intention of founding a religion. Many of the old beliefs were shaken by this criticism.

As the old religious foundations were being weakened by science and democratic ideas, attempts were made to formulate a philosophy to take the place of the old religion. One of these attempts was by a French philosopher, Auguste Comte, who lived from 1798 to 1857. Comte felt that the old theology and dogmatic religions were out of the date, but he was convinced that some kind of religion was a social necessity. He therefore proposed a "religion of humanity" and called it "Positivism". This was to be based on love, order and progress. There was nothing supernatural about it; it was based on science. At its back, as indeed at the back of nearly all current ideas of the nineteenth century, was the idea of the progress of the human race. Comte's religion remained the belief of a few intellectuals only, but his general influence on European thought was great. He may be said to begin the study of the science of sociology, which deals with human society and culture.

A contemporary of Comte's but surviving him by many years, was the English philosopher and economist, John Stuart Mill (1806 - 1873). Mill was influenced by Comte's teaching as well as by his socialistic ideas. He tried to give a new direction to the English school of political economy, which had grown up round the teachings of Adam Smith, and brought some socialistic principles into economic thought. But he is best known as the chief "utilitarian." "Utilitarianism" was a new theory, started a little earlier in England, and brought into greater prominence by Mill. As its name suggests, its guiding philosophy was utility or usefulness. "The greatest happiness of the greater number" was the fundamental principle of the Utilitarians. This was the only test of right and wrong. Actions were said to be right in proportion as they tended to promote happiness, and wrong in so far as they tended to promote the reverse of happiness. Society and Government were to be organized with this point of view – the promotion of the greatest happiness of the greatest number. The view-point was not quite the same as the earlier democratic doctrine of equal rights for everybody. The greatest happiness of the greatest number might conceivably require the sacrifice or the unhappiness of a smaller number. I am merely pointing this difference out to you, but we need not discuss it here. Democracy thus came to mean the rights of the majority.

John Stuart Mill was a strong advocate of the democratic idea of liberty for the individual. He wrote a little book, *On Liberty* [1859], which became famous. I shall give you an extract from this book in favour of freedom of speech and the free expression of opinion.

> But the peculiar evil of silencing the expression of an opinion is, that it is robbing the human race; posterity as well as the existing

> generation; those who dissent from the opinion, still more than those who hold it. If the opinion is right, they are deprived of the opportunity of exchanging error for truth; if wrong, they lose, what is almost as great a benefit, the clearer perception and livelier impression of truth, produced by its collision with error...We can never be sure that the opinion we are endeavouring to stifle is a false opinion; and if we were sure, stifling it would be an evil still.

I have given just a few names of important thinkers in western Europe during the nineteenth century to show the way ideas were developing and to serve as landmarks in the world of thought. But the influence of the people, and the early democrats generally, was more or less confined to the intellectual classes. To some extent it percolated through the intellectuals to the others. Although the direct influence on the masses was slight, the indirect influence of this democratic ideology was great. Even the direct influence in some matters, such as the demand for the vote, was great...

Socialism and Anarchism

I have written about the advance of democracy; it was a hard-fought advance. People who have interests in an existing order do not want change, and resist it with all their might. And yet progress or any betterment means such change; an institution or a method of government has to give place to a better one. Those who desire such progress must necessarily attack the old institution or the old custom, and thus their path leads to constant repudiation of existing conditions and conflict with those who profit by them. The ruling classes in western Europe resisted all advance step by step.

These democratic ideas were, during the first half of the nineteenth century, largely confined to the intellectuals. The common people had been powerfully affected by the growth of industrialism and driven from the land to the factories. An industrial working class was growing, huddled up in ugly insanitary factory towns, usually near the coalfields. These workers were changing rapidly and developing a new mentality. They were very different from the peasants and artisans who had flocked to the factories, urged by starvation. The conditions in the factories were appalling, the workers' houses or huts were even worse. There was great misery among them. Little children and women worked incredibly long hours. And yet all attempts at improving these factories and houses by legislation were stoutly opposed by the owners. Was not this a shameful interference, it was said, with the rights of property? Even the compulsory sanitation of private houses was opposed on this ground.

There arose a man among the factory-owners of Manchester [England] who was a humanitarian and who was pained at the shocking conditions of the workers. This man was Robert Owen. He introduced many reforms in his own factories and improved the condition of his workers. He carried on an agitation among his own class of employers and tried to convert them by argument to a better treatment of labour. Partly because of him, the British Parliament passed the first law to protect the workers against the greed and selfishness of the employers. This was the Factory Act of 1819. This Act laid down that little children of nine should not be made to work more than twelve hours a day.[2]

It was Robert Owen, it is said, who first used the word "socialism" somewhere about 1830. Of course the idea of a levelling up between the rich and the poor, and a more or less equal distribution of property, was not a new one. Many people had advocated it in the past. In the early communities there had even been a kind of communism, the whole community or village holding land and other property in common. This is called primitive communism, and is to be found in many countries, including India. But the new socialism was something much more than a vague desire to equalize people. It was more definit and, to begin with, it was meant to apply to the new factory system of production. It was thus a child of the industrial system. Owen's idea was to have workers' co-operative societies, and that workers should have a share in the factories. He established model factories and settlements in England and America with more or less success. But he failed to convert his brother employers or the government. His influence during his time, however, was great, and he gave currency to a word, socialism, which has since captivated millions.

All this time capitalist industry was growing, and as it recorded success after success, the problem of the working class grew with it. Capitalism resulted in more and more production, and because of this the population grew with enormous speed, as more people could now be supported and fed. Huge businesses were built up with intricate co-operation between their different sections, and at the same time the competition of little businesses was crushed out. Wealth was poured into England, but much of this went to start new factories or railways or other such concerns. The Workers tried to get better conditions by strikes, which usually failed miserably, and then joined the Chartist movement of the forties. This Chartist movement collapsed in the year of revolution, 1848.

The successes of capitalism dazzled people, but still there were some radicals or people with advanced views, or humanitarians, who were not happy at its cut-throat competition and the suffering it caused the workers in spite of the country's growing wealth. In England and Germany and France these people considered various alternatives to it. Several solutions were suggested, and they are all grouped together under the name of socialism or collectivism or social democracy, each of these words vaguely meaning the same thing. There was general agreement among these reformers that the trouble lay in the private ownership and control of industry. If instead of this the State could own and control this, or at any rate the principal means of production, like the land and the chief industries, then there would be no danger of the workers being exploited. So, rather vaguely, people sought an alternative to the capitalist system. But the capitalist system had no intention of collapsing. It was going from strength to strength.

These socialistic ideas were started by intellectuals and, in the case of Robert Owen, by a factory-owner. The workers' trade-union movement developed on different lines for a while, merely seeking higher wages and better conditions. But it was naturally influenced by these ideas, and in its turn it greatly influenced the development of socialism. In each of the three leading industrial countries in Europe – England, France and Germany – socialism developed somewhat differently, in accordance with the strength and character of the working class in each country. On the whole, English socialism was conservative and believed in evolutionary methods and slow progress; Continental socialism was more radical and revolutionary.

In America conditions were different because of the vastness of the country and the demand for labour, and so no strong working-class movement grew up for a long time.

On the Continent of Europe a new creed was finding enthusiastic and ardent support. This was anarchism, a word which seems to terrify many people who know nothing about it. Anarchism meant a society with, as far as possible, no central government and with a great deal of individual freedom. The anarchist ideal was extraordinarily high: "Faith in the ideal of a commonwealth based on altruism, solidarity, and voluntary respect for the other fellow's rights." There was to be no force or compulsion on the part of the State. "That government is best which governs not at all; and when men are prepared for it that will be the kind of government which they will have," said an American, Thoreau.

This seems a very fine ideal-perfect freedom for everybody, each person respecting the other, unselfishness all round, willing co-operation–but the present-day world, with all its selfishness and violence, is far removed from it. The anarchists' desire for no central government or a minimum of government must have arisen as a reaction from the autocracy and despotism under which people had suffered for so long. Governments had crushed them and tyrannized over them, therefore let there be no governments. The anarchists also felt that under some forms of socialism, the State, being master of all the means of production, might itself become despotic. The anarchists were therefore socialists of a kind, laying great stress on local and individual freedom. Many of the socialists, on the other hand, were prepared to agree to the anarchist creed as a distant ideal, but were of opinion that for some time it would be necessary to have a centralized and strong State government under socialism. Thus, although there was a great deal of difference between socialism and anarchism, there were many shades of each, gradually approaching and overlapping each other.

Anarchism, by its very nature, could not be a well-organized movement. Anarchistic ideas therefore had little chance of spreading in industrialized countries where trade unions and the like were growing up. England thus had no appreciable number of anarchists, nor had Germany. But southern and eastern Europe, which were backward in industrialism, were more fertile ground for these ideas. As modern industry spread to the south and east, anarchism became weaker and weaker. To-day it is practically a dead creed, but even now it is represented to some extent in a non-industrialized country like Spain.

Anarchism as an ideal may have been very fine, but it gave shelter not only to excitable and dissatisfied people, but also to selfish individuals who tried to seek profit for themselves under cloak of the ideal. And it led to a type of violence which has now become associated with the word in every one's mind and which has brought much discredit on it. Unable to do anything on a big scale to change society as they wanted, some anarchists decided to do propaganda in a novel way. This was the "propaganda by the deed," the influence of courageous example, brave deeds to resist tyranny and sacrifice one's own life. There were risings in various places. Of course [they] were put down. This foolish violence was obviously a sign of growing weakness and despair. Gradually, anarchism as a movement faded away.

Communism, Dictatorship and Fascism

Benito Mussolini's example of setting himself up as a dictator in Italy seemed to be a catching one in Europe. "There is a vacant throne," he had said, "in every country in Europe waiting for a capable man to fill it." Dictatorships arose in many countries. Among the other countries besides Italy and Spain that gave up the democratic forms of government and established dictatorships were: Poland, Yugoslavia, Greece, Bulgaria, Portugal, Hungary, and Austria. In Poland Pilsudski, the old socialist of Tsarist days, was the Dictator, owing to his control of the army, and he was in the habit of using the most amazingly offensive language to the legislators of the Polish Parliament, and sometimes indeed they were arrested and bundled away. In Yugoslavia, the King Alexander, is himself the Dictator. It is stated that in some parts of the country conditions became worse, and there was more oppression than there ever was even when the Turks governed them.[3]

All the countries I have mentioned above have not been continuously under open dictatorships. Sometimes their parliaments wake up for a while and are allowed to function; sometimes, as recently happened in Bulgaria, the government in power arrests any group of deputies it does not like, such as the communists, and removes them forcibly from the Parliament, leaving the others to carry on as best they can. Always they live either under dictatorship or on the verge of it, and such governments of individuals or small groups, resting on force, must find support in continuing repression, murders and imprisonments of opponents, a strict censorship, and a widespread system of spies.

Dictatorships sprang up outside Europe also. [In Turkey there was] Kemal Pasha. In South America there were many dictators, but they are an old institution there, for the South American republics have never taken kindly to the processes of democracy.

I have not included the Soviet Union in the above list of dictatorships, because the dictatorship there, although as ruthless as any other, is of a different type. It is not the dictatorship of an individual or a small group, but of a well-organized political party basing itself especially on the workers. They call it the "dictatorship of the proletariat." Thus we have three kinds, of dictatorships--the communist type, the fascist, and the military. There is nothing peculiar about the military one; it has existed from the earliest days. The communist and fascist types are new in history, and are the special products of our own times.

The first thing that strikes one is that all these dictatorships and their variations are the direct opposite of democracy and the parliamentary form of government. You will remember that the nineteenth century was the century of democracy, the century when the Rights of Man of the French Revolution governed advanced thought, and individual freedom was the aim. Out of this developed the parliamentary form of government, in varying degrees, in most countries of Europe. The twentieth century, or rather the post-War years, put an end to this great tradition of the nineteenth century. And with this fall of democracy the so-called liberal groups everywhere suffered a like fate.

Why has this happened? Why did democracy, which was for a century or more the ideal and inspiration of countless people, and which counted its martyrs by the thousand, why did it fall into disfavour? Such changes do not happen without sufficient reason; they are not just due to the whims and fancies of a fickle public.

I have referred to democracy as "formal." The communists said that it was not real democracy; it was only a democratic shell to hide the fact that one class ruled over, the others. According to them, democracy covered the dictatorship of the capitalist class. It was plutocracy, government by the wealthy. The much-paraded vote given to the masses gave them only the choice of saying once, in four or five years, whether a certain person, X, might rule over them and exploit them or another person, Y, should do so. In either event the masses were to be exploited by the ruling class. Real democracy could only come when this class rule and exploitation end and only one class exists. To bring about this socialist State, however, a period of the dictatorship of the proletariat was necessary so as to keep down all capitalist elements in the population and prevent them from intriguing against the workers' State. In Russia this dictatorship was exercised by the Soviets in which all the workers and peasants and other "active" elements were represented. Thus it became a dictatorship of the 90 per cent or even 95 per cent over the remaining 10 or 5 per cent. That is the theory. In practice the Communist Party controls the Soviets and the ruling clique of communists control the Party. And the dictatorship is as strict, so far as censorship and freedom of thought or action are concerned, as any other. But as it is based on the good will of the workers it must carry the workers with it. And, finally, there is no exploitation of the workers or any other class for the benefit of another. There is no exploiting class left. If there is any exploitation, it is done by the State for the benefit of all. Russia, it is worth remembering, never had the democratic form of government. It jumped in 1917 from autocracy to communism.

The fascist attitude was entirely different. [The Fascists] did not seem to possess any fixed principles. But they were opposed to democracy, and their opposition was not on the communist ground that democracy was not the real article but a sham. Fascists objected to the whole principle underlying the democratic idea. Mussolini called it a "putrefying corpse!" The idea of individual liberty was equally disliked by the fascists, the State was everything, the individual nothing. (Communists also do not attach much value to individual liberties.) What would poor Mazzini, the prophet of nineteenth century-democratic liberalism, have said to his fellow-countryman Mussolini!

Not only communists and fascists, but many others became dissatisfied with the old idea of giving a vote and calling it a democracy. Democracy means equality, and can only flourish in an equal society. It was obvious enough that the giving of votes to everybody did not result in producing an equal society. In spite of adult suffrage and the like, there was tremendous inequality. Therefore, in order to give democracy a chance, an equal society must be created, and this reasoning led [the critics of democracy to propose] various other ideals and methods.

Let us look a little more deeply into fascism. It gloried in violence and hated pacifism. Mussolini wrote in the *Encyclopedia Italiana:*

> Fascism does not believe in the necessity or utility of perpetual peace. Therefore it repudiates pacifism, which conceals a refusal to struggle and an essential cowardice-in face of sacrifice. War, and war only, raises human energies to the maximum of tension and seals with its nobility the peoples who have the courage to accept it. All other trials are substitutes; they do not place the individual before the choice of life and death.

Fascism was intensely nationalistic, while communism was international. Fascism opposed internationalism. It made of the State a god on whose altar individual freedom and rights must be sacrificed; all other countries were alien and almost like enemies. In spite of certain anti-capitalist slogans and a revolutionary technique, fascism was allied with property-owning and reactionary elements.

These were some odd aspects of fascism. The philosophy underlying it, if it has any, is difficult to grasp. It began, as we have seen, with the simple desire for power. When success came, an attempt was made to build up a philosophy round it. Giovanni Gentile was considered the official philosopher of fascism; he was also a fascist minister in the government. Gentile said that people should not seek self-realization through their personality or individual selves, as in democracy, but, according to fascism, through the acts of the transcendental ego as the world's self-consciousness (whatever this may mean – it is wholly beyond me). Thus in this view there was no room for individual liberty and personality, for the true reality and freedom of the individual was that which he gained by losing himself in something else – the State.

> My personality is not suppressed, but uplifted, strengthened, enlarged by being merged and restored in that of the family, the state, the spirit.

Again Gentile said:

> Every force is moral force in so far as capable of influencing the will, whatever be the argument applied, the sermon or the cudgel.

All these were subsequent attempts to justify or explain a thing that happened. It was also said that fascism aimed at a "Corporative State," in which I suppose everybody pulled together for the common good. But no such State has so far appeared in Italy or elsewhere. Capitalism functioned in Italy more or less in the same way as in other capitalist countries, though some restrictions have been introduced.

As fascism spread in other countries, it became clear that it was not a peculiar Italian phenomenon. Whenever the workers became powerful and threatened the capitalistic State, the capitalist class naturally tried to save itself. If the owning and ruling class could not put down the workers in the ordinary democratic way by using the police and army, it adopted the fascist method. This consisted in creating a popular mass movement, with some slogans which appealed to the crowd. The backbone for this movement came from the lower-middle class, suffering from unemployment, and many of the politically backward and unorganized workers and peasants were also attracted to it by the slogans and hopes of bettering their position. Such a movement was financially helped by the big bourgeoisie who hoped to profit by it, and although it made violence a creed and a daily practice, the capitalist government of the country tolerated it to a large extent because it fought the common enemy socialist labour.

Fascism thus appeared when the class conflicts between an advancing socialism and an entrenched capitalism became bitter and critical. The owning class had no intention of giving up what it had, and so the conflict became intense. So long as capitalism could use the machinery of democratic institutions to hold power and keep down labour, democracy was allowed to flourish. When this was not possible, then capitalism discarded democracy and adopted the open fascist method of violence and terror.

Nationalism vs Internationalism

Nationalism by itself, unconnected with some wider concept, is a narrow creed. It is also obvious that without nationalism we are rootless. We just have no deep roots anywhere. On the other hand internationalism is not only good but essential in the world today. And yet some kind of vague internationalism without definite contacts and bonds with nationalism, is almost an airy nothing. How to combine the two? What are the essential features of the two? And what are the conflicts between the two? Apparently there are, though possibly in reality, there are not. You know in the past many years internationalism has grown as life's activities have tended that way with the increase not only of rapid communication, but with the growth of almost everything that we see around us today.

So people think that nationalism is something fading off and giving place to internationalism. We see internationalism in many aspects, even in the activities of what I might call proletarian elements of the world. On the other side of the scale we see internationalism developing perhaps more concretely, though with less shouts, in the realm of finance, trade and commerce and cartels, and in between we see this internationalism in the development of science, in the new commerce of ideas, in so many ordinary things which meet us at every turn of the road, the radio, cinema, etc.

People think that internationalism is obviously the thing of the future, and nationalism must fade away. And there is a great deal of truth, I suppose, in this and yet whenever a country or the world faces a crisis, nationalism becomes immediately dominant. We have had a very big crisis during the last five or six years of the world war. One of the lessons of this crisis is how, when deeply stirred, the people turn to nationalism immediately. Every country that was involved in this war became tremendously nationalistic. It forgot its internationalism. Even in cases of countries with proletarian bias, which thought and resolved in terms of internationalism and workers of the world holding together against other elements oppressing them, nationalism is intensely a dominant passion.

In spite of this development of internationalism all over the world, which is an inevitable development influencing human life, man's mind continues to function to a very large extent, especially in times of crisis, on a nationalistic basis. So, I suppose, one of the problems of today and tomorrow is how to fit in these two conception-nationalism and internationalism. Nationalism obviously is something deep down in human nature. We cannot uproot it and there is no reason why we should try to uproot it, because nationalism ultimately depends on all that is best in us.[4]

Evolution from Capitalism

Much can be said about socialism, but I should like to stress one thing. The whole of the capitalist structure is based on some kind of an acquisitive society. It may be that, to some extent, the tendency to acquisitiveness is inherent in us. A socialist society must try to get rid of this tendency to acquisitiveness and replace it by co-operation. You cannot bring about this change by a sudden law. There have to be long processes of training the people; without this you cannot wholly succeed. Even from the very limited point of view of changing your economic structure, apart from your minds and hearts, it takes time to build a socialist society. The countries that have gone fastest have also taken time. I would like you to consider that the Soviet Union, which has gone fast in industrialization, has taken thirty-five years or more over it. Chairman Mao of the People's Republic of China – which is more or less a communist state-said, that it would take China twenty years to achieve some kind of socialism. Mind you, this in spite of the fact that theirs is an authoritarian state, and the people are exeedingly disciplined and industrious. Chairman Mao was speaking as a practical idealist.

Capitalism in India

There has been, there often is, a kind of argument against capital, against labour, and much is said about what the capitalists do or do not do. I should like this House to consider this question apart from the personal equation that capitalists are good and capitalists are bad. As a matter of fact, the state of India is such today that capitalism is very immature here; it has not developed as in the other countries of the world. But the point is that our capitalists are the product of our history of our economic system and the rest of it. They are not to blame. You change your system, if you like, gradually or rapidly. It is no good blaming them. But I will say this, that our capitalists, good and bad-and many of them I have no doubt are very patriotic-do lack what I call a social outlook.[5]

Welfare State

Our national aim is a Welfare State and a socialist economy. Neither of these can be attained without considerable increase in national income and neither is possible without a much greater volume of goods and services and full employment. In order to attain this Welfare State of a socialist pattern, it is not enough to pass a resolution or even law or to limit our thinking to nationalisation of existing industries. We have to increase production and aim at an economy of plenty. We have to see that there is equitable distribution and that the privileged position of individuals and groups is not favoured.

Everything, therefore, that leads, to fuller production and fuller employment is to be encouraged, provided it does not take us away from the ultimate objective of a socialist pattern of society. If we cannot have fuller production and fuller employment, then there will be neither welfare nor socialism, even though we might nationalise some industries or pass brave laws and decrees. If we aim at mass production, this is only possible if this production is for the masses and the masses have the purchasing power to consume it. We have to introduce a certain dynamism in every sector of our economic and national life in order to achieve this goal. The test must always be the results to be achieved and not some theoretical formula.[6]

This test should be applied to the argument that has been going on as to the relative importance of the public or state sector and the private sector or non-state and voluntary enterprise. It is obvious that, in a socialised economy,there will be social control of the means of production and distribution. It is equally obvious that in any planned approach to a socialised economy the public sector must grow and become the dominant feature of the landscape. But, in our present state, to limit resources to the public sector means restriction of our opportunities of production and growth. The main purpose of a socialised pattern of society is to remove the fetters to production and distribution. If, however, we adopt a policy, in the name of socialism, which actually maintains some fetters or encourages them, then we are moving away from our objective and preventing the growth of full dynamism. It becomes necessary, therefore, to have a private sector also and to give it full play within its field, provided always that it is coordinated with our planned approach. Many of us, because of past fears or comparisons with some other countries, are afraid of a private sector functioning. There need be no such fear if we are vigilant and keep our objective in view. Planning will necessarily have strategic controls and, as I have said, the public sector will inevitably grow, more especially in the basic industries. But there is a wide field which the public sector cannot touch for a considerable time and growth in that field will therefore, have to be left to public enterprise. In the present state of our development, there is, or should be, an integral and essential relationship between the public sector and the field of private enterprise. This does not at all mean our accepting the out-of-date and discredited policy of laissez-faire as that is opposed to the very conception of planning. In present circumstances, the public sector itself will fail to function adequately if it is not helped by private enterprise in many ways, chiefly in the consumption of power and the products of heavy, medium and light industries. We shall require a network of well-spread out industries of all levels and types. It will, of course, always be open to the state to enter into any field for economic or social reasons, but in no event will it be in a position for a long time to come to cover the entire field of the nation's economy. As a matter of fact, land, which is the biggest industry of all in India, will remain essentially in the private sector. Small-scale and cottage industries will also remain largely in the private sector, though it is highly desirable to organise them on a cooperative basis. So also most of the lighter industries. It may be advantageous to allow some heavier industries to be organised by private enterprise, if the state is not prepared to assume that burden.

If this is so, then we must adopt a healthy attitude towards the private sector, keeping always in view the main objective of achieving a socialist pattern and preventing the growth of any tendency which might come in our way later. The existence of state enterprise side by side with private enterprise may also prove healthy in the present circumstances as providing some kind of a competition between the two. We have to remember always that within the large framework that we lay down, the test always is fuller production and fuller employment.

We are, I believe, on the eve of a great expansion in our industry. This will require a straining of all our resources to the utmost and we cannot afford to waste any. The financial aspect is important, but far more important is the training of personnel for the industrial revolution which is coming our way. The danger is that we may have to slacken our pace for lack of trained personnel. We have manpower enough and sometimes manpower can take the place even of capital. But, without trained manpower, we cannot go far. We have, therefore, in our planning, to think ahead and train an adequate number of persons for all branches of national activity.

However vast we may develop our big industries, it is inevitable that great emphasis should be laid on the widespread development of small-scale and cottage industries. The Congress has always stood for cottage industries. Today the need for their growth is even more important as in no other way can we absorb the unemployed and add substantially to our production. I see no basic conflict between big industry and cottage industry provided our approach is a balanced and planned one.

May I say that a welfare state and a socialistic pattern of economy are not synonymous expressions? It is true that a socialistic economy must provide for a welfare state but it does not necessarily follow that a welfare state must also be based on a socialistic pattern of society. Therefore the two, although they overlap, are yet somewhat different, and we say that we want both. We cannot have a welfare state in India with all the socialism or even communism in the world unless our national income goes up greatly. Socialism or communism might help you to divide your existing wealth, if you like, but in India, there is no existing wealth for you to divide; there is only poverty to divide. It is not a question of distributing the wealth of the few rich men here and there. That is not going to make any difference in our national income. We might adopt that course for the psychological good that might come out of it. But from the practical point of view, there is not much to divide in India because we are a poor country. We must produce wealth, and then divide it equitably. How can we have a welfare state without wealth? Wealth need not mean gold and silver but wealth in goods and services. Our economic policy must therefore aim at plenty. Until very recently economic policies have often been based on scarcity. But the economics of scarcity has no meaning in the world of today.

REFERENCES

1. Glimpses of World History, 1939.
2. Nehru, J.L. on World History.
3. Nehre, J.L., Glimpse of World History, 1939.
4. A Convocation Address at the Visva-Bharati University, Santiniketan, December, 23, 1945.
5. Lok Sabha speech 3 Feb. 1950.
6. Extract from the Report presented at the 60th Session of the Indian National Congress *Avadi,*, January, 21-23 1955.

DEMOCRATIC IDEALS

1. The Chosen Path:

Individual and Social Quality of Life;

Demands of Parliamentary Democracy;

Rights and Duties;

Ordered Liberty;

Self-Discipline;

Peaceful Methods;

Change and Continuity;

Wider Concept

2. Combining Democracy with Socialism

3. Coping with Work

4. Civic Bodies;

The Acid Country Planning;

The Grassroots Level

5. Institutions Reflects People

FOUR

DEMOCRATIC IDEALS

The Chosen Path

We choose this system of parliamentary democracy deliberately; we choose it not only because, to some extent, we had always thought on those lines previously, but because we thought it was in keeping with our own old traditions also; naturally, the old traditions, not as they were, but adjusted to the new conditions and new surroundings. We choose it also–let us give credit where credit is due–because we approved of its functioning in other countries, more especially the United Kingdom.[1]

Individual and Social Quality of life

We have definitely accepted the democratic process. Why have we accepted it? Well, for a variety of reasons. Because we think that in the final analysis it promoted the growth of human beings and of society; because, as we have said in our Constitution, we attach great value to individual freedom; because we want the creative and the adventurous spirit of man to grow.[2]

Democracy . . . is a means to an end. What is the end we aim at? I do not know if everybody will agree with me, but I would say the end is the good life for the individual. What form it should take can be argued about but the good life certainly must imply a certain satisfaction of the essential economic needs, which will release him from continuous oppression, and which will give him a chance to develop his creative faculties.[3]

In the past, democracy has been taken chiefly to mean political democracy, roughly represented by the idea of every person having a vote. It is obvious that a vote by itself does not mean very much to a person who is down and out and starving. Such a person will be much more interested in food to eat than in a vote. Therefore, political democracy by itself is not enough except that it may be used to obtain a gradually increasing measure of economic democracy. The good things of life must become available to more and more people and gross inequalities must be removed.[4]

Demands of Parliamentary Democracy

Now, parliamentary democracy demands many things, demands of course, ability. It demands a certain devotion to work as every work does. But it demands also a large measure of co-operation, of self-discipline, of restraint. It is obvious that a House like this cannot perform any functions without the spirit of cooperation, without a large measure of restraint and self-discipline in each Member and in each group. Parliamentary democracy is not something which can be transplanted in a country by some wand or by some quick process. We talk about it but we know very well that there are not many countries in the world where it functions successfully. I think it may be said without any partiality that it has functioned with a very large measure of success in this country. Why? . . . I do think, because of the background in our country, and because our people have the spirit of democracy in them.[5]

Rights and Duties

We live in an age of democracy, and India is committed to the democratic ideal. For the first time in history we were brave and courageous enough to give the vote to the dwellers in the jungle, even as to the dwellers in the cities. We did not deny the vote to any person in India. We did not attach any property qualification or education tests. We treated every one as a human being, with a right to say what his Government should be. So we put our faith in democracy to the fullest extent. And democracy only flourishes, as freedom flourishes, when the responsibilities of freedom are understood and carried out. If the responsibilities are not understood and carried out, then freedom itself tends to slip away. There is no right without a corresponding responsibility and obligation. We claim rights, but we forget the obligations that accompany the rights and such rights will not be a blessing to us, and may even be a cures.[6]

Ordered Liberty

I should like this country to develop the democratic process and grow on democracy and of liberty. And those words are dear to us because most of our lives we have fought for freedom and liberty; and yet when you talk of democracy it means some kind of ordered liberty because a disordered liberty is not democracy, and it leads ultimately to the suppression of that liberty. We have seen–those of us who are acquainted with recent history–how too much talk of liberty has led to licence and has led to suppression of liberty. The history of Europe will show that; the history of other countries too. So let us not be too sure of the liberty and freedom we possess. Let us cling to them and guard them jealously. But we will not guard them or preserve them by loose talk or loose action. Only by stern discipline and sternly understanding the limitations of freedom can we preserve them, for everything has its limitations, even freedom and even liberty. Without those limitations we endanger the very thing we stand for.[7]

Self Discipline

We believe in democracy. Speaking for myself, I believe in it, first of all, because I think it is the right means to achieve ends and because it is a peaceful method. Secondly because it removes the pressures which other forms of Government may impose on the individual. It transforms the discipline which imposed is by authority largely to self-discipline. Self-discipline means that even people who do not agree–the minority–accept solutions because it is better to accept them and then change them, if necessary, by peaceful methods. Therefore, democracy means to me an attempt at the solution of problems by peaceful methods. If it is not peaceful, then to my mind, it is not democracy. If I may further elaborate the second reason, democracy gives the individual an opportunity to develop. Such opportunity does not mean anarchy, where every individual does what he likes. A social organization must have some discipline to hold it together. This can either be imposed from outside or be in the nature of self-discipline. Imposition from outside may take the form of one country governing another or of an autocratic or authoritarian form of government. In a proper democracy, discipline is self-imposed. There is no democracy if there is no discipline.[8]

Peaceful Methods

Parliamentary democracy involves naturally peaceful methods of action, peaceful acceptance of decisions taken and attempts to change them through peaceful ways again; it is not parliamentary democracy otherwise. It is essential that we, who talk and who believe in the quest of peace so much, should remember that the quest of peace and the quest of democracy can only be made through methods of peace and not through methods of peace and not through any other. We have a great united country, a country which is dear to us, and of which we are proud. But being proud of it does not mean that we should close our eyes to the grave problems we often have to face in the country and the disruptive tendencies that raise their heads and challenge the democratic process which this Parliament represents ...

We prize the parliamentary form of government because it is a peaceful method of dealing with problems. It is a method of argument, discussion and decision, and of accepting that decision, even though one may not agree with it. However, the minority in a parliamentary government has a very important part to play. Naturally, the majority, by the mere fact that it is a majority, must have its way. But a majority which ignores the minority is not working in the true spirit of parliamentary democracy.

In a period of dynamic change, the institution of parliament has to function with speed. Does the parliamentary form of government enable a country to move with speed when a speed becomes essentials? Take an emergency like war. When a war occurs, parliaments continue to function but with certain limitations because of the emergency. A great deal depends on the conditions of the times, on the environment and on the problems which a country has to face.

Change and Continuity

This system of parliamentary democracy embodies, I think, these principles of change and continuity, both. And it is up to those who function in this system, Parliament, Members of the House and the numerous others who are part of this system to increase the pace of change, to make it as fast as they like, subject to the principle of continuity, because the moment that continuity is broken we become rootless and the system of parliamentary democracy breaks down. Parliamentary democracy is a delicate plant and it is a measure of our own success that this plant has become sturdier during these last few years.

Wider Concept

Parliamentary government is a democratic conception. It means the gradual widening of the franchise till it becomes adult franchise. It is only in very recent times that any country has had adult franchise. The effects of adult franchise are being felt in full only now. This political change having fully established itself, it has become obvious that a political change by itself is not enough.

From political democracy we advance to the concept of economic democracy. First of all, that means working for a certain measure of well-being for all, call it Welfare State. Secondly, it means working for a certain measure of equality of opportunity in the economic sphere. Every country, whether it is communist, non-communist or anti-communist, is going that way.

We can hardly have a political democracy without mass education. In other countries full-blooded political democracy came after education had spread a good deal as a result of the economic revolution which had prepared the ground for it. But in most Asian countries certainly in India, we have taken a huge jump to hundred per cent political democracy without the wherewithal to supply the demands which a politically conscious electorate makes. That is the essence of the problem in all the Asian countries. All our political life is really concerned with how rapidly we can bridge this hiatus between desires and their fulfilment.[9]

Combining Democracy with Socialism

We have definitely accepted the democratic process. Why have we accepted it? Well, for a variety of reasons. Because we think that in the final analysis it promotes the growth of human beings and of society; because, as we have said in our constitution, we attach great value to individual freedom; because we want the creative and the adventurous spirit of man to grow. It is not enough for us merely to produce the material goods of the world. We do want high standards of living, but not at the cost of the man's creative spirit, his creative energy, his spirit of adventure; not at the cost of all those fine things of life which have ennobled man throughout the ages. Democracy is not merely a question of elections. The question before us is how to combine democracy with socialism, through peaceful and legitimate methods.[10]

I look upon socialism as a growing, dynamic conception, as something which is not rigid, as something which must fit in with the changing conditions of human life and activity in every country. I believe that socialism can be of many varieties. Socialism in a highly developed industrial community may be of one type. I do not see why we should try to imitate another country, although we should take advantage of the experience gained elsewhere. If I wish to industrialize my country, I have to learn not only higher techniques of industrialization from the countries where such techniques have been adopted and are flourishing, but many other things, such as the way they industrialized. It would sometimes be useful to copy what other countries have done; sometimes it would be useful to avoid it. I do not see why I should be asked to define socialism in precise, rigid terms. What I want is that all individuals in India should have equal opportunities of growth, from birth upwards, and equal opportunities for work according to their capacity.

We must realize that the process of bringing socialism to India, especially in the way we are doing it, that it, the democratic way, will inevitably take time.

Coping with Work

The problems of government have grown so enormously that sometimes one begins to doubt whether the normal parliamentary procedures are adequate to deal with them. I remember reading discussions about the growing difficulty in the British Parliament thirty years ago. They were not finding time to deal with these problems in detail and suggestions had been made from time to time for powers to be transferred to large committees of Parliament which could deal with legislation in detail and finalize it once the principle had been laid down by Parliament. That is one way of getting over the difficulty, but I do not know whether any satisfactory solution has been found.

Parliaments now-a-days have to work much harder than they used to. Members of Parliament get a vast number of papers to study which they can hardly read. They have to sit late hours to grapple with the problems. If the average Member has to carry this great burden of printed paper and sit late hours, with select committee and all kinds of other committees functioning, you can very well imagine what the poor members of the government have to carry. In addition to the papers given to private Members, they have to carry the burden of decisions and many other loads which are part of the day-to-day government of the country not coming up before Parliament. The business of Government and the business of Parliament become more and more complicated and it becomes a little doubtful how far parliamentary democracy can carry on its work and solve such problems. Some kind of a division of authority may become necessary; otherwise problems might remain unsolved, unsolved problems are dangerous . . . . How far can parliamentary democracy be adapted to meet these new burdens and functions of government satisfactoril, effectively and in time? Time is the overriding consideration and that is why the question has arisen whether democracy which ensures that these problems can be dealt with rapidly and effectively.

Civil Bodies

The Acid Test

. . . . I go to a great city and find great palatial buildings there, I always form my opinion of the city not from the palaces, but I form my opinion of the city from from things that are happening behind these palaces–the mud-huts in which are living thousands of people, living in misery and unhappiness, missing education, sanitation, hygiene, cultural development, parks, libraries and so many other things for which the municipality is set up and so many other things. This is undoubtedly the look-out of the municipality. An efficient municipality is also ultimately responsible for their maintenance and if there is no work for the people to do, it is its duty to provide them with employment.

A poor man, a starving man, is a disgrace to a municipality. It is not good for the municipality to say that we have no money to do this or to do that. I think it is the essential function of a municipality to see that there is no unemployment. If you cannot fulfil this function, it must be understood that something is wrong either in the municipality or in the social structure under which it functions.[11]

I have been going up and down several times a day the long artery of traffic which leads from here to Raj Bhawan, and it is a very fine and attractive road with attractive buildings. Every time I pass, large number of people line up and very considerable number of them are little children, attractive cheerful as they ought to be. It seems to me that the first duty of the Corporation must be to these children–almost everything else would come after that–and to see that they are properly fed, housed, clothed and schooled. I should like to think of the day when every child in India will have good schooling and also a square meal or if not a square meal at least a cup of good fresh milk, as they have given by such bodies in some countries of the west. Perhaps we may not be able to do that yet for lack of resources; but I think it would make a tremendous difference if we could gradually bring that about, beginning with the cities and later taking it to out rural school also.[12]

Town and Country Planning

In the India of today, the growth of cities, big and small ones, is quite anarchic. It is ugly, it is horrible, in fact it is painful to see it. I am surprised how it is tolerated by great corporations and city municipalities. The same thing applies, in a smaller sense, to the small towns and the larger villages, etc. You go to any of the these big cities, even the good ones. You find their outskirts growing as if there were nobody to govern it. The corporation is busy dealing with the heart of the town, and not with what happens on its outskirts. No road should be built in the edge of a town which is not wide enough to contain all the traffic in the next 50, 60, 100 years, if you like. Sufficient room should be left for a widening of the road on either side. Nobody should be allowed to build there.[13]

This is a very minor instance that I have placed before you. Town planning is becoming more and more important in India, not only planning of great cities like Delhi or Calcutta, which is very important, but smaller cities and smaller towns. Planning now means not only producing something more livable but possibly doing away with many of the difficulties and dangers that may come later. You must think of that. You must build for the future. Build for the present, by all means, but build also for the future with schools and hospitals and playgrounds, markets and roads. All these things do not cost much except a little extra labour and thought. I am afraid the habit of thought is not particularly obvious among our Municipal Councillors. They are so busy with their day-to-day difficulties that they seldom think of the future. Planning means thinking of the future, and I think it is very important that in your conference you should give thought to the future. You have to think of what you want your towns and villages to be like, so that gradually you may approach the ideal. You cannot accomplish it quickly.

The Delhi Master Plan has taken us about six or seven years to prepare, even with some of the most competent men that we could obtain. They worked hard for the planning of Delhi and they have produced a plan. Naturally, they cannot write on a plain surface. They have to accept Delhi city as it is and then plan for its future. That limits one's efforts but they have produced a plan which I think is a good plan and they expect it to be given effect to in the course of the next 15 or 20 years. We must work to that end as far as we can and gradually it will take shape. Of course, you can make changes in between, when you want. Whatever the Corporation and the Municipality do must fit into that plan.

I would suggest some things which you must concentrate upon at all costs. Water supply is very important. Water supply for villages its even more important than for the towns and important cities. It is astonishing that there are still areas in India where good water is not available and men and women specially have to go long distances to fetch a little water. Good water and clean surroundings will probably do more for the health of the country than all the medicines and other things that you may import or manufacture here. So I would suggest your making a special effort to ensure such things.

Houses suitable for the villages should be so designed that they can be built with local material. This will not be difficult, and it is being done in some places . . . . Oddly enough, we see the lack of civilized living at both ends of the social scale. The very poor–it is obvious enough. The very rich–it is also equally obvious. Flaunting their wealth in front of other people's poverty is vulgar, it is not a civilized thing. Both these have to be improved, and conditions created in which neither of these things is tolerated, but everyone has a chance according to his quality, according to the work he does, according to what he contributers to the community.

Good life is more important possibly than what all Assemblies and Parliaments do. Planning of towns and countryside is equally important to make them good look at, to make them yield as much as they can and, consequently, to these subjects which you will consider are of basic importance for the growth of country. I hope you will look at them from this larger point of view and lay down, as far as possible, objectives which you can achieve year by year, and not make vague, pious declarations of your wishes. Declarations are good provided they are tied up with the actual things. Let it be a definite goal that there should be no village in India where water is not available and housing does not progress rapidly.

The Grassroots Level

. . . . We have the Panchayati Raj. The concept behind Panchayati Raj has attracted us and we have given it the utmost importance because the test of success in India is not the construction of few buildings but how human being grow. The whole object behind the Community Development Movement and the Panchayati Raj is to create opportunities for human beings to grow, to be able to think, to be able to act, to be able to co-operate with each other and act together.

—

We say that out aim is a socialist pattern of society. That is no doubt our aim, and that is the only aim which ultimately any civilized society must have. It is not a dogmatic socialism but something which affects the whole community, helps all the people in the country to raise their level on living and reduces the big differences that may exist. Today there is, in India, a certain vulgarity about the difference in people's standards; there are the very well-to-do and the very poor. It is inherent in the circumstances. You cannot get rid of that by simply cutting off the heads of the tall people. You want people to grow, you do not want to shorten all of them.

Municipalities, by and large, are not shining examples of efficiency in doing any kind of good work. A very dangerous situation confronts us now when we have also the Panchayati Raj and new Councils and Parishads have been elected. Are they also going down the drain like our third-rate municipalities? It would be a terrible thing if that were to happen. We have to pull them up and make them set an example to the people. I am quite sure that if the Panchayati Raj institutions flourish properly, everything else, including the top institutions, all your State Assemblies and your Parliament, will function rightly. They are the base, and if the base is strong, the upper structure will largely be conditioned by it. But if the base itself is not good, then we do not make much progress. Ultimately, the improvement of that base will come about through education. Fortunately, education is spreading–not perhaps of an ideal type– but still it is some manner of education and it is doing a lot of good. It is bringing discipline, some knowledge, some habits, and if we pay more attention to the schools, it will give a strong basis for the new community that is growing up.

In our Local Self-Government we see the grass roots of community life. I would wish that all our legislators who come up to Assemblies and Parliament are made to serve for some time in this type of Local Self-Government before they are allowed to stand for higher bodies. That would give them knowledge and experience, and in every way it will give them good training. Whichever way we look at things, the importance of this foundation is very great, whether it is in the rural or in the urban areas . . . .[14]

Institutions Reflect People

All our institutions, including the parliamentary institutions, are ultimately the projections of a people's character, thinking and aims. They are strong and lasting in the measure that they are in accordance with the people's character and thinking. Otherwise, they tend to break up.

You have been the leaders of the youth movement in India and you have built up a strong and living organism. But remember that organisations and institutions are passive instruments of man. They become living and vital only when they are pushed onward by the strength of great ideas. Have great ideals before you and do not lower them by ignoble compromise. Look deep down to where the millions toil in field and factory and look across the frontiers of India to where others like you are facing problems similar to yours. Be national, the sons and daughters of your ancient motherland working for her liberation; and be international, members of the Republic of Youth, which knows no boundaries or frontiers or nationalities and work for the liberation of the world from all thraldom and injustice. "To do great things", said a Frenchman many years ago, "a man must live as if he had never to die'. None of us can evade death, but youth at least does not think of it. Old men work for the span of years that still remains for them, the young work for eternity.[15]

REFERENCES

1. Speaking by way of valedictory references at the conclusion of the term of the First Lok Sabha (1952-57).
2. Speaking at the All India Congress Committee, Indore, January 4, 1957.
3. Speaking at a Seminar on Parliamentary Democracy, Feb. 25, 1956.
4. Speaking at a Seminar on Parliamentary Democracy, Feb. 25, 1956.
5. Speaking at a Seminar on Parliamentary Democracy,Feb. 25, 1956.
6. Speaking at a reception at Pondicherry, January 16, 1955.
7. Speaking on the Constitution (First Amendment) Bill, 1951.
8. Speaking at a Seminar on Parliamentary Democracy, Feb. 25, 1956.
9. Inaugurating a Seminar on Parliamentary Democracy of New Delhi on December 6,1957.
10. A Speech at the AICC Session Indore, January 4, 1957.
11. An Address at the Calcutta Corporation, November 9, 1936.
12. Speaking at Madras, October 11, 1952.
13. Speech at the Ninth meeting of the Central Council of Local self-Government, New Delhi, September 6, 1963.
14. Government, New Delhi, September 6, 1963.
15. Speaking at a Seminar on Parliamentary Democracy, Feb.25, 1956.

NATIONAL RECONSTRUCTION

1. Planning in India:

Essence of Planning;

Indian Genius Strategy of Planning;

Watege of Planning

A Continuous Process;

Perspective Planning;

Social Objectives;

Popular Support

2. Setting the Sights

3. Economic and Social Justice

4. Nationalisation

5. Private and Public Enterprise

6. Cooperative Movement

7. Cooperative Development Programme

8. Community Development Programme

9. The Land and the Tiller:

Agrarian Reform

Agricultu al Production

10. Defence Underpinning

FIVE

NATIONAL RECONSTRUCTION

Planning in India

Essence of Planning

The essence of planning is to find the best way to utilize our resources of man power, of money and so on, we want to arrive at a stage when we can assess accurately what the next stage is going to be, visualise our problems in advance and take appropriate action before events force our hands. That is after all the object of planning..... There is no other way but planning for an under-developed economy like ours.

Indian Genius

Some people charged the Government for coming under the influence of communist planning while others had charged them with coming under the influence of somebody else. The real point was that an attempt was being made to evolve an approach, consistent with India's own thinking, while profiting by other's thinking and experience.

Watege of Planning

We talk about planning. As you all know, planning is essential and without it there would be anarchy in our economic development. The conception of planning today is not to think of the money we have and then to divide it up in the various schemes but to measure the physical needs, that is to say, how much of food the people want, how much of clothes they want, how much of housing they want, how much of education they want, how much of health services they want, how much of work and employment they want, and so on. We calculate all these and then decide what everyone in India should have of these things. Once we do that, we can set about increasing production and fulfilling these needs. It is not a simple matter because in calculating the needs of the people, we have to calculate on the basis not only of an increasing population but of increasing needs. I shall give you an instance. Let us take sugar. Our people now consume much more sugar than they used to, with the result that our calculations about sugar production went wrong. Now, why do they eat more sugar? Evidently because they are better off. If a man getting a hundred rupees finds his income increased to a hundred and fifty, he will eat more sugar, buy more cloth, and so on. Therefore, in making calculations, we have to keep in mind that the extra money that goes into circulation because of the higher salaries and wages, affects consumption. So we find out what in five years' time will be the needs of our people, including even items needed by our Defence Services. Then we decide how to produce those things in India. In order to meet a particular variety of needs we have now to put up a factory which will produce the goods that we need five years hence. Thus, planning is a much more complicated process than merely drawing up some schemes and fixing a system of priorities.

Behind all this is another factor – finance. Finance is important but not so important as people think. What is really important is drawing up the physical needs of the people and then working to produce things which will fulfil such needs. If you are producing wealth, it does not matter very much if you have some deficit financing because you are actually putting money back through goods and services. Therefore it does not matter how you manipulate your currency so long as your production is also keeping pace with it. Of course there is the fear of inflation. We must avoid it. But there is no such fear at present in India. On the other hand, there is deflation. Nevertheless, we have to guard against inflation. We have to produce the equivalent of the money pumped in. Sometimes there is a gap between investment and production, when inflation sets in. For example, let us say we put in a hundred crores of rupees in a river valley scheme which takes seven or eight years to build. During the years it is being built we get nothing out of it but expenditure. This can be balanced in cottage industries, in which the gap in time is not large. The additional money that you have put in is not locked up for long. Therefore in planning we have to balance heavy industry, light industry, village industry and cottage industry. We want heavy industry because without it we can never really be an independent country. Light industry too has become essential for us. So has cottage industry. I am putting forward this argument not from the Gandhian ideal, but because it is essential in order to balance heavy industry and to prevent the big gap between the pumping in of money and production.

But production is not all. A man works and produces something because he expects others to consume what he produces. If there is no consumption, he stops production. Therefore whether it is a factory or a cottage unit, consumption of what is produced should be taken care of. Mass production inevitably involves mass consumption, which in turn involves many other factors, chiefly the purchasing power of the consumer. Therefore planning must take note of the need to provide more purchasing power by way of wages, salaries and so on. Enough money should be thrown in to provide this purchasing power and to complete the circle of production and consumption. You will produce more and consume more, and as a result you standard will go up.

A Continuaus Process

Planning is a continuous process and cannot be isolated for short periods. Thus the third plan is a projection and combination of the first and second plans and it will lead to fourth and the subsequent plans. Planning is a continuous movement towards desired goals ... indeed perspective planning is of the essence of the planning process. As the process develops, there is a certain rhythm of expansion in the development of the people and a sense of enterprise and achievement comes to them.

Perspective Planning

Long term planning does not mean planning in terms of five years only, but planning for fifteen years and twenty years ahead, keeping in view the broad picture of the social structure we want so attain twenty years hence.... it is only by keeping this broad picture in view, that our current planning can fit into the structure. Otherwise we would be lost in current planning, and plan in a wrong direction.

When the second five year plan was drawn up there was a good deal in it about the perspective for the future... anyhow, the idea then was that we should prepare for the third plan and get ready for further advance along certain lines. Similarly, now that we are considering the third plan, we had really, to keep in mind the Fourth plan and possibly the fifth plan.

Social Objectives

We have kept in view two social objectives (a) We are to build up, by democratic means, a rapidly expanding and technologically progressive economy; and (b) we are to establish a social order based on social justice and offering equal opportunity to every citizen. These objectives have to be kept in view all the time. Therefore, it is necessary for us to have not only a Five Year Plan, but a plan with longer perspective. We propose to have the perspective plan approach. We have been making that approach all these years, but hereafter it will be a more definite one for the next 15 years. One of the principal activities of the Planning Commission is going to be the preparation of a Fifteen Year Plan.

Popular Support

Plan would make the people to come out of their narrow grooves of thought and action, to think of problems in relation to one another and develop to some extent at least a wider cooperative outlook.[1]

We can bring about social changes and developments by the pressure of democracy and also by friendly cooperative approach rather than the approach of struggle and elimination.[2]

It is clear that so far as country is concerned, we cannot attain this ideal by conflict or violence.[3]

...If people thoroughly understood the plan and so the direction in which it would take them and the result it was likely to achieve they would put a larger measure of effort.[4]

...It was therefore essential that the people should join them in their thinking about the plan. If the Government or the Planning Commission, brought out the plan themselves and placed it before the public, the latter might not understand many things and might not accept some of them. On the other hand, when they appreciate the difficulties and know that if they want something worthwhile they have to pay for it and by hard work. In that way it became easier, to tackle the question of resources.[5]

The mighty task that we have undertaken demands the fullest co-operation from the masses of our people.[6]

...That co-operation cannot come unless we put forward an objective which is acceptable to them and which promises them results. The change we seek necessitates burdens on our people, even those can least bear them, unless they realise that they are partners in building up of a society which will bring them benefits. They will not accept these burdens or give them full co-operation. What is called "free enterprise" will never appeal to the masses of our people, it will lead to the use of resources often for purposes that are not of primary importance.

Setting the Sights

In the past few years I have had occasion to express my general views on this subject many times, and for some years I was Chairman of the National Planning Committee[7] where all such matters came up for discussion. We did a lot of good work in that committee. Unfortunately, this work did not bear fruit in the shape of a final report, but the reports issued by a large number of subcommittees and a considerable number of our own resolutions bear witness to the work that has already been done. I am glad to say that many of these reports of the sub-committees are now available for such persons as are interested in them. If they read these reports as well as the other materials which we have, they will find that these questions are extraordinarily intricate and overlapping, and that they cannot be solved by a mere formula.[8]

Production is perhaps one of the most important things before us today: that is, adding to the wealth of the country. We cannot overlook other factors. Nevertheless, production comes first, and I am prepared to say that everything that we do should be judged from the point of view of production first of all. If nationalisation adds to production, we shall have nationalisation at every step. If it does not, let us see how to bring it about in order not to impede production. That is the essential thing. It is not so easy as the honourable member seems to think that we can legislate and then, by some kind of jugglery, we can produce results. To take such a step may possibly lead to some kind of disaster, actually a graver crisis may follow. So it is not merely a question of adopting a certain economic outlook, but also of timing, of priorities, of how to do it, in what manner and when to do it-these are the most important factors. It is not enough to put aside or break up a certain system, but you have to put another system in its place. All these factors have to be borne in mind.

In judging of the circumstances in our own country, we have to consider all manner of factors and we have to plan accordingly and go ahead, step by step, so as not to break up something we have without replacing it immediately by something better. It is fairly easy to break things up.

It is not so easy to construct. It is quite possible that, in an attempt to change the economic system, you may have a period of semi-disaster. You may even stop production which we aim at. Ultimately, perhaps very gradually, you may build up a new kind of apparatus. But for the moment you will break up the existing apparatus. That is undesirable when all our energies have to be concentrated on production.

In so far as the National Congress is concerned, it accepted this principle about 17 years ago the nationalisation, ownership or control of defence and key industries and public utilities, and I do believe that such industries will have to be nationalised some time or other. Then, again, the Congress in its various resolutions has also indicated that this process of nationalisation should go a little further in other directions. But when you come down to giving effect to this, you have to think of which to choose first and how to do it without upsetting the present structure and without actually interfering with production.[9]

The use of the word 'key' industries is very vague. Opinions may differ as to what is a key industry, whether we are referring to a few or many. Deliberately it has been left vague, because the stage of defining these industries will come later, when the matter is considered by the Planning Commission. Quite apart from defining them, the question of nationalising them and the timing of it, would also depend on the commission or whatever authority that might consider the problem.

There is another matter which has been referred to in this report. We have specifically stated that, apart from certain obvious industries of vital importance, we consider that the state should nationalise or start nationalising new industries of a particular type, that is to say, we should not waste our resources at the present moment in trying to nationalise existing industries, except where it is absolutely necessary, but rather conserve our resources and start new industries. I thought that a very sound principle, because, after all, whatever we may do, it will have to be limited by our own resources. We have to choose which to take up first. If we squander our resources in merely acquiring for the state existing industries (that we have acquired them may be for the nation's good), for the moment we have no other resources left, and we would have rather spoiled the field for private enterprise too. So it is far better for the state to concentrate on certain specific, vital, new industries than to go about nationalising many of the old ones, though, as I said, in the case of some specific vital industry of national importance that might be done.

This has many advantages, one advantage being, as I said, that the state's resources are applied to new industries, according to the requirements of production, without interfering with the existing apparatus except where it is absolutely necessary. All the work that the state would do would be to add constructively to production rather than merely effect a changeover. After a period (which is hinted at in this report), after five years or so, the state may reconsider the problem and see what else it can do, how far it can go.

Now, what is the point in putting in this five-year period? As a matter of fact, whatever period might be put in has little significance in the present changing, dynamic world. One does not know, and I doubt if any member of this House can say, what will happen in India two years hence or three years hence, in either the political or economic domain, so that putting down any time-table or programme does not help much, except that it gives us some picture in our minds to which we can work up to.

Why five years was the time put down was really to give a kind of assurance to those who might be somewhat put out by the prospect of these changes, that is to say, that we are not going to upset existing things, we are leaving them as they are more or less, but that we are enlarging the domain in other fields, more or less specified fields, so that there may be no grievance that something is done which upsets the existing structure.[10]

The progress of technology and of science is so enormous and so rapid that within a fairly short space of time, let us say fifteen years, the whole conception of modern industry will change completely. New sources of power will be discovered and those sources of power will upset the methods of production that exist today much more so than the Industrial Revolution did 150 years ago in England and in the rest of Europe. All these enormous changes are going to take place and I find that many of us, whether we call ourselves Socialists, Communists or Capitalists or by any other name, are singularly unaware of the big changes that are taking place. We are so unaware of this that we think merely in terms, not of the greater wealth coming into existence by fresh methods, but rather only of changing the ownership of industry which, of course, may be important from the point of view of advancing towards equality. Distribution is very important, but what is far more important is the dynamic future. In the changed situation all over the world, new sources of power might completely revolutionise our agriculture as well as our industry. Therefore what I think most important for the state is that whatever may happen to the existing sources of production, these new and novel sources of production should always remain in the hands of the state. We should not allow them to go into private hands and thus become private monopolies. And in regard to the existing sources, we should proceed step by step, and avoid any drop in production or disturbances of the economic structure as far as possible.

We have a large number of big schemes or projects dealing with river valleys. These schemes deal with construction of big reservoirs, hydro-electric works, irrigation canals, prevention of erosion, prevention of malaria and so on and so forth. These schemes are going to require a vast deal of money and by far the most important thing is that they will be the basis of all future growth. They will go a long way to solve our food problem, to provide that power which is essential for industrial growth. Once you have that power you can go ahead pretty fast. So the Government decided to concentrate on the rapid development of these river valley schemes and not to fritter away their energy on temporary expedients here and there.

If we are going to concentrate on these big schemes are we going to divert our energy from them in acquiring this or that little industry which may make only some or no difference at all, which will create upsets here and there and not lead to that basic foundation on which all industry should rest in the future? Therefore, even from the point of view of socialisation, we should proceed with the foundations first, lay them down, have a system of priorities and timing, take over a sector of the national economy and socialise it only when the time is ripe for it. When the time will be ripe I cannot say. We require not only money but, what is far more important, trained human material. In fact, in the ultimate analysis, that is the only essential thing whether it concerns industrial or any other department of life. Let us admit we do not possess a sufficient quantity of that trained human material in any field of life in India today. We have produced competent persons in every department of life in science, in industry. We have some of the finest scientists in the world. Nevertheless, they are few. They are not enough. The House may remember that the Government appointed a Scientific Manpower Committee a little time ago because we attach the greatest importance to using the scientific manpower we have, to increasing it and rapidly augmenting it. That Committee reported and its report was considered by the Government. Many of its recommendations were adopted. We are trying our best to increase our technical and other personnel by sending people abroad, and getting people from abroad to teach our students here. All this is the real basis, the foundation, that is being laid down for future progress, and the other approach, that is a theoretical and doctrinnaire approach, merely stating we are going to make these big changes, does not help much. On the other hand, it gives a completely wrong picture to the people, who do not realize what is to be done or what preparations have to be made before the various steps can be taken.

In regard to the land system, our general policy has been to put an end to what is being called the zamindari system. The pace has been slow, not due to any lack of effort, but because all manner of difficulties have cropped up. Still, I hope that the matter will be gone through fairly soon. That again is one of the foundations on which we can build everything else. There has been talk about collective and cooperative farming. I should like to have collective and cooperative farming in this country. I hope that, in any event, if not on a large scale, at least on a small scale, we shall begin soon with cooperatives, and, may be, with collectives. But it is obvious that before you can think of them, you have to put an end to the present land system which prevails in the greater part of India first of all the big zamindari system, and then perhaps other aspects of it, and that is not such an easy matter. It is not a matter of a few, whom you might call, capitalists, disliking it, but possibly a very large number of peasant proprietors disliking it. Obviously, whatever decision we may make must have the consent of the large number of people. We cannot force it down the throats of the vast majority of our peasants. We have to convert them. The best way to do that is to give them a living example in cooperatives, and show them how they will function; and then only can they be converted. India is a huge country. We may have various types of agricultural economy side by side, and gradually the one that is best suited to the land will prevail. Even in cooperatives, there are so many types. I cannot say immediately which is the most suitable; it may be that one type may be suitable in one part of the country and another in another part.[11]

Whatever we may do, we want to put production first. We think it is most essential. Production obviously depends on a very great deal of cooperation among those people who are most concerned with production. Obviously, we want the goodwill of the industrialists of the country. The question is often asked, "Have you the personnel to nationalise industries?"..... The question rather surprises me, because it is the same personnel that might be used whether industry is nationalised or not. The personnel which function in private industry will not leave the country when it is nationalised. It is the same personnel, including the captains of industry, who will also be utilised because of their very special ability managerial, executive, etc. Now, the point is that in any programme that we put forward, we must have the largest measure of goodwill. We must not allow it to affect production. At the same time we must lay the foundations of future progress in the direction we aim at.

Economic and Social Justice[12]

The dominating urge today is that of social justice and the wiping out of the vast inequalities that exist. We have said so in our Constitution, but our progress has been slow. Unfortunately that Constitution, fine as it is, rather comes in the way of swifter progress. Recently we had to amend the Constitution so as to remove an obstacle that had come in the way of land reform. The abolition of the big zamindari system had been the major plank of our programme for many years and we had laboured to that end. But difficulties cropped up continually and years passed without achievement. I am glad that a recent decision of the Supreme Court has removed many of these difficulties and I hope that progress now will be swift. Some of our states have gone ahead with land reforms, others have lagged behind. This is a programme which applies to the whole of India and we must put an end as rapidly as possible to all such rights in land which bear down upon the people and come in the way of their growth.

Whatever plan we might make, the test of its success is how far it brings relief to the millions of our people who live on a bare subsistence level, that is the good and advancement of the masses of our people. Every other interest must be subordinated to this primary consideration. Our Constitution has rightly laid stress on our raising our Scheduled Castes and Tribes and other economically backward classes. This is a duty not only to them but to the nation because only so can we raise the general level of our people. The unfortunate fact must be remembered, however, that, from any economic point of view, probably eighty per cent of our people can be called backward classes.

Our fight against poverty and unemployment and our attempt at the economic betterment of the people thus become major objectives. This is the next vital stage of our journey after political independence. This can only be achieved by social and economic planning so that our resources can be used to the best advantage and increased as rapidly as possible. It cannot be achieved by leaving things to chance or to the vagaries of private enterprise or by the encouragement of the acquisitive instinct. We have had unfortunately an abundance of anti-social practices in this country during the last wâr and after. This has to be combated on a planned basis and with controls where necessary....

Nationalisation[13]

The issue of nationalisation is a complex problem. There should be complete clarity on this point so that the whole country knows what our policy is. There should be no apprehension in people's minds about these things. I am firmly convinced that there should be clarity on this matter. It is one thing to adopt a high-flown principle of socialism or something else. But it does not seem wise to me for anyone, especially in the India of today, to say that we shall follow this 'ism' or that. In this changing world we must understand the circumstances and try to follow some principles. There is no use talking in the air. The principles that we follow must be relevant to the circumstances in the country. It is obvious that we have neither the strength nor the resources to nationalise everything on a large scale immediately, apart from the fact that in the process we could be killing public enterprise. Therefore we have to be careful about what we choose to nationalise. It is obvious that for a long time now this has been in the air though you may not have paid attention to it. As far as the Congress is concerned, it had declared nearly 17 or 18 years ago, at the Karachi Congress, that the big industries should be under state control. This has been an accepted fact for a long time now all over the world except in one or two countries. In short, the question before us is what should be nationalised first and what can be done a few years hence. There may be other sectors which we have no intention of nationalising, though we cannot give a permanent guarantee about that. Another problem that arises in this connection–you have also hinted at–concerns the big river valley schemes and projects which the Government is taking up. The question is whether we ought to use our resources in these new tasks or carry on some of the old ones. It is obvious that it would be better to utilise them for these new tasks. So we have to take a decision. In some sectors of industries, there will be no private enterprise, especially in the key industries as in defence, etc. In some others, there can be both public and private enterprises. In yet others, it can be left wholly to private enterprise. Even in the sectors in which we wish to ban private enterprise eventually, it is better not to interfere just now because we wish to utilise our resources in new enterprises instead of in the old ones though planning will certainly mean a certain amount of interference in all industries.

...Now in regard to nationalisation, I should like to add one thing, that is, even when the industry is nationalised, I think it should be run by some kind of a statutory corporation, more or less on the lines, if you like, even of private business, that is to say, not on a departmental level. I do not like departmental running of industry at all. So that it will approximate to the same ways of carrying on business as any efficient private industry might.

Private and Public Enterprise[14]

May I say here that while I am for the public sector growing, I do not understand or appreciate the condemnation of the private sector? The whole philosophy underlying this plan is to take advantage of every possible way of growth and not to do something which suits some doctrinaire theory or imagine we have grown bcause we have satisfied some textbook maxim of a hundred years ago. We talk about nationalization as if nationalization were some kind of a magic remedy for every ill. I believe that ultimately all the principal means of production will be owned by the nation, but I just do not see why I should do something today which limits our progress simply to satisfy some theoretical urge. I have no doubt that at the present stage in India the private sector has a very important task to fulfil, provided always that it works within the confines laid down and provided always that it does not lead to the creation of monopolies and other evils that the accumulation of wealth gives rise to.

...While the public sector must obviously grow–and even now it has grown, both absolutely and relatively–the private sector is not something unimportant. It will play an important role; though gradually and ultimately it will fade away. But the public sector will control and should control the strategic points in our economy. The private sector, as we have stated in the Industrial Policy Resolution, will be given a fairly wide field subject to the limitations that are laid down. It is for us to decide, from time to time, how to deal with that sector. The point is that since we are an under-developed country, the scope for industrialization and advance is very vast...

The way a government functions is not exactly the way that business houses and enterprises normally function. A government rightly has all kinds of checks, as it deals with public money. Usually it has time to apply these checks. But when one deals with a plant and an enterprise where quick decisions are necessary, which may make a difference between success and failure, the way a government functions is not sometimes suitable. I have no doubt that the normal governmental procedure applied to a public enterprise of this kind will lead to the failure of that public enterprise. Therefore, we have to evolve a system for working public enterprises where, on the one hand, there are adequate checks and protections, and, on the other, enough freedom for the enterprise to work quickly and without delay. Ultimately it has to be judged by the results, though one cannot judge a government by financial results alone. In judging a big enterprise, one has to judge by the final results.

Sometimes it is said that parliamentary democracy is inevitably combined with a system of private enterprise. Private enterprise may be good or bad, but I do not see what parliamentary democracy has to do with private enterprise. I do not see any connection between the two except the connection of past habit and past thinking. In fact, the arguments about socialism, private enterprise and public sector, important as they are, have tended to become less and less valid. There is no country in the world where some middle way between the extremes has not been or is not being found. In the U.S.A. which is said to have a highly developed form of modern capitalism and private enterprise, there is more public enterprise than in most countries which apparently have a different objective and ideal.

In Europe, we see many countries having advanced very far on the road to socialism. I am not referring to the communist countries but to those which may be called parliamentary, social democratic countries. There is no conflict between socialism and parliamentary democracy. In fact, I would venture to say that there is going to be an increasing degree of conflict between the idea of parliamentary government and full-fledged private enterprise.

Cooperative Movement[15]

...It is the peasant who has borne the burden of India for ages past. It is on the growth and betterment of our peasantry that the future of India must necessarily depend.

Today we are laying the greatest stress on two lines of advance–greater food production and more cottage and small-scale industries. Food has become the cornerstone of our planning and this means more intensive growth. We have made many appeals in the past for this purpose and they have brought results. The time has now come not merely for general appeals but for a specific and planned approach to each village and almost to each family, so that targets may be laid down and we may work up to them.

What is the future of our peasantry? The great number of them have barely one or two acres of land to cultivate. It is possible and necessary to increase the yield of this little patch of land and thus to better somewhat the condition of the peasant. But there is a limit to this–the limit laid down by the smallness of that holding.

There are too many people in India subsisting on land. This means that many people must take to other activities and occupations. Some of these can be whole-time activities and some part-time allied to agriculture. Herein is the importance of our cottage and small industries programme. No doubt, as large industries grow up, many people from the rural areas will be attracted to them. But however speedy the growth of large industries, the major problem of unemployment and other occupations will not be solved by them. It can only be progressively solved by the development of cottage and small-scale industries.

Even so, how will the peasant function with his small patch of land? It is not possible for him to take advantage of modern techniques or the facilities offered by new methods unless he works in co-operation with others of his kind. Co-operation is the key to his future growth[16] and the co-operative movement thus must spread all over the country and comprise all the villages and peasants of this vast land.

What kind of co-operation? There are the so-called service cooperatives, there are those which deal with credit. We have in the past laid stress mostly on credit co-operatives and they are no doubt helpful, but they are not enough. We must cover a much larger field through our co-operative movement. Indeed, the co-operative movement should enter into the life of the peasant in as many ways as possible and, together with the panchayat, must be the main bulwark of our rural structure.

The next stage of co-operation is joint farming and there has been some argument about this. I have no doubt that joint farming, wherever possible and agreed to, will be good, but it must be clearly understood that this can be no imposition and can only be brought in by the agreement of the parties. To begin with, there must be the service co-operatives and as these succeed, the next step may well be some joint farms. Where new land is brought into cultivation, it may be possible to have the joint cultivation to begin with.

I would prefer relatively small co-operatives comprising one or two or three villages. It seems essential to me that a co-operative should not be controlled from above, not too officialized, but should represent the spirit of self-reliance and self-growth of the people. Also there should be an intimacy about its members, otherwise it becomes impersonal and difficult for the villagers to consider as something of their own.

This whole movement, as our entire political and economic structure in India, must be conditioned by the democratic process.

Cooperative Farming[17]

It should be clearly understood that progress in agriculture and the development of a sounder basic structure necessitate our going towards co-operative farming. The development of modern science cannot be brought to the individual small farmer easily. It will be much easier for a co-operative to take advantage of these developments which are ever growing. This does not mean mechanization of farming, that is, the use of tractors and the like. Tractors may be used occasionally with profit, but I do not think it is feasible or desirable to think of any widespread mechanization. We should rather aim at simple improvements of technique in farming and in processes associated with it. At the same time we may well have some demonstration farms where we can experiment otherwise.

Community Development Programme

We have to deal with a people who have for many centuries or many millennia been used to certain traditional ways of doing things. We cannot uproot them. We have to convince them and bring them round to new thinking and new ways of action. In particular, attention should be paid to what might be called local culture and social life which should not be uprooted. Indeed it should be encouraged except where it is obviously bad...

In the world as it is today, the lack of co-operation between independent nations has brought us to the verge of disaster. It is recognized that even separate nations have to fall in line and co-operate. How much more is this necessary within a nation and in regard to the basic activities of that nation?

I have welcomed the decision to bring about a close co-ordination in the activities of the Central and State Social Welfare Boards and the community development movement. I think that this is essential. There is inevitably a lack of this approach to women and children in our community programmes. Women are not only important in themselves, but are probably more important from the point of view of creating reactions in the public. Also they are the mothers of the next generation. As for children, I do feel that the greatest attention should be paid to them. They can learn more easily and grasp this new spirit. It is probably easier to influence their parents through the children. And, after all, it is the children for whom we are working, and who will constitute tomorrow's India.

I think we are gradually changing our men in rural areas as a result of many years of Community Development. Therefore, we have now introduced what we call Panchayati Raj. Groups of villages have been given a great deal of authority and resources. The taxcs they pay are returned to them and village elected councils deal with them. We look upon this as a tremendously educative process. As far as possible, we want to get rid of the bureaucratic element coming from the towns and cities, petty officers ordering about everything. We want the people to have the sensation of doing things for themselves. Great many difficulties come in the way. But, still, I think it is basically the right approach and it will do good. I do think that some change in the mentality of the millions of our farmers is coming. In some parts of the country, as in Punjab, it is very far advanced. In fact, parts of Punjab are today right in the middle of the industrial revolution–both in agriculture and industry. You can see it with your own eyes. Curiously enough, no big plants have been put up in Punjab. There are only small industries. People put them up. Government has helped them sometimes. On the other hand, in areas like Bihar, where there is a concentration of heavy industry, the average farmer lives as he lived a thousand years ago. He has not been affected by it. It is rather extraordinary.

The Land and the Tiller

Agrarian Reform

The first problem we took up, inevitably, was the land problem, because most of the peasantry were oppressed by the land tenure system in India. It was a varied system–sometimes completely feudal, sometimes something less than feudal but, nevertheless, bearing down heavily upon the tenant. So, right from the beginning in our programme, the reform of the land tenure system occupied a very prominent place.

The land problem, we wanted to solve with all speed, too. That is a much more difficult problem but in a great part of India–in three of our biggest provinces–it is practically solved or in the process of being solved. It meant acquiring the land from big landlords on payment of compensation. That meant rather big sums by way of compensation. Therefore, it was complicated; otherwise there was no difficulty. The actual cultivators will keep their land and the absentee owners will be paid compensation for giving up such right as they might have had. We are proceeding with that. This is important because the biggest problem of Asia–taken as a whole–is the land or the agrarian problem. There are many other problems is Asia but the basic problem, before you can make progress in an agricultural country, is obviously the agrarian problem. I think that many of the troubles of Asia can be understood only if you keep in mind this fact; the agrarian problem is the most important.

We tackled the agrarian problem in India and, if I may say so, the basic stability of the Indian Government is due to the fact that we have dealt with the agrarian problem in a way satisfactory to the peasant in India. I might also mention in this connection that the peasantry suffered tremendously in the past with everybody sitting on their backs. Our cities grew at the expense of our peasantry. For the first time in their lives, the peasantry had a tolerably fair deal during the last war. That is, the high prices of agricultural produce brought them much more money than they had ever seen.

This resulted in their paying off the very heavy agricultural debt which was bearing down upon them. And again, for the first time also, they began to eat a little more because they got a good price. They were not forced to sell every bit of grain or other produce, as they were previously, to pay their rent. Previously, they had to sell almost everything just to hang on to their land. Because they got much higher prices for their produce, they could pay their rent easily and have something left over. So they began to eat more.

Agrarian reform is basic to every plan. What is the good of an institution for a few persons here and a few persons there when millions of people in the rural areas do not have a life worth living? This is the basic problem. Other problems are there, of courses that of industrial workers and such other problems. But, in India, the basic problem still remains agrarian. If we were to think purely in terms of output, all the big and important factories in India are not really so important as agriculture. Of course, from the point of view of future growth and all that, it is essential for us to industrialize, but the very basis of industrialization is agricultural progress. Forgetting the basic fact that 90 per cent of the population need to be uplifted and looking after selected people who suffer most would give us a wrong perspective...

Agricultural Production[18]

We are passing through a grave crisis in regard to food. This crisis is not of today. It is a continuing one. Therefore, the first priority has to be given to increasing the production of foodgrains. This is vital from every point of view, including our industrial growth. It is out of our surplus in agricultural production that we shall build the resources for industrial growth.

Agricultural production is a most vital thing because it provides enough food and raw material for industry. If you don't have enough food, you have to import it and all your resources go into it. We must not only have food, but also surplus food. That would require not only machinery and fertilizers and the like, it would also mean dragging a few million farmers out of their old ruts. People seem to imagine that it is merely a question of providing fertilizers. You have to change the men who grow food. That is a big job.

Defence Underpinning[19]

What is the equation of defence? In what lies the strength of a people for defence? Well, one thinks immediately about defence forces–army, navy, air force. Perfectly right. They are the spear-points of defence. They have to bear the brunt of any attack. How do they exist? What are they based on? The more technical armies and navies and air forces get, the more important becomes the industrial and technological base of the country. You may import a machine or an aircraft or some other highly technical weapon and you may even teach somebody to use it, but that is a very superficial type of defence because you have not got the technological background for it. If spare parts go wrong, your whole machine is useless. If somebody from whom you bought it refuses to supply a part of it, it becomes useless, so that in spite of your independence you become dependent on others, and very greatly so.

From that point of view probably there are very few countries in the world that are really independent, able to stand on their own feet against the military strength of others. Therefore, apart from the army, navy and so on, you have to have an industrial and technological background in the country.

Supporting all this is the economy of the country. If the country's economy is not sound, it is a weak country....

The equation of defence is your defence forces plus your industrial and technological background, plus, thirdly, the economy of the country, and fourthly, the spirit of the people.

REFERENCES

1. Nehru Jawaharlal: The Discovery of India, Asia publishing House, Bombay, 1945, p.418-425.
2. Government of India: New Delhi, *Jawaharlal Nehru's Sspeeches*, 1953-57, Volume III. p. 76-78.
3. Nehru Jawaharlal, Speech, First Plan in Parliament 1950.
4. Government of India; New Delhi, *Jawaharlal Nehru's* Speeches, Volume III, May, 1955.
5. *Ibid*.
6. Nehru on Socialism: Selected speeches and Writings, New Delh, 1964, p.38-39.
7. The committee was constituted in October 1938. Its work, suspended in 1940 when Nehru was imprisoned, was resumed in 1945. It dissolved itself on 26 March 1949 having published 26 volumes containing the reports of the sub-committees.
8. Speech in the Constituent Assembly (Legislative), February, 17, 1948. *Constituent Assembly of India (Legislative) Debates, Official Report*, Vol.II. 1948, pp. 825-834.
9. The reference is to the Economic Programme Committee which had submitted its report to the Congress Working Committee on 25 January 1948. The report was endorsed by the A.I.C.C. on 22 February 1948.
10. The Government's decision to nationalise the Reserve Bank and the Imperial Bank was announced on 4 February 1948. While the Bill to nationalise the Reserve Bank was passed on 2 September 1948, the Government announced on 1 February 1949 that it was not feasible as yet to nationalise the Imperial Bank of India.
11. The resolution embodying the Government's industrial policy was placed before the Constituent Assembly on 6 April 1948 and approved on 7 April.
12. Presidential Address at the 57 Session of the INdian National Congress, New Delhi, October 19, 1951.
13. Inaugural Speech at the Annual Session of the Federation of Indian (Chambers of Commerce and Industry, New Delhi, March 28, 1948).
14. Speech in the Lok Sabha, May 23, 1956.
15. National Herald October 3, 1957.
16. National Herald October 3, 1957
17. A note on C.D. Scheme, April 1957.
18. A Note on the Community Development Scheme, April 1957.
19. A Speech in the Lok Ssabha, March 21, 1956.

NATIONAL INTEGRATION

SIX

NATIONAL INTEGRATION

Unity of India

Geographical Factor

Throughout the ages geography has made us one great land, history has made us one land, the common culture has made us one land and our common aspirations, our common hopes and fears, victories and defeats, have made us one. That is the past. In the present, by our common labours, common sacrifice and common struggles, we gained the freedom of India.

How then can we today, when we are at last politically united and when we are a free country, allow ourselves to destroy that unity which we have inherited and disturb that freedom which we have struggled to achieve? The past and present have provided a common ground to us. So also must the future be common to us, the future that we are striving to attain, the future of millions of our people, their welfare. In whatever region we may live, this calls for unity of purpose, unity of endeavour and sacrifice.

United But Composite

We are not going to reach our goal through crookedness or flirting with evil in the hope that it may lead to good. The right end can never be fully achieved through wrong means.

Let us be clear about our national objective. We aim at a strong, free and democratic India where every citizen has an equal place and full opportunity of growth and service, where present-day inequalities in wealth and status have ceased to be, where our vital impulses are directed to creative and co-operative endeavour. In such an India communalism, separatism, isolation, untouchability, bigotry, and exploitation of man by man have no place, and while religion is free; it is not allowed to interfere with the political and economic aspects of a nation's life. If that is so, then all this business of Hindu and Muslim and Christian and Sikh must cease in so far as our political life is concerned and we must build a united but composite nation where both individual and national freedom are secure.

India is made up of a number of States but these divisions represent not differences but administrative arrangements to subserve a common purpose. These shall not divide us. Similarly, the many languages we have in India shall not divide us.... Language should not be a dividing factor but it should bring us together, and each language can help the other languages of India to grow through contact and exchange of ideas. Language joins. Language does not separate. Likewise, India is a country of many religions, but in the past religion has not been a dividing factor. Why should it be so in the present?

1. India has for ages past been a country of pilgrimages. All over the country you find these ancient places, from Badrinath, Kedarnath and Amarnath high up in the snowy Himalayas down to Kanyakumari in the South, and throughout the ages people have gone on pilgrimage from north to south and south to north, and mixed with each other. For, from the very beginning of history, the people of India always thought of themselves as a people belonging to one great country.

2. What has drawn out people from the north to the south, and from the south to the north in these great pilgrimages? What is the common thought that has made them travel from one region to the other? It is the feeling of one country and one culture, and this feeling has bound us together. This sense of a common urge and a common thought came to us hundreds, may be thousands of years ago. Our ancient books have said the land of Bharat is the land stretching from the Himalayas in the north to the Southern seas.

3. This conception of Bharat as one great land which the people considered a holy land has come down the ages and joined us together, even though we have had different political kingdoms and even though we may speak different languages. This silken bond still keeps us together in many ways.

4. Throughout these thousands of years, this land has been ours, ours in mind, ours in heart, and ours in spiritual heritage. I who come from the north feel at home here, because I am in a part of my country, among friends, among colleagues, and among people who have the same ideas, same thoughts and same urges. Similarly, the north does not belong exclusively to those who live there, but belongs to you also, even though you live in the South of India. The Himalayas are yours as much as they are mine, and Kanyakumari and Madurai are mine as much as yours. This land is a common heritage of ours, where we have been, born and which we seek to serve.

Cultural Synthesis[1]

Often I ask myself: What is India? What is the essence of India? What are the forces that have gone to make India and how are they related to the major dominating influences of the world in the past and in the present? The subject is a vast one and covers the entire field of human activity, not only in India but elsewhere, and I suppose no single person can do ustice to it. But we can take up some particular aspects of it and try to understand them. We can at least try to understand our India, although that understanding will be limited if we do not have the wider picture of the world before us.

What is culture? I look it up in the dictionary and I find a variety of definitions. One great writer has called it "the acquainting ourselves with the best that has been known and said in the world." Another definition says that it is "the training, development or strengthening of the powers, mental or physical, or the condition thus produced; improvement or refinement of mind, morals, or tastes; enlightenment of civilization". Culture in this sense, is something basic and international. Then there are the national aspects of culture and there can be no doubt that many nations have each developed a certain genius and individuality.

Where does India fit in? Some people have talked of Hindu culture and Muslim culture and Christian culture. I do not understand these terms, although it is true that the great religious movements have influenced the culture of a race or a nation. If I look at India, I find, ...the gradual growth of composite culture of the Indian people. The origins of this culture may be traced back on the one hand to the pre-Aryan period, the civilization of Mohenjodaro, etc., and the great Dravidian civilization. On the other hand, it received a powerful impress from the Aryans who came to India from Central Asia. Subsequently, it was influenced by repeated incursions from the North-West and later by the people who came across the seas from the West. Thus, this national culture gradually grew and took shape. It had a remarkable capacity for synthesis and for absorbing new elements. So that as it did so, it was dynamic and living. In later years it lost the dynamic quality and became essentially static which led to weakness in all fields. Throughout India's history we see two sets of contradictory forces at work–those in favour of a synthesis and absorption and those fissiparous tendencies which separate. Today we face the same problem in a different context. There are powerful forces working for unity, not only political but cultural also. There are also forces that disrupt and lay stress on separateness.

The question, therefore, for us today is not an academic one but a vital issue, on the understanding and solution of which depends our future. Normally, it is the business of the intellectuals to give a lead in dealing with such problems, but our intellectuals have failed us. Many of them do not even seem to realize the nature of this problem, others suffer from frustration and a crisis of the spirit, not knowing where to turn.

Marxism and its progeny attracted many of the intellectuals, and there is no doubt that it gave a certain analysis of historical developments which helped us to think and to understand. But even that proved too narrow a creed and, whatever its virtue as an economic approach, it failed to resolve our basic doubts. Life is something more than economic growth, though it is well to realize that economic growth is a basic foundation of life and progress. History shows us two principles at work, the principle of continuity and the principle of change. They appear to be opposed to each other and, yet, each has something of the other. We notice that we consider sudden changes in the shape of violent revolutions or an earthquake. Yet, every geologist knows that the major changes in the earth's surface are gradual, and earthquakes are trivial in comparison to them. So also revolutions are merely the outward evidence of a long process of change and subtle erosion. Thus, change itself is a continuous process, and even a static continuity must yield to gradual change so long as it is not overcome by complete stagnation and death.

There are periods in history when the processes and tempo of change are more in evidence. At other times, the appearance is much more static. The static period in the life of a nation is a period of gradual deterioration and weakness, leading to the decay of the creative arts and tendencies and often to political subjection.

Probably the most powerful cultural element in India came from the union of the Aryan with the older elements in India, chiefly the Dravidian. Out of this arose a mighty culture, chiefly represented by our great classical language, Sanskrit. That language, though it had its origin together with old Pahlaviin a common parent in Central Asia, became the national language of India. Both the North and the South contributed to its growth. Indeed, in later days, the South played a very important part. Sanskrit became the symbol not only of our people's thought and religion but the embodiment of the cultural unity of India. Ever since the Buddha's time, it has not been the spoken language of the people and yet it continued to exercise this powerful influence all over India. Other great influences came in, which led to new avenues of thought and expression.

Geography made India, in her long past, almost a closed country. Surrounded by the sea and the mighty Himalayas, it was not easy of entry. Migrations took place in India in the course of thousands of years but probably there was no big migration of peoples after the coming of the Aryans. We must contrast this with the tremendous movement of peoples right across Asia and Europe, one tribe driving the other and changing the texture of the population. In India, after the Aryans came, these incursions were relatively limited. They produced their effect but did not change over much that basic population. It must be remembered, however, that there were marked changes even in India. The Scythians and the Huns and the many others who came to India later developed into branches of the Rajputs and claimed ancient lineage. The fact that India was for long a closed land gave it its peculiar character. We became as a race somewhat inbred. We developed some customs which are unknown and not understood in other parts of the world. Caste, in its innumerable forms, is a typical product of India. Untouchability, the objections to inter-dining, inter-marriage, etc., are unknown in any other country. The result was a certain narrowness in our outlook. Indians, even to the present day, find it difficult to mix with others. Not only that, but people of each caste tend to remain separate even when they go to other countries. Most of us in India take all this for granted and do not realize how it astonishes and even shocks the people of other countries.

Thus, in India, we developed at one and the same time the broade tolerance and catholicity of thought and opinion as well as the narrowest social forms of behaviour. This spilt personality has pursued us and we struggle against it even today. We overlook and excuse our failings and narrowness of custom and habit by references to the great thoughts we have inherited from our ancestors. But there is an essential conflict between the two, and so long as we do not resolve it, we shall continue to have this spilt personality.

In a more or less static period these opposed elements did not come into conflict with each other much. But, as the tempo of political and economic change has grown faster, these conflicts have come to more in evidence. In the atomic age, at the threshold of which we stand, we are compelled by overwhelming circumstances to put an end to this inner conflict. To fail to do so is to fail as a nation and lose even the virtues that we have possessed.

We have to face, therefore, this crisis of the spirit in India, even as we have to face great political and economic problems. The industrial revolution is coming rapidly to India and changing us in many ways. It is an inevitable consequence of political and economic change that there should be social changes also if we are to remain as integrated human beings and an integrated nation. We cannot have political change and industrial progress and imagine that we can continue unchanged in the social sphere. The stresses and strains will be too great and if we do not resolve them, we shall crack up.

The picture of India, as we see it, in the first millennium after Christ and indeed even before that, is very different from its later appearance. We see in those early days an exuberant, vital people, full of the zest of life and adventure, carrying their message to far countries. In the realm of thought, they dared to scale the highest peaks and to pierce the heavens. They built up a magnificent language and in the realm of art, they showed creative genius of the highest order. That early period does not indicate a closed-in-life or a static society. We see also then the same cultural impulses surging throughout the land of India. It was from South India that the great colonizing expeditions went out to South-East Asia. It was also from the South that the great Bodhidharma went to China with the message of Buddhism. North and South joined in this great adventure of life, each nourishing the other.

Then come the later centuries when a process of decay sets in, visible the growing artificiality of language and the ornateness of our architecture. Our thoughts become largely a repetition of what has been said and the creative spirit grows less and less. We become afraid of adventure either of the body or mind, and we develop the caste system and a closed-in society. We talk still, as of old, in the highest terms, but we act differently.

It is extraordinary how our professions run far ahead of our practice. We talk of peace and non-violence and function in a different way. We talk of tolerance and construe it to mean our way of thinking only and are intolerant of other ways. We proclaim our ideal to be philosophic detachment even in the midst of action, that of a *sthitaprajna*, but we act on a far lower plane and a growing indiscipline degrades us as individuals and as a community.

When the Westerners came here across the seas, the closed land of India was again thrown open in a particular direction. The modern industrial civilization gradually crept in a passive way. New thoughts and ideas invaded us and our intellectuals developed the habit of thinking like British intellectuals. That shaking up and opening out was good in its own way and it began to give us some understanding of the modern world. But it cut off these intellectuals from the mass of the people who were little affected by this new wave of thought. Our traditional thinking was displaced and those who still clung to it did so in a static and uncreative way, totally unrelated to modern conditions.

Now this faith in Western thought is itself being shaken and so we have neither the old nor the new, and we drift not knowing whither we are going. The younger generation has no standards left, nothing to direct their thinking or control their actions.

This, a dangerous situation, if not checked and improved, is likely to lead to grave consequences. It may be that we are passing through an age of transition, political, economic and social, and these are the inevitable consequences of such a period. But in the atomic age no country is likely to be given many chances to correct itself, and failure may well mean disaster.

Even if we do not understand fully the mighty forces that are at work in the world, we must at least endeavour to understand what India is and how this nation has developed its composite personality with its many facets and yet with an enduring unity. No one section of the community in India can lay claim to the sole possession of the mind and thought of India. Each part has contributed its share in making this country what it is. If we do not understand this basic fact, we do not understand India at all and if we do not understand India, we cannot function adequately or render any effective service to this country of ours.

Communal Malaise[2]

I. The tragedy of Cawnpore is an object lesson that violence, though we may use it with the best of motives, is apt to recoil on us and lead to internecine conflict. The only people who profit by it are our opponents. Today, we cannot settle any vital problem in the country, much less the communal problem, by violence; nor can we settle it by temporary pacts or arrangements. Only by attacking the root of the disease can we eradicate it. Young men must envisage a new order of things and remove the evils which make progress impossible. Young men must remember that 'freedom' and 'independence' are mere words till a new order is fashioned which ends inequalities, exploitation, and religious bigotry.[3]

II. The want of clear ideals and objectives in our struggle for freedom undoubtedly helped the spread of communalism. The masses saw no clear connection between their day-to-day sufferings and the fight for swaraj. They fought well enough at times by instinct, but that was a feeble weapon which could be easily blunted or even turned aside for other purposes. These was no reason behind it, and in periods of reaction it was not difficult for the communalists to play upon this feeling and exploit it in the name of religion. It is nevertheless extraordinary how the bourgeois classes, both among the Hindus and the Muslims, succeeded, in the sacred name of religion, in getting a measure of mass sympathy and support for programmes and demands which had absolutely nothing to do with the masses, or even the lower middle class. Every one of the communal demands put forward by any communal group is, in the final analysis, a demand for jobs, and these jobs could only go to a handful of the upper middle class. There is also, of course, the demand for special and additional seats in the legislatures, as symbolizing political power, but this too is looked upon chiefly as the power to exercise patronage. These narrow political demands, benefiting at the most a small number of the upper middle classes, and often creating barriers in the way of national unity and progress, were cleverly made to appear the demands of the masses of that particular religious group. Religious passion was hitched on to them in order to hide their barrenness.

In this way political reactionaries came back to the political field in the guise of communal leaders, and the real explanation of the various steps they took was not so much their communal bias as their desire to obstruct political advance. We could only expect opposition from them politically, but still it was a peculiarly distressing feature of an unsavoury situation to find to what lengths they would go in this respect. Muslim communal leaders said the most amazing things and seemed to care not at all for Indian nationalism or Indian freedom; Hindu communal leaders, though always speaking apparently in the name of nationalism, had little to do with it in practice and, incapable of any real action, sought to humble themselves before the government, and did that too in vain. Both agreed in condemning socialistic and such like 'subversive' movements; there was a touching unanimity in regard to any proposal affecting vested interests. Muslims communal leaders said and did many things harmful to political and economic freedom, but as a group and individually they conducted themselves before the government and the public with some dignity. That could hardly be said of the Hindu communal leaders.

Breaking the Barriers[4]

We can see disruptive forces at work in India. Some people are deliberately disruptive. Others are unconsciously disruptive and they become parochial or provincial or communal. They forget the large purposes that we have in view, forget the great destiny before India, forget that India aims high, that India never aimed low.

We should not become parochial, narrow-minded, provincial, communal and caste-minded, because we have a great mission to perform. Let us, the citizens of the Republic of India, stand up straight, with straight backs, and look up at the skies, keeping our feet firmly planted on the ground and bring about this synthesis, this integration of the Indian people. Political integration has already taken place to some extent, but what I am after is something much deeper than that–an emotional integration of the Indian people so that we might be welded into one, and made into one strong national unit, maintaining at the same time all our wonderful diversity. I do not want this diversity to be regimented and taken away, but we must be wary of losing ourselves in petty quarrels. We may often have to accept somebody else's opinion even though we do not like it; that is the way of democracy...

The main thing we have to keep in mind is the emotional integration of India. We must guard against being swept away by momentary passion, whether it is religion misapplied to politics or communalism or provincialism or casteism. We have to build up this great country into a mighty nation, mighty not in the ordinary sense of the word, that is, having great armies and all that, but mighty in thought, mighty in action, mighty in culture and mighty in its peaceful service of humaanity.

In view this question of national integration as a challenge to us, because we in India are passing through a period of the greatest transformation in our long history. It is not surprising that in the course of this transformation things happen which are not always to our liking. We cannot go through this tremendous period without having to face perils and, occasionally, even stumbling.

Some of our difficulties are inherited from the past but others are the result of the very progress that we are making... In fact, the way these difficulties are occurring is an indication that we are marching ahead and that we are fighting the evils which come in our way.

What these evils are is fairly well known: they are, broadly speaking, communalism, casteism, regionalism and linguism. Or, we may simply call them the various things that narrow us. It is bad enough to be narrow-minded at any time, but it is worse in the world as it is today to be narrow-minded when there is a tendency for the whole world to shrink. It is obvious that all these things come very much in our way when we are trying to change India economically, socially and otherwise...

The question of integration covers in a sense almost everything in life. Above all it covers education, which means the training of the individual from childhood up...

Essentially, I have not a shadow of doubt that whether politically or otherwise the Republic of India stands on firm foundations and we need not imagine that even the wrong tendencies which we see are going to undermine us in any way. In spite of our failing, weakness and difficulties, India is a stable country going ahead, which can compare very favourably with any other country.[5]

All the same the problems before us are undoubtedly of giant stature. I have no doubt that the people have the capacity to solve them and that they will solve them, not suddenly but in due course. It involves an attitude of mind. Essentially, these big problems have to be approached, logically, reasonably and as a matter of faith. Faith in whom? Faith in ourselves, in our people and in our capacity to work together and to solve big problems together.

Secular Administration[6]

I do not think we can ignore the political aspect. Indian, in spite of its overwhelming Hindu population, is a composite country from the religious and other points of views. It is a vital problem for us to solve as to whether we are to function, fundamentally in regard to our general policy as such a composite country, or to function as a Hindu country rather ignoring the viewpoints of other groups. It is inevitable that the majority Hindu sentiment will affect our activities in a hundred ways. Nevertheless it does make a difference whether we try of think of India as a composite country or as a Hindu country. It should be remembered that the stoppage of cow-slaughter means stopping non-Hindus from doing something which they might do. For economic reasons steps can always be taken because they are justified on economic grounds. But if any such step is taken purely on grounds of Hindu sentiment, it means that the governance of India is going to be carried on a in a particular way, which thus far we have not done...

This question, therefore, raises rather vital issues in regard to our approach to almost all our problems. As you know, there is a very strong Hindu revivalist feeling in the country at the present moment. I am greatly distressed by it because it represents the narrowest communalism. It is the exact replica of the narrow Muslim communalism which we have tried to combat for so long. I fear that this narrow sectarian outlook will do grave injury not only to nationalism as such but also to the high ideals for which Indian and Hindu culture has stood through the ages. We are facing a crisis of the spirit in India today and a false step may have far-reaching consequences.

Sir, before this debate proceeds any further I should like to indicate, the attitude of Government in regard to this Resolution.[7] The Government welcome this Resolution and desire to say that they wish to do everything in their power to achieve the objective which lies behind this Resolution; as a matter of fact, it is an inevitable policy which an independent country must adopt. There might have been in the past various reasons which came in the way of such policy being given effect to, although I think that even in the past those of us who accepted any measure of communalism erred and acted unwisely, and we have suffered greatly for our unwisdom.

However, in the past, conditions were different; but when a country is functioning independently there is no alternative except to follow this. The only alternative is civil conflict. We have seen as a matter of fact how far communalism in politics has led us; all of us remember the grave dangers through which we have passed and the terrible consequences we have seen. In any event now there is no alternative; and we must have it clearly in our minds and in the mind of the country that the alliance of religion and politics in the shape of communalism is a most dangerous alliance, and it yields the most abnormal kind of illegitimate brood.[8]

We have talked a great deal about politics being allied to ethics; that is something which, I hope, we shall always stand for. During the last quarter of a century or more Mahatma Gandhi taught us to place politics on an ethical level. How far we succeeded is for the world to judge and for future generations to decide. But it was something at least that we placed that great ideal before us and tried in our own weak and halting way to give effect to it. But the combination of politics and of religion in the narrowest sense of the word, resulting in communal politics, is--there can be no doubt--a most dangerous combination and must be put an end to. It is clear, as has been pointed out by the hon. Mover, that this combination is harmful to the country as a whole; it is harmful to the majority, but probably it is most harmful to any minority that seeks to have some advantage from it. I think even the past history of India will show that. But in any event a minority in an independent State which seeks to isolate and separate itself does some injury to the cause of the country, and most of all it injures its own interests, because inevitably it puts a barrier between itself and the others, a barrier not on the religious plane but on the political plane--sometimes even to some extent on the economic plane; and it can never really exercise the influence which it legitimately ought to aspire to exercise, if it functions in that way...

Whereas it is essential for the proper functioning of democracy and the growth of national unity and solidarity that communalism should be eliminated from Indian life, this Assembly is of opinion that no communal organization which by its constituion or by the exercise of discretionary power vested in any of its officers or organs, admits to or excludes from its membership persons on grounds of religion, race and caste, or any of them, should be permitted to engage in any activities other than those essential for the bona fide religious and cultural needs of the community, and that all steps, legislative and administrative, necessary to prevent such activities should be taken.

The Education Ministry have suggested that the Inspectorates of Education in the States should be utilized to promote communal understanding in educational institutions. I think this is an excellent suggestion. I think also that our senior students, during their holidays, might well devote themselves to this highly important task. Whatever our views may be about political or economic problems, any man or woman with any sense will realize that no progress can be made unless we have this communal understanding. This is a challenge to us, and if we fail in this challenges we dub ourselves as backward and little-minded people lacking the culture that makes a nation grow and prosper.

REFERENCES

1. Foreword in Hindi to *Samskriti Ke Char Adhyaya* by Ramdhari Sinha 'Dinkar', September 30, 1955.
2. Speech at All India Convention, Karachi, March, 27, 1931.
3. Speech at All India Students Convention, Karachi, March, 27 1931.
4. Speech at Bangalore, October 6, 1955.
5. Speech at National Integration Conference, New Delhi, September 28, 1961.
6. A letter to Dr. Rajendra Prasad, August 7, 1947.
7. Speech in the Constituent Assembly (Legislative), New Delhi, April 3, 1948. Resolution moved by Mr. Ananthasayanam Ayyangar, Member of the Constituent Assembly:
8. Letter to Chief Minister, May 2, 1950.

EDUCATION

1. Function of Education

Social Relevance of Education;

Process of Education;

Education - Real and Superficial.

2. Basic Education

What it is;

Nai Talim;

The Basic Approach.

3. Higher Education

A Place of Culture;

Role of Universities;

Providing Environment for Creativity;

Reforms in University Education;

University Administration;

Universities and Research Institutes.

SEVEN

EDUCATION

Functions of Education[1]

Social Relevance of Education

The ideal of education has long been the improvement of the individual. The ideal must inevitably hold, for without individual advancement there can be no social progress. But even that care of the individual must today be considered in terms of the mass of the people or else the enlightened individual will be submerged in the unenlightened mass. And, in any event, is it right or just that a group of individuals should have opportunities of advancement and growth which are denied to the many?

But, even from the standpoint of the individual, a vital question has to be faced. Can an individual truly advance, except in the rarest cases, if the environment that surrounds him is pulling him back all the time? If this environment is evil or injurious to him, the individual battles in vain against it and must inevitably be crushed by it. What is this environment? It consists of inherited ideas, prejudices and superstitions which restrict the mind and prevent growth and change in a changing world. It is the pressure of political circumstances that keeps the individual and the group in enforced subjection and thus starves his soul and crushes his spirit. It is, above all, the stranglehold of economic conditions which denies opportunity to vast masses of people. It is this complex of prejudice and superstition, political and economic conditions, that form our environment which holds us in its grip.

Through your educational system you may teach all the well known virtues, but life today teaches something else, and the voice of life is louder and more effective. You may teach the advantages of co-operative effort, but our social structure is based on cut-throat competition, and each one tries to rise on the dead selves of others. The glittering prizes go to him who is most successful in knocking down and crushing his rivals. Is it any wonder that our youth should be attracted by these glittering prizes, and should hold acquisitiveness as the most desirable quality in an acquisitive society?

We swear by non-violence in this country, yet violence envelopes us not only in its more obvious forms of warring nations but in the very social structure in which we live. Out of this violent environment no real peace or non-violence can ever come, unless we change that environment itself.

Our educational system, in spite of the ideal which it may profess, is itself an outcome of and a part of this environment. It seeks sustenance from it and, consciously or unconsciously, supports it. Yet if there is anything clear in the world today, it is this: that this environment is the cause of most of our troubles, and to leave it as it is, is to head straight for disaster.

Indeed, it may already be too late to prevent that disaster, and the war that is raging in Europe may yet shatter the edifice of modern civilization. We shall not escape this tragedy, and even if we survive this general collapse our own problems threaten to overwhelm us, unless we see aright and act aright. Recent events have shown how strong the forces of evil and disruption and narrow-minded bigotry are in this country. We have seen also how the dominant political and economic interests resent and combat change.

...All education must have a definite social outlook and must train our youth for the kind of society we wish to have. Politicians may strive for political and economic changes in order to bring that society into existence, but the real basis of that society must be laid in the teaching of our schools and colleges. The real change will have to come in the minds of men, though that change can and will be helped greatly by external changes in the environment. The two processes go together and should help each other.

Our present-day social fabric is a decadent and dying thing, full of its own contradictions, and leading continually to war and conflict. This acquisitive and competitive society must be ended and must give place to a co-operative order, where we think in terms not of individual profit but of the common good; where individuals co-operate with each other and nations and peoples work in co-operation for human advancement; where human values count for more and there is no exploitation of a class or group or nation by another.

If this is the accepted ideal of our future society then all our education must be fashioned to that end and must not pay homage to anything that is against this conception of the social order. That education will always have to think in terms of the hundreds of millions of our people, and not sacrifice their interests for any group or class. The teacher will then be not just a follower of a profession which gives him a livelihood, but one who has chosen his vocation in the ardent spirit of a missionary in a sacred cause which fills his being.

Process of Education[2]

In the final analysis, no subject is of greater importance than that of education. It is the men and women in a country that make and build a nation and it is education that is supposed to build those men and women.

The process of education, therefore, must help to build men and women suited to the age and the tasks they have to perform. It should presumably deal with certain basic factors in the development of boys and girls to give them strength of character and the right outlook on life. I do not mean by this that they should be conditioned only in one particular way, but rather that they should develop, apart from the essentials of character, a trained receptive and tolerant mind which is capable of considering problems in their entirety and trying to arrive at solutions. They should in effect develop into integrated human beings. Integration means not only a process within themselves, which of course is highly important, but also a measure of integration with the environment.

The part of training that deals with the environment will necessarily vary with the age and the kind of work that these people may be called upon to do. We live, as is well known, in an intensely transitional age. We cannot go back upon it and we can only try to understand it and look forward to the changes that are likely to come.

Education - Real and Superficial[3]

I suppose everyone is concerned in every country because more and more it is realized that it is through education that you can ultimately influence people's minds and thereby events. I think in the Preamble of the Constitution of UNESCO it is stated that warss begin in the minds of men. Well, if wars begin in the minds of men as they surely do, then one has to influence the minds of men and women. That seems obvious enough and therefore, whether we look at it from the narrower point of view of imparting education say, in the scientific or technological fields which is so essential or other fields, the basic thing that should be necessary is to direct people towards thinking in terms of let us say, peace and co-operation and understanding and not in terms of the type of international life that we lead today.

But we find that the most highly educated nations and peoples in the world, who have all the advantages of technical education, advantages of education in humanities and who have succeeded in a large measure in getting rid of some of the ancient evils from which humanity has suffered like poverty, etc. in another context not only do not get on with each other but are full of violent hostility towards each other.

Now, is that the result of different types of education or lack of education? Does education lead to greater hostility in spite of greater understanding? It is a problem which, I will submit to you, deserves consideration. I am quite sure that education is essential and I am not decrying education but the fact is education or, if I may say so, that the type of education that we have had has not led to that peaceful and co-operative international approach which has become so essential to the world's growth or even to the world's survival. That troubles me.

And in thinking about our own-educational problems in this country–as we do very often, even a layman like me–we may argue as to greater stress sometimes on scientific training, technological training or may stress about humanities, the importance of the humanities.....

How far does education help in creating that atmosphere, I venture to submit, that it is worthy of your consideration. You are going to discuss training for responsibility which is a very good and desirable subject, an important subject that we, each individual have a measure of responsibility in discharging his obligations and duties. We claim rights but no right is ever divorced from a duty or an obligation and it is right that we should be trained in that.

But still responsibility for what? Responsibility for doing an odd job. Well, that is one thing and very necessary. Responsibility to our fellow-citizens, our neighbour, responsibility for not only our neighbour but the man who lives the next door to him, may be further away, may be in another country, national responsibility or international because the world as it is too compact, too close together for us to ignore or to live apart from any one else. The whole concept of national sovereignty indeed becomes weaker and weaker when you indulge in flying across numerous countries in a jet plane in a few hours and more so when you are on the threshold of the space age, all this business of national boundaries becomes rather out of date and yet our minds function in that previous age which is past, looking at things in a narrow way, narrow even from the nationalist concept.

It does surprise me that while education is obviously desirable, inevitable and essential, I do not find the educated person always so desirable. He is often, in spite of his education, rather narrow-minded and throws his weight about on others whom he considers inferior to him, whether he does it as an individual, as a group or as a nation, but he does it. And in some ways he has got, inspite of his education, rather a closed mind. He does not look into other people's minds, peep into it and understand it because he starts with the presumption that he has got all that he wants to have in his mind and does not open it to others' impressions. That surely cannot be a good result of education. Education should open the mind and enable a person to understand other human beings and be understood by them...

Big revolutionary changes are taking place in the minds of the people. Education, I think, is the most revolutionary factor in India and is changing the face of India. It is not so suddenly obvious but any person who goes and sees the changes taking place is tremendously impressed by it.

Basic Education

What it is

...Basic education* laid stress on various factors of importance, notably the coordination of the mind with manual work. That is an essential feature which we have to encourage...

*Basic education, started at Wardha in 1937, was designed to develop the basic abilities of the child and therefore gave a primary place to manual training in the child's education. With the mother tongue as the medium of instruction, it was to be free and compulsory, and of seven-year duration at the school level. It was believed that such education apart from stimulating the intellect, "would be a kind of insurance against unemployment."

Nai Talim

In regard to refugee children. I am very anxious that proper arrangements for education should be made. Indeed, I am more anxious about the children than about the grown-ups and I must confess sorrowfully that we have not done our duty to these children. Our educational methods are slow, cumbrous and expensive. Apart from this, they seem to train people for a career of unemployment. Obviously they are not suited for these refugee children. The only proper method for them was and is the Sevagram basic school method, that is, the *Nai Talim*.

The Basic Approach[4]

Looked at from the purely educational point of view, I think, any modern educationist is bound to accept the system called the Basic method of Education. Yet, unfortunately, and to my great surprise, some educationists in our country have chosen to criticize it, saying that this is a throw-back to some primitive stage of instruction. I can only say that they have not taken the trouble to understand what basic education is. Further, they have not quite understood what India is aiming at today. Now, the whole pattern of education, as is wellknown, was originally devised by the British 150 years or so ago with the purpose of getting a large number of Indians trained to help them in the administration of the country in the lower grades.

It is true that since then our education has progressed, and it is also true that even under the old mode of education India has produced some very fine specimen of humanity, very finely educated, cultured and trained. Great men and women have been produced by India. That is, however, not an argument that it is a perfect type of education. For my part. I think that given the opportunities, India ought to produce a large number of very high-class persons, both men and women. I have no doubt in my mind-and I am not, if I may say so, merely talking casually about this - that given opportunities, India can produce hundreds of thousands of absolutely first-class people in various spheres of work and knowledge. They do not have this opportunity now. I tell you that nothing saddens me so much as when I go abroad and return and see more especially our little children who are denied education or the proper education. They are sometimes even denied food and clothing. If our children are today denied these, what is the India of tomorrow going to be? It is the duty of the State to provide good education for every child in the country. I would add that it is the duty of the State to give education, free education for every child and also make provision for it. Unfortunately, we cannot do all these things quickly and promptly for lack of resources, lack of finances, lack of trained personnel, lack of trained teachers and for lack of many things. But we have to get going, because after all, whatever the pattern of society we are visualising, it must contain trained human beings, not people who have just learnt to read and write, but trained men and women whose character has been developed, whose mind has within it some elements of culture and whose hands can do something.

In our country there has, unfortunately, been a tradition that manual labour is something degrading and meant merely for the lower classes of people. I doubt if anything has done more harm to India than this peculiar and fantastic notion that manual labour is meant for the lower classes and a higher class person should not move his hand but only do what is called mental, intellectual work. That idea is still persisting. I can only describe it not only as a wrong idea, but a pernicious idea. I do not think any nation that feels that way can really progress. Apart from everything else, from the point of view even of physical development, manual work is essential... I have always attached a good deal of importance to the body; I like to be fit and strong. I have an acute dislike for illness, anybody's illness. I do not sympathise with illness. I say so, because I am afraid many people here think that it is rather aristocratic to be ill, to be feeble. I do not like feebleness, frailness, sickness, weakness or illness. I want our people, young people and old, to be healthy and strong and agile. I want them to be physically able, an A-1 nation, because individuals apart, I do not think we can really make much intellectual progress unless we give it a good physical background. This aspect has little to do with this resolution and yet it has much to do with it.

The type of education which concerns itself only with the reading of books is, from the human point of view, from any point of view, incomplete. You may become a high-class mathematician or something else as an individual, but you will find that you will be a better mathematician if your body functioned adequately and properly. It has, therefore, become necessary in our country to lay greater stress on physical fitness. I do not like any person going about with a bent back. I want them to be straight like a ram-rod. I want them to be quick in their walking, not sauntering as many of us do. It has thus become a matter of extreme importance, this stress on two things–physical culture and physical fitness and ability of the hands to do something. You can take it from me that if your hands can do something, your mind will work much more satisfactorily. I have no doubt about it.

When we talk about basic education, as you will see in this resolution, we say something that is of very great significance. We say that we require an education for the purpose of achieving the national aims and social objectives of free India and, in particular, for training the right type of personnel for the speedy execution of development plans. After all, you want to educate a person for something. What for? Perhaps, previously it was to get a post or job in the Government. Well, Government service is an honourable calling, nothing wrong about it, in free India certainly. But, obviously, only a handful can get into Government service and the vast majority of people have to do something else. You can become lawyers, and others. Ours is a free country and anybody can become a lawyer, even though I do not think it is profitable from the national point of view for us to have too many lawyers. However, that is a matter of personal opinion. I want you, each one of you, to produce something. You are a consumer, each one of you. You eat, you clothe yourself, you consume what society produces. Unless you produce at least the amount you consume, you are burden, on society. You are consuming something that others have produced. A French man said: "You are a thief on society; you are thieving other people's wealth". You talk about a rich man who lives on other people's wealth. It may be true, and yet possibly, the rich man is perforing apart from his riches, an important part, having his organising capacity and all that. He is doing something which somebody else may not be able to do. But it is only thieving if the person who is not rich and produces nothing, yet lives on other people's production.

We want a society in which every body is a producer. In some way or other everybody is a consumer, and he must also be a producer. If he is to be a producer, an effective producer, he must know his job well; he must learn. We want absolutely first-rate men at the job. We want everyone to be good at a particular job he does. There are hundreds of thousands of ways of working. I do not confine you to this or that, but you must in some field of activity or other be a producer.

Now, if this is our objective, then our whole training must be aimed at that, ideological training, intellectual training as well as physical training.

The whole concept of basic education, as I understand it, is that for a period of seven years, everybody in India, boy and girl, say, from the age of 7 to 14, must go through this course of basic training. That training must give the person a background, an adequate background, to do something. He may, at a later stage, go for higher studies. Higher studies do not necessarily mean a degree, like B.A. or M.A. It will probably mean study at some technical institute or some scientific institute where he can go and specialise. But, seven years of basic training will be common for all. That will give him some cultural attainment, some character, some capacity to work hands and feet and co-ordinate his manual activity with his mental process, some intellectual ability and character. We want that type of basic education throughout. Before basic education - we do not say that in this resolution, but what I consider very essential is the pre-basic training, that is the training of the child from the very moment almost of birth, or after the child is a year or two old, some vital training, simple but of the highest importance, more important than any training you can give afterwards, since the child's character is largely formed in the first 9 or 10 years. We have to do that in India. It is a tremendous task. Now, for the present, let us have the second, that is, basic education and try to give it to everybody in India, every child of this age.

The next step will, of course, be that this basic training should be fitted into the post-basic training, for you cannot have a full-stop after basic training. It has to go on. No doubt, many people after that may not go for additional training. One may become a farmer, a worker, a shop-keeper or an artisan. They are important things. While most people may not need to go to a college or university, those who have the capacity, can go and have higher technical training, scientific training, medical training or engineering training that will diversify occupational pattern. The basic training and the other training should, therefore, be linked, should be dovetailed. At present, they are not. There is some difficulty. So, here is a subject of the highest importance, the training of our youth, training them in body and mind and hand and all these, and getting rid of this extraordinary notion that manual work is something degarding. There is nothing more ennoble than manual work, nothing better for your physical or mental health...

Higher Education[5]

A Place of Culture

I take it that a university is essentially a place of culture, whatever 'culture' might mean... There is a great deal of culture all over the place and I, normally, find that those people who talk most loudly of culture, according to my judgment, possess no culture at all. Culture, first of all, is not loud; it is quiet, it is restrained, it is tolerant. You may judge the culture of a person by his silence, by a gesture by a phrase or, more especially, by his life generally. The peculiar, narrow idea of culture that is spreading is that culture depends on the kind of headgear you wear or the kind of food you eat or on similar superficial things which, I do not deny, have a certain importance but which are very secondary in the larger context of life.

Each country has certain special cultural characteristics which have been developed through the ages. Similarly, each age has a culture and a certain way of its own. The cultural characteristics of a country are important and are certainly retained, unless, of course, they do not fit in with the spirit of the age. So, by all means, adhere to the special culture of your nation. But there is something that is deeper than national culture and that is human culture. If you do not have that human culture, that basic culture, then even that national culture of which you may be so proud has no real roots and will not do you much good. Today more especially, it has become essential for us to develop, in addition to such national culture as we may have, something that can only be called a world culture. There is much talk of One World and I believe that, at some time or other, that talk must bear fruit or else this world will go to pieces. It may be that we will not see that One World in our generation but if you want to prepare for that One World you must at least think about it. You have at least a culture to sustain you; and there is no reason why you should live your lives in narrow grooves, trying to think yourselves superior to the rest of the world.

Role of Universities[6]

The universities have much to teach in the modern world and their scope of activity ever enlarges. I am myself a devotee of science and believe that the world will ultimately be saved, if it is to be saved, by the method and approach of science. But whatever path of learning we may pursue, and however profitable it might seem to us, there is a certain basis and foundation without which the house of learning is built on shifting sands. It is for a university to realize and to lay stress on this essential basis and foundation, those standards of thought and action which make an individual and a nation. Above all, this is necessary today, during this phase of extremely rapid transition, when old values have almost left us and we have adopted no new ones...

A University stands for humanism, for tolerance, for reason, for progress, for the adventure of ideas and for the search for truth. It stauds for the onward march of the human race towards even higher objectives. If the universities discharge their duty adequately, then it is well with the nation and the people. But if the temple of learning itself becomes a home of narrow bigotry and petty objectives, how then will the nation prosper or a people grow in stature?

A vast responsibility, therefore, rests on our universities and educational institutions and those who guide their destinies. They have to keep their lights burning and must not stray from the right path even when passion convulses the multitude and blinds many amongst those whose duty it is to set an example to others.

Providing Environment for Creativity

...We have to accept the present and think of the future. How shall we shape the present? How are you, young men and women of this University, going to conduct yourselves? I do not know what you have in your minds or what desires and urges influence you. I try to study the millions of faces I see wherever I go and I have seen a good proportion of India's vast population. Although I see them in crowds and in groups, I look into their eyes and try to read what lies behind those eyes. I do this, especially when I meet young men and women, because I am deeply concerned with the future of India which they represent to me. The future of this country ultimately depends on her young men and women, most of whom are in colleges and universities today. I am very anxious to find out what stuff they are made of. They are large in number; but what really counts, if our country is to progress, is the quality of our human material. The future of India does not depend on her numbers or even on her past, except in so far as the future grows out of the present and the present grows out of the past. It is possible for a country to make progress to some extent even with people of mediocre quality. India has a large number of them. Obviously, that is not enough. If a great country like India is to be greater, it is essential for her to have men and women who must be more than mediocre. I have no doubt that you try to play a good game when you go in for sports. You perhaps run a hundred yards in ten seconds; but if you want to be an athlete of real quality you have to surpass and outdistance others. It makes a lot of difference whether you do a hundred yards in ten seconds or in eleven seconds. The difference is only one second but it is very important. That applies to everything.... We produced men and women of quality in the past. Subsequently, however, that quality seemed to have worn off and we became a nation that more or less lived on its inheritance. Of course, nothing is more advantageous and more creditable than a rich heritage; but nothing is more dengerous for a nation than to sit back and live on that heritage. A nation cannot progress if it merely imitates its ancestors; what builds a nation is creative, inventive and vital activity. I seek the creative mind. How do creative minds come to be? In many ways, I suppose. I know that... what the University can do is to provide an environment in which creativeness and vitality of mind and body have a place and can prosper.

India seems to me an odd mixture of traits and characteristics. Some fill me with joy and faith and others with alarm. I cannot predict which will prosper and which will ultimately win. That, the future will tell. All I can say is that I have a great deal of faith in my country and in my people. At the same time, what is wrong with our country is also quite obvious. We are narrow in mind and vision; we not only lack creativeness of mind but the atmosphere in which it can flourish. I am astonished at the way the word 'culture' is bandied about in India. To me this only means that there is no culture where this is done. Culture is not something that can be bandied about. It does not talk too much and does not shout too much. The other day, I read one of Rabindranath Tagore's poems or rather a translation of it, which spoke of the wonderful variety of India where innumerable streams have flowed, producing the culture we now possess. The capacity to absorb these various streams of culture is a part of the creativeness of India. Therefore, there is no reason why we should adopt the narrow outlook of pride and folly which makes us think that we have every thing and that we need receive nothing from outside. South-East Asia and the Far East have borrowed freely from India's cultural inheritance. Similarly, we find evidence of other cultures in India. Of course, the basis of Indian culture remains unchanged even though it has absorbed other cultures. Such was the country of our distant ancestors. Gradually, a change came. We became afraid of others and shrank into ourselves. We did not want either to go out ourselves or to let others come in. We developed narrow grooves of thought and narrow divisions amongst ourselves, each division isolating itself from other castes or groups. We practically imposed a ban on travel abroad. People were afraid they would lose their caste or religion if they went out of India.

To be dynamic and creative is the practical policy or the higher view of culture. It is fatal to sink into narrowness of mind in spite of the fact that India has had a tremendously rich inheritance. How many of you have that dynamic approach and how many of you are thinking in terms of getting jobs here and there under the Government? Whether you go into Government service or take up any other occupation, what is you ideal? Just to earn a few hundred rupees? Or is it to achieve something creative and good? Are you just dragging on an unworthy existence for a number of years and doing nothing else? That is a big question facing India. Whatever our virtues and failings–and a long list can be prepared of both–I believe in facing life in an adventurous way, in meeting life more than half way without making a noise and without shouting. Whether Nature adapts itself to you or you to Nature ultimately depends on whether your approach to life and to its problems is going to be an adventurous and active one or a static one. What is your ambition? What I seek in the eyes of the innumerable men and women when I go round the country is great and high ambition to do great things. Sometimes, I see some eyes which rather thrill me; there is something of quality in them. The more I see such eyes or faces, the more I am assured of the future, which depends on the men and women who have the spirit of adventure and who do not flinch from difficulty.

Reforms in University Education[7]

...The whole question of university education has recently been considered by the Universities Commission of which Dr. Radhakrishnan was Chairman... This Commission was composed of very eminent educationists from India, the United States, and England. They have done a remarkably good piece of work in a short time... They have pointed out the evils of tying up our examination system with government appointments. These examinations of ours and the education that lies behind them are looked upon just as stepping-stones to employments by government. Nothing could be worse for education. Our universities turn out tens of thousands of graduates who do not know what to do and appear to be incapable of doing anything except in some office. Our education has been described, perhaps a little uncharitably, as a training for unemployment. That may be an exaggeration. But there is a great deal of truth in it. So it is suggested that university examinations should be completely divorced from official appointments for which there should be separate tests.

One other matter to which I attach great importance, and about which I think I have previously written to you, is the necessity of some kind of manual labour for each student. I think it should be a good thing if every graduate, before he got his degree, was expected to put in a full year's labour in a factory or field or some other place. It might be some kind of social work. This is not a novel idea, as something like this has been tried with success in other countries. Many countries go in for conscription for military service. Why should we not have conscription for social service and labour? That would include, of course, some kind of elementary military training without arms. That discipline is badly needed in this country.

University Administration[8]

The question of education has been much in my mind recently. We all realize the importance of it from every point of view and indeed it is essential for our social and economic development. We want mass education as well as higher education, more particularly technical education.

When we talk about the emotional integration of India, we think immediately of the educational process which will help in this integration. No doubt it will do so, and it has become important that our textbooks and courses should be prepared accordingly.

And yet, there is an obvious danger that faces us if certain present trends in educational matters are allowed to continue. It may be that these linguistic trends might actually lead to greater provincialism and feelings of separateness among the states. This is not merely a linguistic matter although that is important enough, but certain other trends which lay stress on the state and not on the country as a whole. The gods we pay homage to become tied up with our conception of the state and not the nation.

I am myself convinced that the medium of education must be the mother tongue of the child, boy and girl. Only then can his or her mind develop adequately. But unless the larger ideal of India and its unity is always kept in view, this may well lead us to a form of separatism which will impede both our unity and our progress. Our universities, adopting, if they do, the regional languages, will get more and more isolated from each other. Professors and teaching staff will not be easily exchangeable and generally speaking, the outlook that will inevitably grow out of these surroundings, will be a narrow one and not so much an all-India one. There are, of course, strong urges in favour of Indian unity. I do not mean to suggest that they will be easily overcome, but while intellectually we may continue to think of that unity, emotionally we will be conditioned otherwise.

How are we to get over this dilemma? The universities are supposed to build a certain intellectual atmosphere in the country. If there is no common approach in the universities, then this atmosphere itself will be not a common one but a somewhat disruptive one. As a matter of fact, while standards of education are going up in other advanced countries, our own standards are said to be deteriorating. It has become important to pull these standards up by an attempt at a more effective organization of resources which are in many cases spread out too thinly to be really effective. This is particularly applicable to scientific and technological studies, but it applies to the humanities also.

In science or in any of the higher studies, it is not the brilliant individual who counts so much now, but the team of able men who work together. If we have done well in atomic energy, it is because we have collected a considerable number of able young men and women to work together as a team. In our universities, this kind of thing is lacking, even though they may have individual teachers who are good.

It has been suggested that the way to pull standards up in universities is to encourage this team work by having centres of advanced study in as many universities as possible. That is to say, each centre will be for a particular subject, and it should function on an all-India basis. In regard to scientific and technological subjects, such centres should work in close co-operation with national laboratories and institutes.

Each such centre in a university would have a team of professors, lecturers, research fellows, etc. of outstanding ability and qualifications actively engaged in research and advanced teaching, in a particular branch of study. It is considered important that there should be a combination of research and teaching, thus not only maintaining contact with fresh young minds, but also creating a proper academic atmosphere for serious and sustained work. We have found that we have quite an adequate number of bright young students, and given the chance, they will do very well. But that chance is usually lacking.

All this would mean an addition to our professorial and teaching staff. In this matter of team work, a certain minimum number is necessary.

We dare not allow the standards of our universities to go down. For, a university can only justify itself by maintaining high academic and professional standards. It would be an essential part of any such scheme for universities to keep in close touch with each other, exchanging professors, teachers, scholars and senior students, and thus building a corporate intellectual life of India.

If universities are functioning in different languages, how do we bring about this close co-operation and exchange of professors, students, etc. between one region of the country and another? This question has been troubling me and I would like to draw your attention to it. All our progress depends not on the number of factories and plants that are put up, but on the quality of human beings that we produce and train. That quality depends, in the final analysis, on our universities and on their close contact with each other.

I have often noticed that the appointment of vice-chancellors to universities is considered almost entirely from the administrative point of view. Administration is important, but essentially a university is a body of persons devoted to academic pursuits, and this must always be kept in view so that a proper academic atmosphere is maintained and encouraged. If the vice-chancellor, who is the executive head of the university, is merely an administrator, then he cannot enter into that academic life which is so important, nor is he likely to be respected greatly by the large body of students. I think it is essential, therefore, that our vice-chancellors should be men of learning and high academic standards.

Universities and Research Institutes.[9]

...Among the many disappointments that we have had, there is at least one achievement for which we can take credit and that is the advance of scientific research in this country. Our new laboratories are magnificent institutions of which any country can be proud. In this connection, I should like to draw your attention to a certain tendency which is doing harm to science. This is a tendency towards separation of research from teaching. This is accentuated in India by the separation of most research institutes from the universities. Even from the point of view of governmental organization, they are separate. It seems to me essential that there should be the closest co-ordination between research institutes and universities. Also that we should encourage research work in universities. After all, our major research institutes must be fed from the universities and if the universities dry up, then the research institutes cannot survive for long.

REFERENCES

1. Address at the All India Educational Conference, Baradari, December 27,1939.
2. Message to the Hindustani Talims Sangh, November, 8, 1957.
3. Inaugural address to the W.C.O.T.P. Conference at New Delhi.
4. Speech proposing the resolution on education at the Avadi Session of the Congress, January, 1955.
5. Convercation address at University of Ceylon, Colombo, January 12, 1950.
6. An Address at Allahabad University, December 13, 1947.
7. Letter to Chief Minister. September 2, 1949.
8. Circular, July 3, 1961.
9. Extract from letter to chief Minister, 15th April, 1950.

WOMEN

EIGHT

WOMEN

The Essential Spirit of Indian Womanhood[1]

There are two views, among others, about Indian women. One is the typical old Indian viewpoint of the Indian woman being a symbol of purity, faithfulness and submission and devotion to her husband. The great symbols are Sita and Savitri. The other view, mostly to be found in some western countries, is that the Indian women is backward, suppressed and treated almost as a chattel.

Both these views are far from the truth, and deal with some imaginary conceptions little related to life, for life is much more complicated and these simple definitions do not give us much insight into its working. I suppose that none of us can be truly objective in discussing a subject of this kind. In a country like India, with its enormous variety, it is easy to pick up some one aspect here and there and generalize from it. So we can indulge in praise of the women of india and find many examples to justify our praise. We can also condemn their position in Indian life and also find examples to justify this.

For my part, I am partial to the women of India, and the more I have wandered about this great country the more I have felt a certain pride in our womenfolk.

Women in India have played an important part in our social life and in our history. They have played this part in every branch of national activity, from high learning to valour on the battlefield. But it is their unobtrusive work in the household, in the village or in the larger community, that has moulded the nation.

They are essentially feminine, and that is as it should be. But then I have always felt that India, for all her manly qualities, is specially noted for the feminine virtues– gentleness, tendencess, a certain patient resignation and a quiet and sometimes amazing courage of a somewhat passive kind. I say this realizing that I am generalizing when I should not do so, because there are all kinds of men as well as all kinds of women in this country. But I suppose it is true that the idea of women in India is chiefly connected with these feminine virtues as well as, perhaps, with some feminine failings....

Thousands of years have moulded and conditioned our race. Today we pass rapidly through various phases of transition. That is inevitable and not to be regretted. But I doubt if all these coming changes, big as they are, will uproot us from our old foundations. Someone said about another country words which may be applied to India: 'She lives in her own time, in the rhythm of her own history, which does not quite keep time with the clocks of the twentieth century'.

Yet the twentieth century is upon us, with all its destruction of the old and hopes and fears of the future. We live in India simultaneously in almost all the ages and centuries that have preceded this middle of the twentieth century. We are busy co-ordinating them and trying to fit them into each other, to keep the old roots and to have fresh branches and fruits and flowers in this present-day world of ours. The rhythm of our time is an ever-changing one. The clock ticks on often leaving our thinking and our policies behind.

We talk of revolutions, political and economic. And yet the greatest revolution in a country is the one that affects the status and living conditions of its women. It is in so far as our revolution has affected our women that it is basic. I believe it has donc so, not perhaps in a dramatic and aggressive way but rather after the old Indian fashion of combining change with continuity. And yet there have been many dramatic phases of this change even in our time.

It was Gandhiji, that wonderful man and great revolutionary, who brought a dramatic change among our women, when at his bidding they came out in large numbers from the shelter of their homes to take their part in the struggle for India's freedom. Once the old shackles were removed, it was no longer possible to replace them in the same way. Attempts were no doubt made to go back, but they were bound to fail.

Now the full impact of modern life is being felt by our womenfolk in the cities chiefly and in our schools and colleges. I do not know what the final outcome will be except that it will be different from the past, though perhaps not so different as to affect the essential characteristics of India's women.

I can say with considerable confidence that I am proud of the women of India. I am proud of their beauty, grace, charm, shyness, modesty, intelligence, and their spirit of sacrifice, and I think if anybody can truly represent the spirit of India, the women can do it and not the men. Every time that woman has been sent abroad, she has done well; not only done well, but produced a fine impression about the womanhood of India.

I have the greatest admiration–I am not talking about the ancient Indian ideal of womanhood, which I certainly admire–for the women of India today. I have faith in them. I am not afraid to allow them freedom to grow, because I am convinced that no amount of legal constraint can prevent society from going in a certain direction. And if you put too much restraint, the structure breaks.[1]

Women and Politics

(i) Torch bearers of liberty;

(ii) Women's Wing of the Congress;

(iii) Equal Citizenship;

(iv) As Legislators

Torch Bearers of Liberty[3]

Most of us menfolk were in prison. And then a remarkable thing happened. Our women came to the front and took charge of the struggle. Women had always been there of course, but now there was an avalanche of them, which took not only the British Government but their own menfolk by surprise. Here were these women, women of the upper or middle classes, leading sheltered lives in their homes, peasant women, working-class women, rich women, poor women, pouring out in their tens of thousands in defiance of government order and police *lathi*. It was not only that display of courage and daring, but what was even more surprising was the organizational power they showed.

The lot of our womenfolk in prison was especially hard and painful to contemplate. They were mostly middle-class women, accustomed to a sheltered life, and suffering chiefly from the many repressions and customs produced by a society dominated to his won advantage by man. The call of freedom had always a double meaning for them, and the enthusiasm and energy with which they threw themselves into the struggle had no doubt their springs in the vague and hardly conscious, but nevertheless intense, desire to rid themselves of domestic slavery also. Excepting a very few, they were classed as ordinary prisoners and placed with the most degraded of companions, and often under horrid conditions...[4]

I have long been of opinion that a nation's progress depends on the position of women there. The fall of India from her high status was partly at least done due to the deterioration of the status and position of women in India. In a subject country men and women both suffer the indignity of subjection to foreign rule and the numerous disabilities that flow from it. So the first and primary duty of every one is to do his or her utmost to free the country. Indeed it is in performance of the duty that a person or a group gets rid also in some measure of other disabilities. We have seen during the past quarter of a century how the participation of women in the great national struggle in India has in effect raised their status in many ways and opened our opportunities to them.

Now we are on the verge of great changes but before these take place great efforts and sacrifices will be needed. In these I hope women will take a leading part and thus fit themselves for the responsibilities ahead. They will have the future task of getting rid of the many disabilities, legal, social and other, which today attach to their sex, so that they may play an equal part with their menfolk in the building up of a free India.

For the women of India, for all their charm and intelligence and capacity for good work, have been too long neglected. I believe that India has a great future, but I also believe that real and rapid progress in India will only come when our womenfolk get really moving and rid themselves of everything that suppresses them and keeps them back. Because I see clear and definite signs of the movement. I am full of hope for India, and because our national movement has been largely instrumental in releasing women from many an old bond, that movement has demonstrated it essential soundness and vitality.[5]

Women's Wing of the Congress[6]

My own conception of the women's branch of the A.I.C.C. is that it should collect all material relating to women's activities in India, it should keep in touch with all women's organizations in India, it should particularly keep in touch with such women's work as is being done by Congress women and through Congress organisations, it should send such suggestions as may be desirable for the coordination of these various activities, and it should issue special directions to Provincial Congress Committees in this behalf. It cannot undertake direct work of organization etc.

Again in the present crisis attention should not be given to long distant programme but rather to the immediate need. Women should address themselves to the local programmes of self-defence and self-sufficiency as outlined by the Congress. Their work will be chiefly confined to women. It is very important that this approach be made to women as public morale depends greatly on how women feel and act. If they are given some work in their own local areas, they are less likely to give way to a feeling of helplessness and they will feel that they are parts of a larger cooperative enterprise. Immediate problems are arising in some places of molestation of women. This kind of thing is likely to increase as conditions deteriorate. To face this problem women can be of great help, for it is essentially a psychological problem. My own little experience has been that women are anxious to know what they can do at present and any lead given to them will yield results. I am all against treating women as helpless human beings who cannot look after themselves and who must run away from the danger zone. At any time this is bad policy and makes them even more helpless than they are. In present circumstances it is completely pointless as you cannot limit the danger zone. Any and every place may become the danger zone and even the privacy of a house will not be outside this zone. So the only way to tackle the problem is to make women realise that they have to and can face it and to prepare them mentally and otherwise for this.

Equal Citizenship[7]

So far as the women suffrage movement is concerned in its narrow aspect there is not much doing in India. Women have got the suffrage though in a limited way and they are bound to get it extended. But the growing feminist movement in India which deals with other problems also is of course an important later day development. Politically speaking you are no doubt aware that the Congress stands whole-heartedly for equal citizenship of women with men and for the same franchise for both. So far as I am concerned I think that women should be treated on the same level as men educationally and economically and industrially, except in so far as a few occupations are concerned.

Women As Legislators[8]

You are going to have election for the new Parliament very soon. I am writing to you about the necessity of having an adequate number of women members elected. Even in the Constituent Assembly the women members were very few. Of these some dropped out for various reasons and their places were filled by men. I think it is important that we should keep up and add to the number of women in Parliament. From every point of view this is desirable. I have no doubt that a sufficient number of women, at least as competent and suitable as men, are available.

Educational Progress[9]

Girls' Education

I believe education is spreading fast, though the gap between boys'and girls' education is still marked. But it is spreading undoubtedly. Possibly in a few years time, perhaps four or five years, it may well include every boy and girl in the country.

Now, the reasons why girls' education has lagged behind somewhat are fairly obvious-social customs, and other factors too. I do not think those reasons apply with the same force today as they used to, and I have no doubt that this trend will go up. Now it is really for expert educationists and others to suggest what should be done in this matter, and not for an amateur like me who with all his goodwill for what you are aiming at, cannot speak with any authority on the subject. I do not have the figures before me regarding girls' education, but I should think that on the whole they are encouraging, although not so much in comparison with boys' education. Intrinsically, they are satisfactory.

There is one thing that struck me as illustrating the great need for girls' education. You will find that in the past, wherever girls' education was encouraged in India, there was progress. I suppose Punjab is one of the places where girls' education had an earlier beginning than elsewhere. In many respects, Punjab is one of our progressive States. I suppose that might be true of some other places, too. So girls' education is not an end in itself but is intimately connected with the social fabric and with advance along other lines, too.

Therefore, girls' education is very important. Now, of course, conditions are such that they are compelling the advancement of girls' education, irrespective of my desire or your desire to do that. Therefore, whatever you may do or not do, girls' education is bound to advance. I suppose the only difficulty arises in certain rural areas. In towns, the need for girls' education is accepted. In rural areas, too difficulties largely arise from the location of the school. It is difficult for them to walk long distances to go to school. These are the difficulties which have to be got over by the education authorities there.

They are not difficulties which cannot be overcome. There is very little opposition to their education, though there may be a lack of enthusiasm for it here and there. That too will disappear.

...You are, I suppose, thinking of girls' education in the primary and secondary stages. In the later stages, in university stage, girls are fairly successful not only in terms of numbers who pass, but otherwise, too. They are doing fairly well. Ultimately, the future of girls' education depends on the openings available for them in professions and other jobs. Those openings are now increasing daily.

Of course, looking at the mass of the womenfolk, there is no doubt they have been working. They work in the field, they work in the factory. The problem is really of the middle class. Others too have their problems, but different reasons apply to them. But nobody is against education for girls. It is only a question of providing facilities. If facilities are there, they will join schools and colleges in greater numbers.

It seems to me that while the progress of women's education is forging ahead at such a pace, some attention may also be paid to men's education. Truly no argument is required in defence of women's education. For my part, I have always been strongly of the opinion that while it may be possible to neglect men's education it is not possible or desirable to neglect women's education. The reasons are obvious. If you educate the women, probably men will be affected thereby, and in any event children will be affected. For every educationist knows that the formative years of a person's life are the first seven or eight years. We talk about schools, and colleges which are no doubt important, but a person is more or less made in the first ten years of his or her life. Obviously, in that period, it is the mother who counts most of all. Therefore, the mother who has been well trained in various ways becomes essential to education. Most mothers, trained otherwise, I regret to say, are not good mothers. They are too soft. They stuff their children with all kinds of eatables, put too many clothes on them, wrap their necks and heads and ears with all kinds of woollen apparel and make the boy or girl almost an imbecile before he so she grows up. Therefore, it is necessary for women to be educated, if not for themselves, at any rate for their children.

A great French writer once remarked: "If you want me to tell you what a nation is like or what a social organization is like, tell me the position of women in that nation". The status and social place of women will indicate the country's character more than anything else. That applies equally to the educational, social, economic and other fields.

The idea that women should be kept away from most occupations no longer finds favour. It might be that certain occupations are not suited for women, but that is a different matter. There are plenty of occupations which they could engage in and which they do engage in. If we analyse the matter carefully, we shall find that the average women in India works in the field. In fact, both man and woman work in the field. It is only when one gets to the middle class that the question of distinction arises. The great majority of our women have to work because economic circumstances compel them to work. Unfortunately, the ideas has been prevailing -- I am glad to see that it is rapidly fading -- that the less work one does the higher is one's status in society. Thus the person who never works at all has the highest status...

That age is past and everybody, man or woman, has got to be physically good and strong and mentally alert, and do creative, productive work. A time is going to come when people will not tolerate a person who does no work. Therefore, apart from the intrinsic desirability of education, people should have education in sheer self-defence, whether it be defence as a nation against other nations of the world or within the nation itself... It should be the duty the state to provide education of all tests to everybody. I hope a time will come when that will be done. Education is of basic importance, of course; but at the same time it is tied up with the productive capacity of the nation. To increase the productive capacity many things of basic importance have to be done... We have to decide which problem is to be given priority of treatment and draw up a balanced system of priorities. Obviously, in every system, education has to be given a very high place. The problem now is what type of education it should be and also how far we should go in for expensive buildings. Some of the expensive buildings which have been put up for village schools in North India are ugly, futile and in every sense-bad. High structures are put up and charged for by the P.W.D.

when a neat cottage would be infinitely more graceful and useful besides being inexpensive.

We have wrong ideas about many things and sometimes suffer from what may be called the Anglo-Indian conception of things. I am not using the expression in the racial sense but am referring to the mixture of conceptions arising from the impact of the English mind in India. In architecture, housing and other matters, we seem to have lost our foothold, more or less having lost faith in own conceptions. We have accepted many Western ideas, which were partly imposed on us regardless of the fact that India is a country entirely different from England, climatically and otherwise. Of course, the English rulers did not worry much about these matters. They also felt that imperial *izzat* required that they should impose their own conception of things, buildings and the rest of it, even in a small place. But that was really our fault and not the fault of Englishmen. However, the fact remains that we have inherited all kinds of astonishing ideas about buildings and the rest. I am quite sure that education will advance rapidly if we simplify our ideas about buildings and spend more on education and less on bricks. I am all for dignified buildings for educational institutions. I believe that good buildings do produce a strong impression on the person concerned. I do not want shabby, shoddy structures; we should put up dignified, solid buildings, but, meanwhile, if we are to make progress, let us spend what we have on education and its content, rather than on bricks and mortar.

...Only yesterday, Shri. Basheer Ahmed wrote to me a 'private and confidential' letter. Let me whisper it to you: he said in his letter that education among Muslim women was very backward here and that I should say somethings to push it forward. Certainly I am prepared to say a great deal. In fact, whatever I have been saying is meant to stress that aspect. Whatever group or religion one might belong to, education is essential. By education I mean education and not merely learning to be lady-like. Learning to be lady-like may be good in itself but it is not education as such. Education has mainly two aspects, cultural aspect which makes a person grow, and the productive aspect which makes a person do things. Both are essential. Everybody should be a producer as well as good citizen and not a sponge on another person even though the other person may be one's own husband or wife. That is the way we are developing and persons who do not wake up to this fact and prepare themselves for it will just be left behind. So it is highly necessary that we should develop our education, among our girls more especially, because men are provided for to some extent, There are still inhibitions in the case of Muslim girls' education and these should be removed because, apart from any other big reason, common sense tells us so.[10]

Social Shackles[11]

...A great French idealist, Charles Fourrier once said: "One could judge the degree of civilization of a country by the social and political position of its women." And if we are to judge India today, we shall have to judge her by her women. The future that we build up will also be judged by the position of Indian women. I must confess to you that I am intensely dissatisfied with the lot of the Indian women to day. We hear a good deal about Sita and Savitri. They are revered names in India and rightly so. But I have a feeling that these echoes from the past are raised chiefly to hide our present deficiencies and to prevent us from attacking the root cause of women's degradation in India today.

I find from a reference to the report of this institution that it was started to give special instruction to women. It was laid down that since man was the bread-winner, women's place was in the home and her ideal should be that of a devoted wife and nothing more. Her chief delight should be in skilfully rearing her children and serving her revered elders. May I say that I do not agree with this ideal of women's life or education? What does it signify? It means that woman has one profession and one only, that is the profession of marriage and it is our chief business to train her for this profession. Even in this profession her lot is to be one of secondary importance. She is always to be the devoted help-mate, the follower and the obedient slaves of her husband and others. I wonder if any of you here has read Ibsen's[12] *Doll's House*; if so, you will perhaps appreciate the word "Doll" when I use it in this connection.

The future of India cannot consist of dolls and playthings and if you made half the population of a country a mere plaything of the other half, an encumbrance on others, how will you ever make progress? Therefore I say that you must face the problem boldly and attack the roots of the evil. We have *Purdah* and child marriage and denial of rights to women in so many fields. Go to any country and you will see bright-faced boys and girls playing and growing strong in mind and body. Here children of the same age are kept in *purdah*, locked up in cages almost, and denied in a large measure all freedom. They are married just when they should be growing physically and intellectually and are thus stunted and made miserable for life.

If this *Vidyapitha* really stands for the progress of our women it must attack these evil customs. But I should like to remind the women present here that no people, no group, no community, no country, has ever got rid of its disabilities by the generosity of the oppressor. India will not be free until we are strong enough to force our will on England and the women of India will not attain their full rights by the mere generosity of the men of India. They will have to fight for them and force their will on the menfolk before they can succeed.

I hope therefore that this *Vidyapitha* will be instrumental in sending out, into the province and the country, women who are rebels against the unjust and tyrannical social customs of the day and who will fight all who oppose this progress; women who are as much soldiers of the country as the best men.

Freedom of Indian Women from Economic Bondage[13]

Social reform legislation is good and to be worked for and welcomed. But all the good legislation in the world will not make a man or woman a free agent so long as he or she is economically under another's bondage. It is this economic bondage that is the root cause of the troubles of the Indian woman and to the removal of this our energies must be directed. The joint family system of the Hindus, a relic of a feudal age, utterly out of keeping with modern conditions, must go and also many other customs and traditions. But the ultimate solution lies only in a complete refashioning of our society.

If our nation is to rise, how can it do so if half the nation, if our womenkind, lag behind and remain ignorant and uneducated? How can our children grow up into self-reliant and efficient citizens of

India if their mothers are not themselves self-reliant and efficient? Our history tells us of many wise women and many that were true and brave even into death. We treasure their examples and are inspired by them, and yet we know that the lot of woman in India and elsewhere has been an unhappy one, our civilization, our customs, our laws, have all been made by man and he has taken good care to keep himself in a superior position and to treat woman as a chattel and a playing to be exploited for his own advantage and amusement. Under this continuous pressure woman has been unable to grow and to develop her capacities to her fullest, and then man has blamed her for her backwardness.

Gradually, in some of the countries of the West, woman has succeeded in getting a measure of freedom, but in India we are still backward, although the urge to progress has come here too. We have to fight many social evils; we have to break many an inherited custom that enchains us and drags us down. And, above all, the women as well as the men of India have to fight and overcome an arrogant and crushing imperialist that sucks the lifeblood out of us and prevents all growth. Men and Women, like plants and flowers, can only grow in the sunlight and fresh air of freedom; they wilt and stunt themselves in the dark shadow and suffocating atmosphere of alien domination.

For all of us, therefore, the first problem that presents itself is how to free India and remove the many burdens of the Indian masses. But the women of India have an additional task and that is to free themselves from the tyranny of man-made custom and law. They will have to carry on this second struggle by themselves for man is not likely to help them.

Many of them girls and young women present at the convocation will have finished their courses, taken their degrees, and prepared themselves for activities in a larger sphere. What ideals will they carry with them to this wider world, what inner urge will fasion them and govern their actions? Many of them, I am afraid, will relapse into the humdrum day-to-day activities of the household and seldom think of ideals or other obligations; many will think only of earning a livelihood. Both these are no doubt necessary, but if this is all that the Mahila Vidyapitha has taught its students, it has failed of its purpose. For a university that wishes to justify itself must train and send out into the world knight-errants in the cause of truth and freedom and justice, who will battle fearlessly against oppression and evil. I hope there are some such amongst you, some who prefer to climb the mountains, facing risk and danger, to remaining in the misty and unhealthy valleys below.[14]

It is sometimes, said, and I believe the *Vidyapitha* itself lays stress on this, that women's education should be something apart from that of man's. It should train her for household duties and for the widely-practised profession of marriage. I am afraid I am unable to agree to this limited and one-sided view of woman's education. I am convinced that women should be given the best of education in every department of human activity and be trained to play an effective part in all professions and spheres. In particular, the habit of looking upon marriage as a profession almost and as the sole economic refuge for woman will have to go before woman can have any freedom. Freedom depends on economic conditions even more than political and if woman is not economically free and self-earning she will have to depend on her husband or someone else, dependent are never free. The association of man and woman should be of perfect freedom and perfect comradeship with no dependence of one on the other.

What will you do, graduates and others of the *Vidyapitha*, when you go out? Will you just drift and accept things as they are, however bad they may be? Will you be content with pious and ineffective expressions of sympathy for what is good and desirable and do nothing more? Or, will you not justify your education and prove your mettle by hurling defiance at the evils that encompass you? The *purdah*, that evil relic of a barbarous age, which imprisons the body and mind so so many of our sisters-will you not tear it to bits and burn the fragments? Untouchability and caste, which degrade humanity and help in the exploitation of one class by another-will you not fight them and end them and thus help in bringing a measure of equality in this country? Our marriage laws and many of our out-of-date customs which hold us back and especially crush our womenfolk-will you not combat them and bring them in line with modern conditions? Will you not also fight with energy and determination for the physical improvement of our women by games in the open air and athletics and sane living so that India may be full of strong and healthy and beautiful women and happy children? And, above all, will you not play a gallant part in the struggle for national and social freedom that is convulsing our country today?

I have put these many questions to you, but the answers to them have already come from thousands of brave girls and women who have played a leading part in our freedom struggle during the last four years. Who has not been thrilled at the sight of our sisters, unused as they were to public activity, leaving the shelter of their homes and standing shoulder to shoulder with their brothers in the fight for India's freedom? They shamed many a person who called himself a man, and they proclaimed to the world that the women of India has risen from their long slumber and would and be denied their rights.

The women of India have answered, and so I greet you, girls and young women of the Mahila Vidyapitha, and I change you to keep that torch of freedom burning brightly till it spreads its lustre all over this ancient and dearly-loved land of ours.

There was no seclusion of women in ancient India except to some extent among royalty and the nobility. Probably there was more segregation of the sexes in Greece then in India then. Women of note and learning are frequently mentioned in the old Indian Books, and often they look part in public debates.[15]

Whenever I think of the women in *purdah*, cut off from the outside world, I invariably think of a prison or a zoo! How can a nation go ahead if half of its population is kept hidden away in a kink of prison? Tear the *purdah*, and let each one of us see the light of day.[16]

In my own part of the country, you can see a woman working hard in the field or elsewhere with her menfolk, but when the husband begins to earn more, people seem to think that she should retire into *purdah*. Doing no work is considered a sign of high status. The whole conception behind this business is totally unsuited to our time. Of course, in my part of the world, there are strange stories which some of you may have heard, about what the Begums of Oudh used to do or what people thought they ought to have done. They were so delicately nurtured, it seems, that whenever they saw an orange at a distance they caught a cold. It is said that when a doctor. or a *hakim* was called in, he was not supposed to feel the pulse in the normal way. Apart from being improper, it was thought it might hurt the ladies' gentle wrists if the doctor touched them. So it was arranged that a slender threat should run from the wrist to the doctor who should feel the thread and read the pulse. That might have been a good way of proceeding in the matter, because most of these women were neurotics and required no treatment. And so it did not matter what their pulse said.[17]

Marriage and Divorce

...A Hindu marriage is a religious ceremony, undoubtedly. But does it mean that it is a sacrament to tie up people who bite, who hate each other, who make life hell for each other? I think all human relationship should have an element of the sacrament in them. More so the intimate relationship of husband and wife. There is something fine in human relationship provided they are good relationship. Otherwise, the relationship is the reverse of fine. If people have no compatibility, if they are compelled to carry on together, they begin to hate each other and their life becomes bitter. The whole foundation of their existence become bitter...

We are often reminded of the high ideals of Indian womanhood, Sita and Savitri. Well, everyone here, I take it, admires these ideals and thinks of Sita and Savitri and other heroines of India with reverence and respect and affection. Sita and Savitri are mentioned as ideals for the women. I do not seem to remember men being reminded in the same manner of Ramachandra and Satyavan, and urged to behave like them. It is only the women who have to behave like Sita and Savitri; the men may behave as they like. I do not know whether Indian men are supposed to be perfect, incapable of further improvement.

You cannot have a democracy if you cut off a large chunk of humanity, fifty per cent of the people, and put them in a class apart in regard to social privileges and the like. They are bound to rebel, and rightly. I believe some Hon. Members spoke with disdain of what they consider certain trends in the social life of upper-class Indian women. Well, I am not a great admirer of certain types of development which we see in New Delhi. If we do not like these development, let us try to change them. But what exactly does that argument lead to? Does it mean that you should perpetuate or petrify conditions which themselves are leading to these cracks and breakups in Hindu society?[18]

We are often told that divorce is something against the basic conventions and ideas of Hindu society. it seems to me that almost anything can be described that way because Hindu society is so wide, so broad-based and so various that you can say anything about it either historically or as it actually exists today. While we talk about Hindu society, are we talking about a few high-caste people or are we talking and thinking in terms of the 250 or 300 million Hindus in this country? When we want to impress other people with numbers, we shout we are 270 million Hindus. But when we come to brass tacks, as when we talk about reforms, we think of a certain small group at the top. We cannot have it both ways.[19]

Apart from that, what is Hindu society? In order to get the right conception, I say with all deference that you should not read some rigid enactments, like the commandments of Manu. You should rather look into the social life as evolved in our country in the part ages. A better way, probably, is to have some glimpses of the social life as found in our older books. Take one of our old plays, the *Mrichchakatika*. Read it if you have not read it. See the tender humanity that is found in the play. There is in it no rigid puritanism but a human approach to the difficult problems of life. *Mrichahakatika* was probably written in the fifth century A.D. that is, about 1,400 years ago or more. I need not describe the play. The point is that the man who wrote it reflected the life of his day. If you read it, you see a society which is highly cultured. The individual is highly developed. The test of an individual is how he treats his wife, his son or his neighbout. How he behaves towards another how he functions in a social relationship-that is the test of the individual. If this test is applied, our people in those days appear to have been amazingly advanced and tolerant and generous in outlook.

...In the national sphere, we try to settle problems peacefully. In the same way, in the domestic sphere, in the husband-and-wife sphere, cultured society avoids the rod of the policeman, that is, of the law coming down and punishing. It is a sign of the culture of a society or a nation to do away with the use of violence. If that is so in other spheres, much more so is it in this intimate, domestic sphere of the family. Whether it is husband and wife or father and child, the rod is not a good way of dealing with the situation. I use the word rod here for any law which appresses, which constrains, which restricts, which punishes. Our laws, our customs-for the moment I am speaking of the upper strata-fall heavily on the womenfolk. That is who we are introducing this and other pieces of legislation...

Many people seem to imaging that by bringing in divorce you break up the system of marriage. I am absolutely convinced that by bringing in divorce you make for happier marriages, normally. I am not speaking of individual cases.

Divorce must not be looked upon as something which makes the custom of marriage fragile. I do not accept that. If that is so, I say that marriage itself has become a cloak. It is not a real marriage of the minds or bodies. If you compel and force people in this way, it will just be an enforced thing which has no value left in ethics and morality. Certainly stop them from acting rashly. Give them time. Make attempts to bring about a reconciliation. If all that fails, don's permit a state of affairs which, I think, is the essence of evil, which is bad for them, which is bad for the children, bad for everybody. I would particularly beg the House to take the view that this clause about divorce by mutual consent, subject to time, subject to reconciliation, subject to all such approaches, so that nothing may be done in a hurry, is a right and proper clause. It will produce a happier adjustment and a better relationship between the parties than would be produced if one party thinks that he can misbehave as much as he likes and nothing will happen.

The House knows that customs have grown up under which different standards of morality are applied to men and women. You will find women standing up for this right of divorce though some men many challenge it because men happen to be in a dominant position. I hope they will not continue in that dominant position for all time. These different standards of morality cannot be maintained. Therefore, the approach in this Bills is to bring about a certain measure of equality between them. It is true that this cannot be done by law only. It is a question of custom, education, and basically of the economic position of the individual.

Some people say that if we have divorce by mutual conscent, the husband will exploit the wife, will kick her out and force her to give conscent. It is a possibility; it may happen as many worse thing often happen. I do not think it will happen if you give time. If the husband does want to behave in that way, the sooner the wife is rid of him the better.

REFERENCES

1. Forward to *Women of India*', ed., by Tara Ali Beg, 1958.
2. Speech in the Lok Sabha on the Hindu Marriage Bill, New Delh, 5th May 1955.
3. Nehru, *The Discovery of India*.
4. Nehru, *An Antobiography*.
5. Foreword to *Challenge to Women*, Rajkumari Amrit Kaur, by March 7, 1946.
6. Letter to Maulana Abul Kalam Azad, March 5, 1942.
7. Letter to Rani Lakshmibai Rajwade, July 23, 1937.
8. Letter to Chief Minister 4th January, 1950.
9. Speech at a Seminar on Gaps between Boys' and Girls' Education, New Delhi, January 4, 1964.
10. Speech at the Laying of the Foundation of a Women's College at Teynampet, Madras, January 22, 1955.
11. Speech at Mahila Vidyapith, Allahabad, March 31, 1928.
12. Henrik Ibsen (1828-1906); Norwegian dramatist who had a profound influence on the theatre and drama throughout Europe.
13. Review of Katherine Mayo's *Slaves of the God, in The Bombay Chronicle*, April 25, 1929.
14. Massage to the Drayag Mahila Vidyapath, Allahabad July 12, 1934.
15. The Discovery of India.
16. *Glimpses of World History*, Vol. I.
17. Slpeech at the foundation of a women's college in Madras, January 22, 1955.
18. Speech during debate on the Hindu Marriage Bill in Lok Sabha May 5, 1955.
19. Speech in Lik Sabha in the Divorce Clause of the Special Marriage Bill, September 16, 1954.

YOUTH

NINE

YOUTH

Preparing for Nation's Struggles

Role of Students

Students must not take part in politics, some say...[1]

Who are the students? They may be children in the elementary schools or young men and women in colleges. Obviously the same considerations cannot apply to both.

Quite a large number of senior students today possess a vote for the coming provincial elections. To vote is to take part in politics; to vote intelligently necessitates the understanding of political issues; to understand political issues results usually in accepting a certain political policy; and if one accepts that policy it is the duty of the citizen to push that policy, to try to convert others to it. Thus inevitably a voter must be a politician, and he should be an ardent politician if he is a keen citizen. Only those who lack the political or social sense can remain passive and neutral or indifferent.

Even apart from his duty as a voter, every student must, if he is properly trained, prepare himself for life and its problems. Otherwise his education has been wasted effort. Politics and economics deal with these problems and no person is properly educated unless he understands them. Perhaps it is difficult for most people to see a clear path through life's jungle. But whether we know the solution of the problem or not, we must at least know the nature of it. What are the questions that life puts to us? The answers may be difficult, but the curious thing is that people seek to answer without knowing the real questions. No serious or thinking student can take up this futile attitude.

The various isms that play such an important part in the world today – nationalism, liberalism, socialism, communism, imperialism, fascism, etc. – are efforts on the part of various groups to answer these questions. Which answer is correct? Or are they all steeped in error? In any event we have to choose, and in order to choose we must know and have the capacity to choose correctly....

Thus it becomes necessary for all thinking individuals, and more so for the student than for others, to take the fullest theoretical part in politics. Naturally this will apply to the senior students at life's threshold rather than the junior ones who are still far from these problems. But a theoretical consideration is not enough for a proper understanding; even theory requires practice. From the point of view of study alone the student must leave his lecture halls and investigate reality in village and town, in field and factory; to take part to some extent in the various activities of the people, including political activities.

One has ordinarily to draw the line somewhere. A student's first business is to train his mind and body and make them efficient instruments for thought, understanding and action. Before he is trained he cannot think or act effectively. Yet the training itself comes not from listening to pious advice, but by indulging in action to some extent. That action, under normal conditions, must be subordinated to the theoretical training. But it cannot be eliminated or else the training itself is deficient.

It is our misfortune that in India our educational system is thoroughly lop-sided. But an even greater misfortune is the highly authoritarian atmosphere that surrounds it. Not in education alone, but everywhere in India, red-liveried, pompous and often empty-headed authority seeks to mould people after its own pattern and prevent the growth of the mind and the spread of ideas...

They do not like the qualities that are encouraged in free countries, the spirit of daring, the adventures of the soul in uncharted regions. Is it surprising then that we do not produce many men and women who seek to conquer the Poles or Everest, to control the elements and bring them to man's use, to hurl defiance at man's ignorance and timidity and inertia and littleness and try to raise him up to the stars?

Must students take part in politics? Must they take part in life, a full wholesome part in life's varied activities, or be of the clerkly breed, carrying out orders from above? As students they cannot keep out of politics; as Indian students, even more so they must keep in touch with it. Yet it is true that normally the training of their minds and bodies must be their principal consideration during this period of their growth. They must observe a certain discipline but that discipline should not be such as crushes the mind and kills the spirit.

So, normally. But abnormal conditions come when all normal rules are swept away. During the Great War, where were the students of England, France, Germany? Not in their colleges but in the trenches, facing and meeting death. Where are the students of Spain today?

A subject country is always to some extent in an abnormal condition. So India is today. And in considering these problems we must also consider our environment and the growing abnormality in the world. And as we seek to understand it we are driven to take part however little it might be, in the shaping of events.

Basic Beliefs

Ever since my return from Europe eleven weeks ago I have seen and felt a new awakening in the youth of India. After long suppression the spirit of youth is up in arms against all forms of authoritarianism and is seeking an outlet in many ways and in many directions. Youth leagues have sprung up in all parts of the country and individual young men and young women, weary of the continual and barren strife of many of their elders, are groping for a path which might lead them to a fuller realization of themselves, a better and more prosperous India and a happier world. They are beginning to realize that communalism is the very negation of what we should strive for and the attempts that are made to remove this canker from our body politic, well meant as they are and sometimes productive of good results, seldom touch the roots of the problem.

It is felt by many that religion, as preached and practised in India, has become a grave danger to the state and octopus-like it spreads its tentacles into every department of life whether it is political, economic or social. The rules and regulations laid down in a bygone age and for an entirely different society are sought to be applied now in all their rigidity to modern life and conditions, with the inevitable result that there is a hiatus, and friction and unhappiness are the common lot of life in India. Like the old man of the sea, religion has mounted our backs and effectively prevented all progress and advancement. Religion was not meant to be this and if it continues to encroach on other departments of life; the reaction may engulf it utterly.

Thinking men and women, and the young specially, cannot help being distressed at the present inequalities between man and man, class and class. Gross and vulgar luxury on the one side and abject misery on the other must produce in all who are sensitive and those who themselves suffer under the existing system, a feeling of intense bitterness and revolt. The present system, has been admittedly a failure and is condemned. As to what should take its place opinions differ but whatever it may be it should provide for the removal of, or at any rate tend to remove, inequalities of class and caste and wealth. It should result in equal opportunities for everyone and not the grossly unfair lack of opportunities which is the lot most people today.

These are the two avenues along which the thought of many people in India is moving today, and a necessary corollary to them is that India must be fully independent to work along the lines of her own choosing.

Many young friends, Hindu and Muslim, have spoken and written to me on these lines and have expressed a desire for an organisation based on these fundamental ideas. We have many organisations already and I am not at all sure that an addition to them is called for. But that depends on the number of people who agree with these ideas and are prepared to cooperate with each other to realise them. In any event it is worthwhile for those who agree on these general principles to get into touch with each other. It will be open to them then to consider whether they should have a loosely-knit or a compact organisation or none at all.

I would therefore beg of those who generally agree with what has been said above to write to me, making such other suggestions as they may consider necessary. To recapitulate, this appeal is addressed to those who:

1. believe in full independence for India,

2. think that religion should be a purely personal matter with each individual and should not be permitted to interfere with the consideration of political, economic and social question and especially that communalism should be fought in all its aspects,

3. desire to remove inequalities of caste, class and wealth, and wish that there should be an equality of opportunity for every one.[2]

Out of the Cocoon[3]

Indian civilisation today is stagnant. It is the duty of youth to convert this stagnant pool into a moving stream. The test of youth is action, rebellion in every sphere. Every youth must rebel. Not only in the political sphere but in social, economic and religious spheres also. I have not much use for any man who comes and tells me that such and such thing is said in *Koran*. Everything unreasonable must be discarded even if they find authority for it in the *Vedas* and in *Koran*. I know there are difficulties in pursuing this path but these difficulties are infinitely better than in action.

Looking at the present conditions everywhere we see that fear is the dominating feeling. It is so in Europe. Everybody is afraid of everybody else. And they are going on arming themselves in the fear that somebody would attack them. It is the same in India. Every group, every community was afraid of the other, each thought that at the next opportune moment the other would swallow it. That was the reason why at the All Parties Conference yesterday we found each community not only asking for its just rights but bargaining for a dominant position, as each community felt that that was the only way in which it could ensure its existence. This feeling of want of security must go. If Indian youth must achieve India's destiny it must be in the words of the great leader of the French Revolution, "daring and daring and still more daring".

Inculcating New Values

...Our educational system must direct itself to the eradication of this unwholesome Semi-fedal outlook. The National Planning Committee, some year ago, suggested that before a person graduated, he must put in a year or so of some kind of manual work or social service. That would take the place of the military service that prevails in countries which have conscription. In the course of that year, the young man or woman, would be given simple training in drill and discipline, and then in disciplined work of any kind, which may include the erection of public works or adult literacy campaigns, etc. This year of physical labour combined with a disciplined life would be good for the individual and would be good for the community. It would result in a new conception of labour. It should apply to every person, whatever his status in life. I think this proposal of the National Planning Committee was a good one and we should try to give effect to it...[4]

Ambition to Achieve[5]

You are young. I should like you to have the pride of youth and the ambition of youth to do something worthwhile and big. All of you may not be geniuses, but some of you might yet do worthwhile things in some department of human activity or other. I do not like people who have no pride and ambition and are just sloppy people.

I am not using the words pride and ambition in a small personal sense. I do not mean the pride of getting money, which is the silliest of all types of pride. Pride should consist in doing your job in the best possible manner. If you are a scientist, think of becoming an Einstein, not merely a reader in your university. If you are a medical man, think of some discovery which will bring healing to the human race. If you are an engineer, aim at some new invention. The mere act of aiming at something big makes you big.

If my colleagues and I and others who function on the public stage today appear big leaders to you, look back on how we became so. We may have had some virtue and some ability, but essentially we became what we were because we had some ambition and pride, because we hitched our wagon to a star, because we tried to do big things and in so trying our stature increased a little.

It is not what you say that matters, but what you do. Think therefore of the vast opportunities that the world offers to those who are keen of mind, strong of character and fleet of foot. Think of the opportunities that India offers. I know better than you of the difficult problems of India, the suffering and misery of numberless people. We are trying to meet those problems and solve them, not by magic but by strong will and hard work. There is no magic in this world except the occasional magic of human personality and the human mind. It takes time and perseverance to do big things. It will not do to be faint-hearted. One meets with failure occasionally, but one has yet to go on. Success does not come suddenly or without setbacks. So you have these great opportunities in India. Prepare yourself for them; grow strong in mind and body. Have that inner urge to do big things and I have no doubt that you will do big things.

Youth Organisation : Small Do's and Do

Need to be Frugal

I have your letter of the 24th March. I am very glad to learn that there is a chance of the youth delegation going to attend the World Youth Congress in Holland. I am afraid however that it is wholly impossible for me to go with the delegation. This is not because I consider the claims of youth on me of secondary importance. I believe in youth movements so much that I am prepared to sacrifice all other work to the organisation of youth in India. I feel however that I will serve that purpose much better by remaining in India at present and not by going on a delegation. You know I have only recently returned from Europe after a long stay and it is not right for me to rush back.

I had a letter from a young friend in Madras suggesting that I should issue an appeal for funds for a youth delegation. I wrote to him that if an All India delegation is sent an all India appeal should be made, but for a provincial delegation, funds should be raised in the province concerned.

I do not think that large funds are necessary. Members of the delegation can travel third class by the French steamers sailing from Colombo. I do not know if there is third class accommodation in the boats going from Bombay. Even second class accommodation in some boats is not expensive. Inquiries might be made from tourist agencies like Thomas Cook or the American Express.[6]

Self-Education

...I had often suggested at public meetings and elsewhere the desirability of starting youth leagues in the U.P. I had also stated that the initiative must come from the youth themselves...

...As for terrorism and communism I do not understand why you should put me the question. Surely you did not imagine that the league would have such a monstrous aim as terrorism or that it should stand for communism! A youth league, as I understand it, should consist of young men who are dissatisfied with present conditions and seek to better them. Any young person, whatever his way of thinking may be, should be welcome if he takes life seriously and wants to discuss its problems and do something. The league should not encourage rigid adherence to creeds and dogmas and any one who is full of self-complacency would not be a desirable member.

The principal object of such a league should be, I think, self-education by discussions, study circles and by developing contacts with the masses. The members should prepare themselves for future work rather than take up active work before they are clear in their own minds what to do and how to do it. The preparation itself may involve some active work but the object should not be so much the work as the training and knowledge that the work gives. Some kinds of activities can be indulged in even at this stage, for example, boycott of foreign cloth and occasional participation in national demonstrations and the like. Occasionally also, activities are thrust on the league by repressive measures of the Government.[7]

Self Reliance

Personally I feel it is impossible for us to make any progress politically or economically if we are chained up to the past customs. The suitability and adaptability of these particular customs to the present age is a question for you to consider. Undoubtedly the world has changed and it is changing day by day at a terrific speed. It is sheer folly on our part not to see that and not to adapt ourselves to it. That does not, of course, mean that we should give up everything that is old and past and copy everything that is Western. But we must try to realise that in the race of life we have been left behind. India is utterly stagnant and static and youth must bring a dynamic change in the country.

Youth wants continuous change for the better and revolution against everything that is evil...

A dangerous tendency in the youth movement in India is only to criticise the elder statesmen and not do what they ask us to do. This tendency is due to the fact that youth is not self-reliant enough, self-conscious enough, and self-disciplined enough. Do not lean on others, but think out problems for yourselves and come to a logical and clear conclusion.[8]

Playing the Part the Democratic Way

...No man ever died of hard work, if he is working in a good cause, if his spirit is in it, but people do die of ennui and other things. So you and I have got to work. What kind of work? What is your conception of work?

Today people seem to imagine that work lies in marching up and down the streets and calling it a demonstration; or stopping work, whether it is in a factory or a school, or somewhere else, calling it a *hartal*; or some other kind of demonstrative activity. It may be that it has its uses sometimes, no doubt it has. But I do tell you, and I tell you in all sincerity, that I can imagine no greater crime to India than the kind of thing that is going on today. I am not joking with you. I have a few more years of activity and I want to see India great and strong, a flourishing state, not only doing its duty to its own people, but to the wide world. And when I see our young men behaving as they do, when I see young men and hysterical young women misbehaving, I am angry, I tell you. Is all the work we have done just going to be lost because some hysterical people talk nonsense in this way, and behave in a nonsensical manner? What is happening here – is that your idea of liberty and democracy and freedom? I am amazed at this business. I want to be frank with you about it. This is not the way we are going to build up our nation. Have you any idea of what the difficulties before our country are?...[9]

...What are the problems? You have to face them, think of them, not only in relation to India but the wide world, which is in a peculiar frame of mind. It is an astonishing spectacle that you see in this world today. You see fine upsurges of the spirit, fine constructive efforts, great men all over the world, probably more men of goodwill all over the world than ever in the history of the world previously. At the same time you see evil forces at work, you see disruptive forces, warlike forces, all kinds of things working. There is conflict between all these things and I do not know and you do not know what the result of this conflict will be. But I do know this, that in this business as long as we have life and strength, we will have evil forces in India and elsewhere. We stand for the good forces for the forces that free the human spirit and not suppress it...

Well, the world is a big place. Nevertheless, you cannot isolate the problem of India from the world problem. You cannot isolate the problem of U.P. or Lucknow from the larger problem. Therefore, you must have at least some vague conception of this wide problem.

And if I may say so at this moment of great transition in human history, if you want to understand any problem you will have to understand it in the sweep of history, of the past, to see how it has developed, what the roots of it are. It is not good enough for you and me to shout out a few slogans now and call that the understanding of a problem, or the solution of a problem. Slogans may be good, because they do sometimes concentrate an idea in a few words; slogans may be used. But to think that a slogan is a problem or an answer to a problem is just to delude oneself.

...Now, having said this, I want to take your minds back to another direction. All these changes that the development of science has brought about in the world have meant the addition of a tremendous deal of knowledge, a vast quantity of it, which very few people, if any, can wholly grasp. It is too much for the human mind to grasp. I do not know, some prodigies may grasp it, but for normally intelligent people it is too much. The whole field of human knowledge is vast. Take the field of scientific knowledge; take only the field of a particular branch of science. There is so much of it that an individual has to specialize in it if he is to be good in that branch. He becomes an authority in his subject, but perhaps not knowing much about other departments of life. Thus it is probably the case with a highly specialized individual, scientist or technician, that he may be ignorant of many important aspects of life. He may, in other words, be a bad citizen, although he is a very good scientist. He may be a good citizen too. With the growth of science, of industrial civilization, there is such a tremendous fund of knowledge, not easy to grasp, that specialization has grown. With the growth of specialization, the synthetic view of human life, what might be called a philosopher's view of human life and all its problems, has receded into the background...

...In a democratic country, you cannot expect the government just to pass laws and do everything for you. It is an astonishing thing how you and I and most of us have not got rid of the habit of mind which we developed under British rule. We have not got rid of the habit of inaction we developed under British rule. This business of walking up and down with half a dozen banners might have been a suitable thing under British rule. It is – I will not say it is never suitable - it is seldom suitable today. I am talking about the habit of mind which the British Government tried to inculcate, talking about themselves as a *ma bap* government; that is, the government is to do everything, the people are merely to send in petitions to some government official and he will graciously pass orders on them. That is not the way that a democratic government functions.

A government which deals with vital social problems has to function very differently from a government which is essentially a police state. A police state has only to keep the peace, collect revenue, more or less, and do a few other little jobs. Today, we have to tackle intricate social and economic problems. Those problems cannot be tackled by a *firman* or ukase or decree from the Government. There must be right laws. I agree that governmental activity must be right and ought to be right. But in such economic matters governmental activity goes only thus far. It is the activity of the people, it is the temper of the people, and the co-operation that the people in general give that will solve these problems this way or that. And I tell you that the best of our laws or activities of government can be, if not nullified, lessened greatly in effect if there is no will to work in the people or to co-operate to that end. And I tell you also that even an enfeebled government, even a bad political government can yield greater results in the country if people co-operate to that end.

So the essential thing is how to develop that psychology of work and co-operation among the people. And today, if we are suffering from anything in India, it is the absence of that right psychology. Whether it is in the worker, whether it is in the owner of the factory or whether it is in the younger generation, it is entirely a wrong psychology. It is a psychology that assumes that results can be achieved by strikes and demonstration and the rest. And I am sorry to say that people who ought to know better are somehow taken in by it and somehow encourage this kind of thing. I tell you I consider nothing more dangerous for India's present and India's future than the continuance of this psychology.

I have infinite faith in India's future, and if I did not have that faith, perhaps I could not have worked as I have done. But having that infinite faith I want to tell you that we have to face pretty hard problems today. Let us not deceive one another. We have to face very difficult problems, and we have to lift ourselves up, almost rise up from our bootstraps in many ways. You are not going to get gold and money and silver from other countries. You have to produce it yourselves. How do you produce it, by *hartals* and the like? How are you going to increase wages and salaries and the rest, as you want to? Where is the money to come from? Where does the money come from? It comes from taxation, your pockets and nobody else's. It is a very simple proposition. Sit down and think it out. You make demands. It just amazes me when a number of students come to me and talk casually that they thought they ought to have been members of the University Commission in order to place their demands before them. They are always talking about demands. Now, there is such a thing as India also having some demands upon you. You seem to have forgotten that. And I think it is about time that you remembered the demands upon you in terms of your gratitude, of your duty and work and hard labour. There are too few people in India who think of it and work hard to that end. Everybody has demands, everybody has objections, everybody has criticisms and everybody thinks that possibly if his demands were met everything would be all right, forgetting that the meeting of his demands means making somebody else give up his demands, because demands clash.

Think of all these problems. It is a fantastic thing that I see. Obviously, we have inherited a certain structure, a certain political structure, administrative structure, judicial structure, economic structure and the rest; we have to change that. Now, how are we going to change that? There can be two ways of changing. One is: smash it to little bits and build anew, break it up, if you like, get a clean slate and write upon it. As a matter of fact, there is no clean slate in life; there never has been, there never will be. You can never get rid of the past completely. Nevertheless, you can have a more or less clean slate. You can have something that follows from the destruction of the existing apparatus of government or economic and social set-up or structure. If we decide that it is essential for the progress of the nation that we should smash up the structure that we have, well, let us set about doing it and smashing it up, understanding the consequences. Because I do not personally agree to that, I want you to realize that one must be clear about it; we should either try to smash up and build anew, right from the bottom up, or we should change as rapidly as we can, as rapidly as we are capable of, the existing structure and bring it nearer to what we think is the right one. We have to choose between the two, because the adoption of a middle course is fatal. You do not completely smash it up, so you never start building again; and you do not allow the changing process to go on. Neither takes place, except a continuous deterioration and a gradual drifting towards collapse. Now, many people favour this business of breaking up, smashing and starting anew. The consequences of that of course are: if you succeed, first of all, it means an enormous conflict, because some resist, some do not. It means a continuous conflict, not an immediate smashing up as we might like. A slow smashing-up takes a mighty long time and prevents other things being done.

It means, if you succeed in smashing up, then you perhaps have a clean slate, but a completely clean slate, as I said, is impossible. The smashing-up process also enfeebles the nation in every sense, from the military, the economic and the financial points of view. Therefore, suddenly, India at a critical phase of her young existence as a free country is enfeebled. I do not know what the consequences might be. As a person responsible for the State of India, I dare not enfeeble my nation and give a chance to evil-minded countries and evil-minded forces to come in and play havoc in this country. I may thereby imperil my freedom. Freedom will be imperilled, not only from the political or military point of view, but from the economic point of view. If we are enfeebled and helpless and in a starving condition, and we cannot do anything, what are we going to achieve? We may take out our processions and shout our slogans. How are we to feed these millions who have no food and who gradually arrive at so low a level that they are too weak really to stand up to the world?

That, I tell you, is an almost inevitable consequence, the immediate consequence, whatever the final emergence may be; the inevitable consequence of any process which aims at smashing up the present structure completely is the enfeebling of the nation, the imperilling of our freedom, and evil forces, evil countries taking advantage of it and exploiting the situation for their own profit and advantage. I do not want that to happen. During this smashing-up process, this generation – and when I say this generation. I do not mean my generation but the younger generation, the generation of the young men and young women who have taken their degrees and will be citizens tomorrow or the day after – I repeat that this generation will be a ruined generation if this smashing-up takes place. As I just said, we are condemned to hard labour. That is the truth. But you have no conception of what you will be condemned to if you start smashing-up the apparatus in India today. It is possible that at the end of this generation, out of the inner strength of India something else will grow.

But, for the moment, you must give up that idea. Therefore, if you give up the idea then you have to be wary, then you have to avoid all actions that lead to a deterioration of the situation and towards smashing-up the present. Smash-up the evil, certainly. Fight the evil. But you have to proceed on lines not of smashing-up the structure, but of changing it as rapidly as you can.

I wish to put another aspect of it and that is in terms of violence and non-violence, peaceful methods and violent methods. That is a good test, because if you employ peaceful methods, I do not think you are likely to go very wrong. Even though you may employ them for wrong purposes, you are safe and you apply your own brake. The peaceful method is itself a brake on too much wrong action. If you have to employ the violent method, however much a violent method might be justified against a foreign enemy and against a foreign dominating nation in a country, that is another argument; as a matter of fact, even against the foreigner we employed peaceful methods on the whole. But the use of violent methods on a domestic issue, not against a foreigner, but against some of yourselves, is a most dangerous thing. I am not prepared at the moment to discuss the philosophy of it. Nor do I rule it out from every country. But I do say in India, situated as she is today, the use of methods of violence is the greatest act of treason that any Indian can be guilty of. We have a strong unifying force, but at the same time we have all kinds of disruptive and fissiparous tendencies among us. We have fought communalism, and we have suffered from communalism. We have provincialism, and we have so many 'isms' and separating tendencies. And now, if in this field violence comes in any shape or form and people take to violent methods, then the result is, of course, that violence is smashed and quickly stopped, as indeed every government must suppress violence. No government can take risks with violence... If I had been in charge, I would have taken stronger action against those who have been misbehaving in the streets of Lucknow. What is this business of young men and young women going and attacking the police and slapping them and throwing bombs and playing about with *lathis*? Are our young men and women degraded to this level of vulgarity and indiscipline and lack of understanding that they behave in this way? And they call that freedom? That is not my conception of freedom, that has never been my conception of freedom. If you are going to act like this, well, you do an ill turn to your city, your country and your nation. I was really astounded by the things I heard of what has been done, and I am surprised that intelligent young men and women do not see the folly of it, not only the folly, but the criminality of it. Are we turning ourselves into a lot of hysterical persons of no understanding, and shouting slogans without realizing what they mean? Is this the idea of freedom? I want you to think about it. Where are we going? No government in the wide world can tolerate this kind of thing; one government may go and another government take its place, but if the government has violence done before its eyes, it must suppress that violence, and it will suppress it so long as it remains a government and has anything to do with administration. Let there be no doubt about it, whether men, women or children, whoever does it, will be picked up. A government simply cannot allow violence to occur. I have to congratulate the police of Lucknow (and I want to say this publicly too) on the way they have behaved here and the restraint they have shown. Some come to me and talk to me and ask me what one is to do if one is slapped in the face. Should one turn the other cheek as Christ said? Well, if we could all do this, the world would be a different place to live in. But obviously the police force is not supposed to turn the other cheek when it is slapped. So please understand these enormous problems that we have to face here, problems that require hard work.

...I want you, even as students, to think about them with all the data before you, to bring out all the facts before you. Nevertheless, you can have and you do have the main things to consider, and your professors can help you. Then prepare yourselves for the burden that you will have to shoulder tomorrow. Students come to me and ask: are we to take part in politics or not? I say, of course, always. But what is politics? It is an astounding conception of politics to go up and down the street in a procession... Now, I can conceive of a crisis coming, of India fighting for freedom, and the colleges closing and the students going out and all that, but that is during a period of crisis and peril for the nation's freedom. If that pattern of behaviour becomes continual, a sort of picture for people to copy, well, of course, whatever good that activity may result in, those people who indulge in it are not training themselves for any future activity of any value. Obviously not, because India is going to be run by a large number of trained people in and if we look after ourselves properly, we shall have opportunities of serving other countries, not in terms of leadership and imposing ourselves on them, but because they themselves will come and seek our service. But before we seek to serve others, or guide others, we must be in a position to do so.

...We must be clear in our minds about this, that we should not stoop to any low means, we should not stoop to any violent means, we should not stoop to any vulgar means. We are not going to make our country great by exhibitions of vulgarity and lowness of action and sporadic violence. Violence is bad enough when nations indulge in it against one another in war. But violence becomes infinitely worse and degrading in the narrow domestic sphere of street violence and the like...

Onward of World Federation

It is realisation of the common bond of humanity that has given rise to the great youth movement of today. Many of you may be too young to remember the despair and feeling of revolt in the minds of youth during, and specially after, the Great War. Old men sat in their comfortable cabinets and banking houses and hid their selfishness and greed and lies under a cover of fine phrases and appeals for freedom and democracy. And the young, believing in these fine phrases, went out by the millions to face death, and few returned. Seventy millions of them were moblised and of the fifteen millions that actually served on the front, over eight millions died and over five and a half million were maimed for life. Think of these terrible figures and then remember that they were all young men with their lives stretching out in front of them and their hopes unfulfilled! And what did this awful sacrifice bring forth? A peace of violence and an aggravation of all the ills that the world was suffering from. You remember well that the first fruits of the peace in India were the Rowlatt Act and Martial Law. You know also how the fine principle of self-determination, which the Allies shouted from the house-tops, has been applied to India and to other countries. A new cloak for the greed of the imperialist powers was created in the shape of mandates and in awarding mandates the "principal consideration" was to be the preference of the inhabitants. This preference was shown unaccountably by rebellion against the British in Mesopotamia and rebellion against the French in Syria. But the aeroplane and the bomb was the British answer in Iraq and the ancient and beautiful city of Damascus was reduced to ruins by the French. In Europe itself the peace created far more problems than it solved.[10]

Is it any wonder that the youth of the world rebelled and cast out their old-time leaders on whom even the terrible lesson of the war was lost, and who still went on intriguing in the old way, and prepared for yet another and a greater war? Youth set about organising itself and set out to find the ways and means of establishing an order of society which would put an end to the misery and conflicts of today.

And so the youth of the world probed deeper into the cause of present-day misery. They studied the economic and the social conditions of the people, and they saw that although science and the changes that science had brought, had in a few generations covered the track of centuries, the minds of men still lagged behind the thought in terms of a dead past. Science had made the world international and interdependent, but national rivalries continued and resulted in war. Science had vastly increased production and there was enough for all and to spare but poverty continued and the contrasts between luxury and misery were more marked than ever before. But if mankind is foolish and errs, facts do not adapt themselves to errors and the world of our imagination conflicts with the world of reality; and is it any wonder that chaos and misery result?

Facts are not to blame for this. The troubles and the difficulties lie rooted in things, in our misconception of them and our misinterpretation of them. Our elders fail frequently because they are rigid in their minds and unable to change their mental outlook or adapt themselves to changing facts. But youth is not hidebound. Youth can think and is not afraid of the consequences of thought. Do not imagine that thought is an easy matter or that its consequences are trivial. Thought is not or should not be afraid of the wrath of heaven or the terrors of hell. It is the most revolutionary thing on earth. And it is because youth dare think and dare act that it holds out the promise of taking out this country and this world of ours from the ruts and the mire in which they have sunk.

Are you, young men and women of Bengal, going to dare to think and dare to act? Are you prepared to stand shoulder to shoulder with the youth of the world, not only to free your country from an insolent and alien rule but also to establish in this unhappy world of ours a better and a happier society? That is the problem before you and if you wish to face it sincerely and fearlessly, you will have to make up your mind to rid yourselves and your country of every obstacle in your path whether it is placed by our alien rulers or has the prestige of ancient custom.

You must have your ideal clear-cut before you. How else can you hope to build the great structure of your dream? Can you build a palace on the foundations of mud-hut, or a fine bridge with straw? With definite ideas of your goal you will gain clearness of purpose and effectiveness of action and each step that you take will carry you nearer to your heart's desire.

What shall this ideal be? National independence and perfect freedom to develop on the lines our own choosing is the essential requisite of all progress. Without it there can be no political, economic or social freedom. But national independence should not mean for us merely an addition to the warring groups of nations. It should be a step towards the creation of a world commonwealth of nations in which we can assist in the fullest measure to bring about cooperation and world harmony.

But there can be no world cooperation as long as one country dominates over and exploits another and one group or class exploits another. Therefore, we shall have to put an end to all exploitation of man by man or women. You cannot have a purely political ideal, for politics is after all only a small part of life, although situated as we are under alien rule, it dominates every branch of our activity. Yours ideal must be a complete whole and must comprise life as it is today, economic, social as well as political. It can only be a social equality in the widest sense and equality of opportunity for everyone. It is notorious that we have neither of these today.

Our womenfolk, in spite of the great examples of old that we are so fond of repeating, are shackled and unfree. Large classes of our countryman have been deliberately suppressed by us in the past and denied all opportunities of growth in the name of religion and ancient practice. And all over India, we see today millions toiling in field and factory and starving in spite of their toil. How can we rid these millions of their dire poverty and misery and make them share in the freedom to come? We hear of the service of the poor and sometimes even of the exaltation of the poor. And by a little act of charity of service we imagine that our duty is done. Having reserved very magnanimously the kingdom of heaven for the poor we take good care to keep the kingdom of the earth for ourselves. Youth at least should be above this hypocricy. Poverty is not a good thing; it is not to be exalted or praised but an evil thing which must be fought and stamped out. The poor require no petty services from us or charity. They want to cease to be poor. That can only come by your changing a system which produces poverty and misery.

In the course of the few months you have seen the whole of India convulsed in labour troubles. Lock-outs and strikes and shootings have followed one after another. Is it amusing, do you think, to the worker to strike and starve and perhaps be shot? Surely no one does so unless his lot becomes unbearable. And indeed the lot of the Indian today in factory or field is past all endurance. In the jute mill of your province, profits and reserve accumulations in ten years before 1926 amounted to nearly 440 crores of rupees. Think of this enormous figure and then see the condition of poor workers in these mills. And yet the jute workers, miserable as they are, have gone there because there was no room for them on the land or their conditions on the land were even worse. Can you expect any peace in the land when there is so much misery and so much contrast between wealth and abject poverty?

You cannot ignore these problems or leave them to a future age for solution. And if you are afraid of tackling them, you will find that facts can only be ignored at your peril. We are sometimes told that we must do justice between landlord and tenant and capitalist and worker, and justice means the maintenance of the *status quo*. it is the kind of justice the League of Nations gives when it maintains the present *status quo* with the imperialist power dominating and exploiting half the earth. When the *status quo* itself is rank injustice, those who desire to maintain it must be considered as upholders of that injustice.

If your ideal is to be one of social equality and a world federation, then perforce we must work for a socialist state. The word socialism frightens many people in this country but that matters little for fear is their constant companion. Ignorant of everything important that has happened in the world of thought since they left their school books, they fear what they do not and will not understand.

It is for you, the youth of the country, to appreciate the new forces and ideas that are convulsing the world and to apply them to your own country. For socialism is the only hope for a distraught world today. It is interesting to note that during the great war when a great crisis threatened to engulf the nations of the West, even the capitalist countries of Europe were forced to adopt socialistic measures to a large extent. This was not only done internally in each country but, unable to resist the pressure of events, even internationally. There was cooperation in many fields and national boundaries seemed to recede into the background. There was economic cooperation of the closest kind and ultimately even the armies of many nations became one army under a single head. But the lesson of the war has been lost and again we drift towards a greater disaster.

Socialism frightens some of our friends, but what of communism? Our elders sitting in their council chambers shake their grey heads and stroke their beards in alarm at the mere mention of the word. And yet I doubt if any of them has the slightest knowledge of what communism is. You have read of the two new measures which are being rushed through the Assembly - one of them to throttle the trade union movement, and the other to keep out people whom the government suspects of communism. Has it struck you that it is a very curious thing that the mighty British Empire with all its tanks and aeroplanes and dreadnoughts should be afraid of a few individuals who come to spread a new idea? What is there in this new idea that the British Empire should collapse like a pack of cards before this airy nothing? Surely you could not have better evidence of the weakness of this giant empire which sprawls over the fairest portions of the earth's surface. It is a giant with feet of clay. But if an idea is a dangerous thing, it is also a very elusive thing. It crosses frontiers and customs barriers without paying any duty and bayonets and men of war cannot stop it. The Government of India must be strangely lacking in intelligence if they imagine that they can stop any ideas from entering India by legislation.

What is the communist ideas before which the British Empire quakes? I do not propose to discuss it here, but I wish to tell you that though personally I do not agree with many of the methods of the communists, and I am by no means sure to what extent communism can suit present conditions in India, I do believe in communism as an ideal of society. For essentially it is socialism, and socialism, I think, is the only way if the world is to escape disaster.

And Russia, what of her? An outcast like us from nations and much slandered and often erring. But in spite of her many mistakes she stands today as the greatest opponent of imperialism and her record with the nations of the East has been just and generous. In China, Turkey and Persia of her own free will she gave up her valuable rights and concessions, while the British bombarded the crowded Chinese cities and killed Chinamen by the hundreds because they dared to protest against British imperialism...

I have placed before you the ideals of internationalism and socialism as the only ideals worthy of the fine temper of youth. Internationalism can of course come to us only through national independence. it cannot come through the British Empire or the British Commonwealth of Nations, call it what you will, for that empire is today the greatest foe of internationalism. If in future England chooses to enter a real world federation none will welcome her more than we, but she will have to shed her imperialism before she can enter. Our quarrel is not with the people of England but with the imperialism of England.

I have laid stress on internationalism although it may be a distant ideal for us. But the world is already largely International, although we may not realise it. And situated as we are, the reaction against foreign rule is apt to make us narrowly national. We talk of the greatness of India, of her special mission to the world and we love to dwell on her past. It is well that we remember our past, for it was great and worth remembering. But it is for the aged to look back; youth's eyes should be turned to the future. And I have often wondered if there is any country in the world, any people who do not fancy that they have a special mission for the world. England has her white man's burden which she insists on carrying in spite of the ungrateful people who object and rebel; France has her mission *civilisatrice*; America is God's own country; Germany has *Kultur*; Italy has her new gospel of Fascism; and Russia her Communism. And it has been so always. The Jews were the elect of the Lord, and so were the Arabs. Does it not strike you as strange that every country should have the identical notion of having a special mission to reform the world, to enrich its culture in some way, and none need lay claim to being the chosen of the Lord?

Self-admiration is always a dangerous thing in an individual. It is equally dangerous in a nation, for it makes it self-satisfied and indorent and the world passes by leaving it behind. We have little enough reason to be satisfied with out present lot, with many of our customs, with our excessive religiosity, with the sad lot of our women and the terrible condition of the masses. What good does it do us to waste our energy and our time in chanting praises of the dead past when the present claims our attention and work awaits us? The world changes and is changing rapidly and if we cannot adapt our society to the new conditions, we are doomed to perish. We have seen what can be done in a brief span of years and even months by a Kemal Pasha or an Amanullah who were not afraid to break through ancient custom and prejudice. What has been done is Turkey and backward Afghanistan can be done in India. But it can only be done in the manner of Kemal Pasha or Amanullah, by fearlessly facing obstacles and removing them and not waiting till the crack of doom for slow reform. it is not a choice for you as it was not a choice for Turkey or Afghanistan, between extinction and immediate action. Turkey and Afghanistan chose the latter path and are reckoned today as great nations. What will your choice be?

The world is in a bad way and India especially is in a perilous state in spite of the glitter and superficial splendour of our great cities. There are rumours of war and awful prophecies that the next war may result in irretrievable disaster to civilisation. But the very excess of evil may hasten the cure.

Does not our Gita state:

> "Yada yada hi dharmasya glanirbhavati Bharata
> Abhyutthannam adharmasya tadatnannam srijamyaham.
> Paritaranaya sadhoonam vinasays ca dushkritam
> Dharma samsthapanarthaya sambhavami yuge yuge".

[Chapter IV, Verses 7 & 8]

> Whenever there is a decline of righteousness and rise of unrighteousness, O Bharata (Arjuna), then I send forth myself. For the protection of the good, for the destruction of the wicked and for the establishment of righteousness, I come into being from age to age.

Great men have come from age to age in this country and elsewhere to help mankind. But greater than any man is the idea which he has embodied. And the conception of *Dharma* changes from age to age, and in a changing world a custom that was good in the past may be parilous to society today. You do not go to Bombay today in a bullock cart or fight with bows and arrows. Why stick to customs which were good only in the days of the bullock cart and bows and arrows?

And the great men who have come have always been rebels against the existing order. Two thousand five hundred years ago the great Buddha proclaimed his gospel of social equality and fought against all privileges, priestly and otherwise. He was a champion of the people against all who sought to exploit them. Then came another great rebel, Christ, and then the Prophet of Arabia, who did not hesitate to break and change almost everything he found. They were realists who saw that the world had outgrown its ancient practices and sought to bring it back to reality. Even so we have outgrown the creeds and rituals of yesterday and as realists we must not hesitate to discard them wherever they clash with reality. The *avatars* of today are great ideals which come to reform the world. And the ideas of the day is social equality. Let us listen to it and become its instruments to transform the world and make it a better place to live in.

I may be a weak instrument capable of doing little by myself in spite of my ardent desire to do much. And you individually may be able to do little. But you and I together can do much and working with the awakened youth of this country we can and will achieve a great deal. For only youth can save this country and the world. I do not admire the Fascists but I admire them for having as their war-cry a hymn to youth: *Giovinezza*. And I wish you would also adopt their motto "Live dangerously". Let our elders seek security and stability. Our quest must be adventure, but adventure in a noble enterprise which promises to bring peace to a distracted world and security and stability to the millions who have it not.

You and I are Indians and to India we owe much, but we are human beings also and to humanity we also owe a debt. Let us be citizens of the commonwealth or empire of youth. This is the only empire to which we can owe allegiance, for that is the forerunner of the future federation of the world.

REFERENCES

1. From Eighteen Months in India, 1938.
2. Letter to the Editor, *The Leader*, March 24, 1928.
3. Speech at a students meeting at Bombay, May 20, 1928.
4. Letter to Chief Ministers, August 15, 1949.
5. 2nd Inter-University Youth Festival, New Delhi October 23, 1955.
6. Letter to Venkatachari, March 28, 1928.
7. Letter to Bhagwat Dayal, April 4, 1929.
8. Speech at Calcutta, August 21, 1929.
9. Convocation Addum Lucknow University, January 28, 1949.
10. Presidential Address at the All Bengal Student Conference, Calcutta, September 22, 1928.

CHILDREN

1 One World of Children

2 In the Image of Man

A Sense of Values

3 Child Welfare

4 Books and Films

Books

Films

TEN

CHILDREN

One World of Children

...I like being with children and talking to them and, even more, playing with them. For a moment I forget that I am terribly old and that it is a very long time ago since I was a child...

...Old people have a habit of delivering sermons and good advice to the young. I remember that I disliked this very much long long ago when I was a boy... Grown-ups have also a habit of appearing to be very wise, even though very few of them possess much wisdom... In any event, people who are wise do not talk about their wisdom and do not behave as if they were very superior persons...

Grown-ups have a strange way of putting themselves in compartments and groups. They build up barriers and then they think that those outside their particular barrier are strangers whom they must dislike. There are barrier of region, of caste, of colour, of party, of nation, of province, of language, of custom and of wealth and poverty. Thus, they live in prisons of their own making. Fortunately, children do not know much about these barriers which separate. They play or work with one another and it is only when they grow up that they begin to learn about these barriers from their elders...

Children everywhere are must the same, it is the grown-ups who imagine they are very different and deliberately make themselves so...

...I thought... of children all over the world, outwardly different in many ways, speaking different languages, wearing different kinds of clothes and yet so very like one another. If you bring them together, they play or quarrel. But even their quarrelling is some kind of play. They do not think of differences amongst some kind of play. They do not think of differences amongst themselves, differences of class or caste or colour or status. They are wiser than their fathers and mothers. As they grow up, unfortunately, their natural wisdom is often eclipsed by the teaching and behaviour of their elders. At school they learn many things which are no doubt useful but they gradually forget that the essential thing is to be human and kind and playful and to make life richer for ourselves and others. We live in a wonderful world that is full of beauty and charm and adventure. There is no end to the adventures that we can have if only we seek them with our eyes open. So many people seem to go about their life's business with their eyes shut. Indeed, they object to other people keeping their eyes open. Unable to play themselves, they dislike the play of others.[1]

...If we meet other people in a friendly way, they also become friendly. But if we are afraid of them or if we show our dislike to them, then they behave in the same manner...

These are simple truths which the world has known for ages. But even so, the world forgets and the people of one country hate and fear the people of another country; and because they are afraid, they are sometimes foolish enough to fight each other...

In the Image of Man

Parents are a curious phenomenon. They seem to live their lives again in their children. I have many wider interests in life which sometimes envelope me and make me forget much else, but still I am not free from that preoccupation of parenthood and I am vastly interested in your growth and preparation for life. The fact that I cannot help you much personally does not lessen this preoccupation. Parents, again, have a tendency to mould their children after their own fashion and to impress them with their own ideas. To some extent I suppose this is inevitable, and yet the fact is that each individual stands out by himself or herself as a new experiment which life is working out. To force a growing person into a particular mould is to stultify him or her and to prevent growth. Bernard Shaw has called this the greatest of crimes. And so I have tried, with what success I cannot say, not to force my ideas and pattern of life on you. I want you to grow and develop after your own fashion and only so can you fulfil your life's purpose. Inevitably you will carry through life certain hereditary habits and ideas which your home life has impressed upon you in your early days, and I am conceited enough to think that your hereditary background is rather good. But the foreground must be your own creation. I have often asked you what particular subjects of study interest you. The object of my questions was not so much to determine these subject as to find out how your mind was working. It matters little what subjects you specialize in, provided they are such as interest you. What I am far more interested in, is yourself. All round us we see people who have had brilliant academic careers and yet who are somehow unable to fit in anywhere. Partly the fault is theirs, but certainly there is something seriously lacking in such a one-sided education.[2]

A Sense of Values

Normally each individual's attitude to life is that of his social group or the more intimate circle in which he or she moves. That lays down the standard to be aimed at with minor variations. When there is revolutionary change in the air, we are affected by it, we talk of it, and yet that talk has little reality behind it, and we find it difficult to pull ourselves out of accustomed ways of life and thought. Sometimes we are compelled to do so by circumstances and we submit, as we must, but unwillingly and rather ungraciously. We become then the slaves of circumstance rather than its masters or even its equals. To a large extent we are all such slaves of happenings which are beyond our individual control. Yet there is a difference.

Every parent wants his or her child to have all the virtues, all the good fortune. But we can seldom, if ever have all of everything. We have to choose or to emphasize some aspects rather than others. There are what are loosely called the masculine virtues and those that are termed the feminine virtues. Both good and desirable and yet just slightly inconsistent with each other. In India, the feminine virtues seem to be more obvious today at any rate, though of course the masculine virtues are present also. Our outlook seems to favour the former.

Then again much depends on the period we are living in. In a more or less static period, certain virtues and accomplishments are more useful: in a rapidly changing period other virtues and capacities assume importance. But whatever the period, self-reliance, fitness of body and keenness of mind and a harmony between the two and a certain basic sense of values are always desirable. If this foundation is provided to the growing child much has already been done...[3]

Problem and suchlike children have I suppose always existed but undoubtedly they are peculiarly common in our present age, especially in Europe and America. They are the products of this age of transition where everything is changing so rapidly that it is difficult to have any standards of values to judge by. Also the small families which are so usual today-one child or two-result in problem children-a larger family, several children, had disadvantages but from this child's point of view it is usually better and he has a more normal life with companions growing up with him. To some extent. But not wholly (except perhaps in a socialist country like Russia), school and a communal life can take the place of family life.

A child has to be treated as an individual and given every opportunity to grow as an individual. But it is at least equally important to treat him as a social being who can live at peace and co-operation with others. That makes one think of the kind of society he will have to live in a difficult business today when society itself is changing. In any event the cooperative habits and traits have to be developed or else he will find it difficult to fit in anywhere. Usually single children, who have been looked after a great deal, have a hard time when they go out into the world and have to fend for themselves. Bertrand Russell says somewhere that parents are wholly unsuited to bring up their children; they are too intensely interested in them to take a dispassionate view or to treat them normally...[4]

Child Welfare

...It is a hateful sight... to see our little children... being put in... contaminating atmosphere of beggardom because, remember that the present generation with all its good and bad points will pass away and the India we are trying to build today will be the India of our children tomorrow. The first duty of all of you and the state should be to protect and nourish this India of tomorrow.

When I see even a single child in India unfed, with hunger in its eyes, not properly clothed or looked after, I am pained, because somehow I regard that not as an individual case of hardship but rather of our forgetting our duty to the India of tomorrow. [5]

...Come to grips with the problem, take a village if you like and try to help the suffering people there. Above everything, keep in touch with the children in those villages and try to take care of them. Nothing has pained me so much as the sight of little children not being properly looked after. Therefore, do develop some social consciousness. On a holiday or at a week-end, go to a village and see that the children there are clad well; you meet them talk to them, clean them, wash them and amuse them, if you do that job, then however big the problem might appear to us all, it will become less. You can get help from outside but make yourself responsible for the children and the poor mothers of those children who have to carry such a terrible weight. There are many things that I can suggest to you this way.[6]

Children are the wealth of a nation and it is the duty of society to take good care of them...

Complaints had been made that in Delhi it had not been possible to take proper care of delinquent children many of whom had to be sent to jail.

...I cannot understand how any court or law can punish a child of five, six or ten years of age. He is not responsible for his actions. If he commits any crime it simply means that his parents did not take proper care of him or that he fell into bad company. To punish a child would be somewhat like punishing a man for falling sick...

To put a child in jail and punish him is something horrible, I cannot understand how society can tolerate it.

...I have had an opportunity of seeing convicts in jails. Only 15 per cent of them are criminals in the real sense of the term, and it is difficult to cure them. Of the remainder, a large percentage can become useful members of the society if they are properly treated...

But to tolerate incarceration of children of five or ten years of age in jail and ruin their lives and make them a burden on society was something unthinkable. It is the bounden duty of society and the Government to remedy the present state of affairs.

That courts dealing with juvenile cases-should be free from the awe and grim atmosphere of policemen. They should be away from uninspiring regular court area. The magistrates should deal with them in a human manner and their primary object should be to wean them away from crime.

The primary responsibility of looking after juvenile delinquents rested on the Municipal Committee and the local administration. The citizens had a responsibility to fulfil which they often seemed to forget. The foundations for the care of delinquent children in the city should be laid on firm footing.[7]

Books and Films

Books

...The Right time for the reading habit to grow is from childhood upwards. Therefore it is particularly desirable to encourage the child to read. They will all read if there are suitable and inquisitive mind. If a book fits in with this spirit of enquiry in the child's mind, then it will be read. Unfortunately, the people who decide as to what book to write and publish seldom take into consideration what a child really wants.[8]

Films

...There is one thing, I feel, India has been lacking in, and that is children's films. Films which are really children's films are of high importance. There is a tendency in our books written for children for the author to consider himself wise and give lectures to children on how they should behave and what virtues they should develop. My own reaction as a child to such lectures, as far as I can remember, was to hit the person lecturing. That is not the way to approach children. By lecturing you inevitably drive children to evil ways. Don't sermonize too much. There are subtler ways of pointing a moral or drawing a lesson. Good children's films can be a very powerful instrument in developing the child and I hope that the Indian film industry will think of this. The Government, not with any intention to compete, is nevertheless likely to compete with private ventures in films; it might on its own produce documentaries or other specialized films, for children and others. There is no desire to compete, but the result to some extent might be a setting up of standards through a certain measure of competition.[9]

REFERENCES

1. For the Children's Number of *Shankar's Weekly*. New Delhi December 26, 1950.
2. Letter to Indira Gandhi, May 6, 1935.
3. Letter to Krishna Hutheesing, April 11, 1944.
4. Letter to Indira Gandhi, June 3, 1944.
5. Speech at Madras-October 10, 1952.
6. Address to Social Workers, Madras, october 10, 1952.
7. Speach at Children Aid Society, New Delhi, May 1950
8. Message to All India Publishers Association, New Delhi, November 11, 1959.
9. Inagurating the Film Seminar, New Delhi, 27th February, 1955.

SOCIAL PROBLEMS

ELEVEN

SOCIAL PROBLEMS

Family Bonds

The large and joint families of the past no doubt served a useful purpose and fitted in with the social structure we had evolved through long ages. But that structure is cracking up now and it cannot survive in its old form. It is pulled in two different directions at the same time–the individual asserting his right to his own way of living, and the larger social group, the community or nation demanding a unified pattern and equal opportunities for all. Between these two pulls, the middle pull of the joint family becomes less and less; it comes in the way of the individual life as well as the larger national life. It does not fit in with the thought and elemental forces that move the world today. so it must fade away, as it is indeed doing. But we are such a huge country and with such deep roots in the past, that major changes take time. Yet in these days time itself moves quickly.

I do believe that the family as a unit is important, especially the smaller family, and fulfils a psychological need. It will survive, But the economic bonds that tie up large numbers of persons in a joint family tend to become real bonds, helping the individual often but also suppressing him and preventing growth. Where a common outlook on life is lacking they become nuisance to all concerned and a constant source of irritation. There is a feeling, and you have mentioned it, that the burden falls on some and not on others, that some are not pulling their weight, that some sow while others reap, and so on. One cannot argue against this for it all depends on our sense of values. Is money-making our test or some other also?[1]

Family Planning

I am wholly in favour of family planning. Certainly one of its principal objects is to lessen the rate of population increase. This is very important. But there are other aspects also: to give a fuller life to the family and more particularly to the mother and children. The standard of living, education, etc. in a large family is likely to be lower than that in a somewhat smaller family.

Any marked success in this movement will depend on two factors: (i) a widespread approach to our rural population, and (ii) simple and cheap methods. We have heard much of oral contraceptives. Undoubtedly, if these are effective, they would go a long way to provide a suitable method.

If we have to approach the rural population, this means (i) a fairly widespread propaganda to create a background of acceptance, and (ii) large numbers of clinics or centres where such information can be given. It would hardly be feasible to have separate family planning centres all over the country. This work will have to be co-ordinated, therefore, with other centres for maternity, child care and various types of medical and health services.

In everything that we do in India, it must be remembered that the organizational structure should not be top heavy and expensive. Otherwise it is limited in scope.[2]

...The planning of the houses and that of the villages can be given some thought, keeping always in view that the population is increasingly impigning on other villages and towns and cities.

...The question of family planning ...is a very important thing. It has to be faced, otherwise, all your efforts at improving the living conditions will fail. Therein comes the role of the so-called organized authority, whether it is Government or Corporation or Municipality of Panchayat, or whatever it is. In order to do that, we constitute this organized authority from those elected by the people. It casts responsibility on the people. That is the democratic method.

It has its failings. Ultimately its success depends upon the quality of the men. If that quality is bad, the best of methods will fail. If it is good, it will succeed wonderfully. That is how we try to create conditions for good civilized living. At present, those conditions are totally lacking.[3]

Scheduled Castes and Scheduled Tribes[4]

Scheduled Castes

...There is another aspect of this matter which must be remembered. We talk about democracy and unity and all that and I hope we shall rapidly have more and more democracy and more and more unity in this country. A democracy is not purely a political affair. The nineteenth century conception of democracy, that is, each person having a vote, was a good enough conception in those days, but it was incomplete and people think in terms of a larger and deeper democracy today. After all there is no equality between the pauper who has a vote and the millionaire who has a vote. There are a hundred ways of exercising influence for the millionaire which the pauper has not got. After all there is no equality between the person who has tremendous educational advantages and the person who has had none. So educationally, economically and otherwise, people differ greatly. People will, I suppose, differ to some extent. All human beings are not equal in the sense of ability or capacity. But the whole point is that people should have equality of opportunity and that they should be able to go as far as they can go.

Now it is patent in India today that there are huge differences between certain groups, classes and individuals. There is a big hiatus between those at the top and those at the bottom. If we are to have democracy it becomes necessary and essential for us not merely to bridge that gap but to lessen it very greatly; in fact to bring them closer together as far as opportunities are concerned, as far ultimately as general living conditions are concerned and in so far as the necessities of life are concerned, leaving out for the moment luxuries and the rest, though ultimately there seems to me to be no particular reason why any particular group or class should be favoured even in regard to the luxuries of life. But that is perhaps a rather distant picture. Now, because there are such great difference in India, it becomes incumbent upon us, not only for humanitarian reasons but from the stand-point of the fulfilment of democracy, to raise up those people who are low down in the social and economic scale and to bring to them every possible opportunity of growth and progress. That has been the generally accepted polity of this country and it is the accepted policy of the Government.[5]

Now in pursuance of that policy, a certain reservation of seats was granted, for instance, to the scheduled castes, and various scholarships, education amenities and so on have been granted. They no doubt will be granted still more, not only to the scheduled castes but also to other backward groups in the country. For there are the tribal people and others who require every help. It is no good for us to say that we have given the vote to every tribal person and we have done our duty by him; having from hundreds and thousands of years not done our duty by him, we consider ourselves absolved of all further duty by giving him a vote. Therefore, we have to think always in terms of raising the level of all those who have been denied opportunities in the past. I do not personally think that the best way to do that is on the political plane by the reservation of seats and the rest. I think the best way, and the more basic and fundamental way, is to advance them rapidly in the economic and educational spheres and then they will stand on their own legs.

There is a great danger, whether you deal with an individual, group or community, of giving certain props to that community which give it a false sense of strength which does not belong to it. The props are external to it, and when they are removed suddenly they make the community weak. A nation ultimately ought to stand on its own legs. So long as it relies on some external prop, it is not strong. It is weak. So these external props, as I might call them-that is, reservation of seats and the rest-may possibly be helpful occasionally in the case of the backward groups, but they produce a false sense of the political relations, a false sense of strength, and ultimately, therefore, they are not so nearly as important as real educational, cultural and economic advance, which gives them inner strength to face any difficulty or any opponent. However, I can conceive that in the present context of affairs in regard to these unfortunate countrymen of ours who have not had these opportunities in the past, special attempts should be made, of course in the educational and economic field and even in the political field, to see that they have a proper place till they find their own legs to stand upon without any external aid.

The Sheduled Tibes

I have always-long before I became Prime Minister-felt very wrongly attracted to the tribal people of this country. This feeling was not the curiosity an idle observer has for strange customs; nor was it the attraction of the charitably disposed who want to do good to other people. I was attracted to them simply because I felt happy and at home with them. I liked them without any desire to do them good or to have good done to me. To do good to others is, I think, a very laudable desire but it often leads to great excesses which do not result in good to either the doer or the recipient.

In the tribal people, I have found many qualities which I miss in the people of the plains, cities and other parts of India. It was these very qualities that attracted me.

The tribal people of India are a virile people who naturally went astray sometimes. They quarrelled and occasionally cut off one another's heads. These were deplorable occurrences and should have been checked. Even so, it struck me that some of their practices were perhaps less evil than those that prevail in our cities. It is often better to cut off a hand or a head than to crush and trample on a heart. Perhaps, I also felt happy with these simple folk, because the nomad in me found congenial soil in their company. I approached them in a spirit of comradeship and not like someone aloof who had come to look at them, examine them, weigh them, measure them and report about them or to try and make them conform to another way of life.

I am alarmed when I see-not only in this country but in other great countries too-how anxious people are to shape others according to their own image or likeness and to impose on them their particular way of living. We are welcome to our way of living but why impose it on others? This applies equally to national and international fields. In fact, there would be more peace in the world, if people were to desist from imposing their way of living on other people and countries.

I am not at all sure which is the better way of living. In some respects I am quite certain theirs is better. Therefore, it is grossly presumptuous on our part to approach them with an air of superiority or to tell them what to do or not to do. There is no point in trying to make of them a second rate copy of ourselves.

Now, who are these tribal folk? A way of describing them is that they are the people of the frontiers or those who live away from the interior of this country. Just as the hills breed a somewhat different type of people from those who inhabit the plains, so also the frontier breeds a different type of people from those who live away from the frontier. My own predilection is for the mountains rather than for the plains, for the hill folk rather than the plains people. So also I prefer the frontier, not only in a physical sense but because the idea of living near a frontier appeals to me intellectually. I feel that it would prevent one from becoming complacent and complacency is a very grave danger, especially in a great country like India where the nearest frontier may be a thousand miles away.

...I would prefer being a nomad in the hills to being a member of stock exchanges, where one is made to sit and listen to noises that are ugly to a degree. Is that the civilization we want the tribal people to have? I hope not. I am quite sure that the tribal folk, with their civilization of song and dance, will last till long after stock exchanges have ceased to exist.

It is a very great pity that we in the cities have drifted so far away from the aesthetic side of life. We still have a good many folk songs and dances when we go to the villages, because modern civilization has more or less left them untouched. The progress of modern civilization in India involves both good things and bad. One of the things we have lost is the spirit of song and dance and the capacity for enjoyment and this is what the tribal people so abundantly have. We seem to pay too much attention to the cinema; it is undoubtedly an excellent medium for many good things but unfortunately it has not proved to be particularly inspiring. We must imbibe something of the spirit of the tribal folk instead of damping it with our long faces and black gowns.

I find that so far we have approached the tribal people in one of two ways. One might be called the anthropological approach in which we treat them as museum specimens to be observed and written about. To treat them as specimens for anthropological examination and analysis-except in the sense that everybody is more or less an anthropological specimen-is to insult them. We do not conceive of them as living human beings with whom it is possible to work and play. The other approach is one of ignoring the fact that they are something different requiring special treatment and of attempting forcibly to absorb them into the normal pattern of social life. The way of forcible assimilation or of assimilation through the operation of normal factors would be equally wrong. In fact, I have no doubt that, if normal factors were allowed to operate, unscrupulous people from outside would take possession of tribal lands. They would take possession of the forests and interfere with the life of the tribal people. We must give them a measure of protection in their areas so that no outsider can take possession of their lands or forests or interfere with them in any way except with their consent and goodwill.[6]

Social Dimensions of Progress[7]

The whole object of development of a country is social welfare in its wider sense and not merely in the sense of aiding the physically handicapped and the weaklings in a society. In a society where even healthy people have no opportunity to get on with the bare necessities of life, the first object of the state is social welfare. What is all our planning for? It aims at improving the standards of living of the people and strengthening the country in various ways. Some people may think that the first object of the state is to make the country militarily strong. That is not our objective. Although we want the country to be strong, ultimately, all this should result in raising the social and other standards of all the people.

...The fundamental problem of India is not Delhi or Calcutta or Bombay but the villages of India, and something has to be done to raise the level of life in villages... Urbanization is taking place fast enough and will go on taking place fast enough. In fact, there is another way of looking at it. The villages are being deprived of their bright persons who go to the cities, leaving the villages rather weak and without any educated or trained persons to help them. You may state the problems in a different way. We want to urbanize the village, not take away the people from the villages to the towns that are growing up, but to bring certain urban standards to the village, and keep the bright persons of the village in the village itself. However well we may deal with the towns, the problems of the villages of India will remain for a long time and any social standards that we seek to introduce will be judged ultimately not by what happens in Delhi city but in the villages of India.

Sitting here, I have been thinking of that specially. My mind was trying to grapple with the problem of what to do with more than 5,50,000 villages of India and the people who live there. After all, our planning is ultimately aiming at higher social welfare - I use to word 'social' in the wider sense, including, of course, economic standards for the 450 million people of India. It is intended not only to benefit the select few who are particularly unfortunate. We should help them, of course. As a matter of fact, we talk about the backward classes, the depressed classes and the scheduled classes in India, who have been given some special privileges in regard to representation, education and such other things. But later we decided that we should not give these privileges as far as possible to particular castes, if I may use the word, but to people who deserve them from the economic point of view. From the economic point of view, about 80 per cent of our people lack these facilities.

Now, if we are going to give special privileges to these 80 per cent, it means practically to the whole lot of our people. It amounts to this that while we do require special institutions to deal with many of these problems, it is ultimately a question of planning with a view to raising the whole level of living in the country. In involves all kinds of things, some of which we have done; many others we have not done, and we should like to do.

I am one of the relics of the Gandhian days. Economists ...used to criticize the spinning wheel. They said: "What has that to do in our age of machinery?" That criticism was right from many points of view. Yet what Gandhiji did was fundamentally right. He was looking all the time at the villages of India, at the most backward people in India in every sense, and he devised something. It was not merely the spinning wheel; that was only a symbol. He laid stress on village industries, which again to the modern mind does not seem very much worthwhile.

What is the place of small industries? We have big plans and all that. I am all in favour of machinery. I like the feel of machinery, the look of it, but more and more, I have felt that from the point of view of balanced development, we have to lay greater stress on many small industries in our villages, make them slightly urbanized, lessen the gap between them and the urban areas and increase the facilities available to the people who live there, instead of concentrating on the towns and cities and drawing out people from the villages, thus creating problems in the cities.

Another point is that we in India live in a very mixed society-mixed in terms of development, in terms of human beings, in terms of the variety in the country and the people. You will find that many people still live as their forefathers lived a thousand years ago or more. You will also find here people who may be said to live in the middle of the twentieth century. So, you see in India a mixture of the tenth, the fifteenth and the twentieth centuries. We have vast areas in India which differ from one another. We have a large number of people whom we call 'tribal people'. Many possibly think that 'tribal people' means some kind of primitive people. Well, some tribes are rather primitive but others are highly developed. They have a different kind of society; they do not have a market economy and do not possess many things that come with the machine age. If I may say so, in many ways, they are far better as human beings than non-tribal people like me. Because they have not developed their economy in the conventional way, they are called tribals. They are a democratic people. They are fine men and women, and possess many cultural qualities which we do not possess.

So, we have all these mixtures of human beings in India, a vast number of them and a growing number of them. How should we deal with them? Broadly, we want them to develop according to their own genius. We do not want to impose things upon them. On the other hand, unless we have some organized scheme of giving them opportunities to develop, they will not develop. Take education, for instance. That is one of the bases of social welfare. At present, we have, I believe, about 55 million students in our educational institutions. That is a considerable number and it is growing every year. I think in two or three years' time it will be 65 million-practically 100 per cent children of the school going age. Although our schools may not be very wonderful to look at, although our teachers may not be perfect, the mere fact that 55 million boys and girls go to schools is a tremendous development. It is a revolutionary development and this fact is changing the whole structure of our society. The children who go to school, specially the girls, influence their parents who may be illiterate, and many of whom live in the villages. Their mothers, grandmothers and earlier to them many generations have never been to school. When the children start going to school, they learn new things and tell their parents about them. They introduce little changes in their homes. There is now a very large number of young women going to our colleges.

So, I should like you to think in terms of providing the basic necessities of life to everybody in a country like India. I am ashamed to confess that even today, in spite of every effort, there are areas of India where it is difficult to get good water to drink, and people have to go miles and miles to fetch a pot of water. If I may put it so, I should think the very first thing to do in social welfare is to provide water to drink. There must be enough food, clothing, housing, education and health. If we could provide all these to every inhabitant, it does bring a certain basic standard of living to everybody. Having provided that, we can try to raise this standard.

Every country has its own problems and it is rather difficult to generalize, but in regard to India, I do feel that we should concentrate on giving the mass of people a share in the progress that India is making. We have put up very fine plants, huge plants, hydro-electric schemes and all that, and they are bearing fruit. Yet there are areas in India where no great changes or improvements have come at all. Gradually, no doubt, these improvements will seep down to them. These areas require help. Of course, such help should be planned in a big way.

There is an important problem which comes up in planning. How should we devote our resources to the development of, let us say, basic industries, mother industries and small industries? A planner usually thinks in terms of scientific development from the base, building up a strong base and gradually extending it till the other smaller industries and plants come up. If you don't have a proper base, there will be delay in building up even the smaller industries. If you don't have enough steel or machine-building capacity, it will come in the way of putting up other industries because you won't be able to make machines and will have to import them. So, we concentrate on the basic industries. If we want electric power, we have to have hydro-electric works. But there are different opinions among our people. Some people have been telling us that we should not have spent so much energy and resources on these big industries. Basically, I don't agree with them at all, though, to some extent, I do see their point of view. I think it is impossible for us to progress without having those basic things. We simply have to have them or postpone our development. At the same time, we have to think all the time also of the social welfare of the mass of our people. We put up huge steel plants and the like, which please us and build up our morale and all that, but hundreds of millions of people cannot be asked to wait for some future age for betterment in their living standards. It is too much for them to do so. Therefore, we have to think also of other kinds of developments for the mass of our people even if it raises them only slightly.

Therein lies the virtue of Mahatma Gandhi's teachings. People think that he was against machinery. I don't think he was against it. He did not want machinery except in the context of the well-being of the mass of our people. What he suggested-cottage industry-was something which immediately benefited the people, not only in regard to employment but also in production.

There is another way of looking at production. If two hundred million people of India, or whatever the number, increase their productive capacity by the smallest sum per day, it will come to a prodigious figure when you total it up. I am not suggesting that you should all take to the spinning wheel. But, not losing myself in grand visions of a machine age, I am suggesting an approach that will directly benefit them immediately, by giving them employment. I personally enjoy such visions, but we must not lose ourselves in them. After all, we have to deal with the betterment of human beings and this aim must always be kept in view. Such a social welfare can only be brought about by State effort, no doubt helped by voluntary agencies. It was with this view that the Central Social Welfare Board was started.

It was with this view, more specially, that the Community Development Movement in India was started. Community Development deals with the villages, the rural population. It has been doing much good, but, still as it often happens in India, things fall into a rut. We all get into a rut. Prime Ministers get into a rut, everybody gets into a rut. The early dynamism of the Community Development Movement became rather spread out. There is too much bureaucracy in it, too many Village Level Workers filling in forms all the time, instead of doing a hard job. It is extraordinary how this disease of form-filling has grown. Everybody in India wants a jeep to do social work. When I was a young boy. I never saw a jeep. Yet we did a lot of work in rural areas. I went about in ramshackle horse carts, in vehicles or on bicycles. Everybody did so, And now nobody can move without a jeep. I am not against jeeps. A jeep is a very useful thing, but this dependence on things which you cannot easily get does come in the way of work.

So the choice has to be made ultimately by the planner–it is a difficult choice-between projects which are important basically and which will lead to further growth but which will not immediately bring relief to the people and some projects which will bring relief to the people much sooner. There are some things which the people must have at all costs. I mentioned an obvious example–water. Every village must have good drinking water. There are many other needs too, like electricity. I do think electricity is perhaps the most necessary and the most revolutionary thing which you can take into the rural areas. The moment you take electricity, all kinds of things begin to move. Petty industries grow up, agriculture is affected; everything is in fact affected. The whole life of the people is changed, they will get longer hours to work because of the lighting and all that. I wish we could concentrate on some of these things. There are, however, many pulls and one has to take an overall view of things.

So, we have to strike a balance; we have to take on major schemes and smaller schemes. Somehow, I feel that the objective should be ultimately the development of the human being. Cities, after all, are moving and they will go ahead. But the villages require very great attention.

Now, there is another thing in our democratic system, adult franchise, in which all men and women vote. Obviously, the average person who comes into our Parliament or our State Assemblies is from the village. If the villages are not adequately looked after, these people are not going to put up with city folk pushing them about. They will insist on having their way. sometimes that way may not be a good way, but still they may insist upon it.

This problems of social welfare might be looked at in many ways. Essentially, I submit, it has to be the point of view of the villages and the towns. Even if a small advance is made *per capita* in a village, in the totality it will amount to a big advance. If we put up big factories, they help in our production, but they do not affect too much the *per capita* income. If the village farmer increases his yield a bit, the *per capita* income immediately goes up and every thing else goes up.

So, although I live in Delhi city, my mind is concerned more and more with the villages of India and how to give them the basic necessities of life, and how to make them self reliant and capable of looking after themselves.

Social Change[8]

...We talk a great deal about doing good to the masses... And yet I would beg to say that we have not as a whole developed that social outlook yet which, if I may say so, is a common factor of communism, socialism and even capitalism in advanced countries. Without that basic things, we talk of bringing about changes at the top by sudden laws. Well, let us have the laws, by all means which will help, but ultimately, laws are the product of a nation's thought, a nation's customs, activities and progress. All the laws in the world cannot make the people honest. You have got the Criminal Code, and yet you talk of corruption - and rightly too. It is not the lack of law that leads to corruption but something else. It is not the lack of law that possibly leads to that lack of social outlook and social sense in many of us, but something else which we have to develop. We have to consider our economic policies carefully and more from the point of view of which economic policy helps in the development of social outlook, and which helps in the hindrance of the anti-social outlook. That, I think, is the test. You cannot change millions of people suddenly. It cannot be done, however rapidly you may progress. You may, if you like, destroy what you have got and have a clean slate. Sometimes, that has to be done. But the process of destruction leads to utmost misery for long periods of time, maybe generations. It is not worth while, unless is is forced down upon you. Therefore, you want to make progress without destruction, except destroying something that is bad.

So we have this vast problem before our country-the problem of raising 340 or 350 million people; raising them economically certainly, raising them educationally and raising them in so many unconscious ways, thus developing a new outlook amongst them. It is all integrated together. It is not merely an economic problem. It is not merely a political problem. It is a social problem and it affects our life in a hundred ways.

The basis of society is some measure of security and stability. With out security and stability there could be no society or social life, but how many today in our present-day society have this security and stability? You know that the millions have it not; they have hardly enough to keep body and soul together. And it is a mockery to speak to them of security. So long as the masses do not share in this security, you can have no stable society. And so you see in the history of the world, revolution after revolution, not because any group or person is a lover of bloodshed, anarchy and disorder, but because of this desire for greater security for larger number of persons. We shall have real security and stability in this world only when it has come to signify the well-being of the vast majority of the people, if not all, and not of small groups only. That time may not be near, but society is continually, sometimes it may even be a little blindly, struggling towards it. And the greater the struggle, the greater the urge to that end, the healthier and more vital the society. If this urge is wholly absent, society becomes static and lifeless and gradually withers away.

So long therefore as the world is not perfect, a healthy society must have the seeds of revolt in it. It must alternate between revolution and consideration. It is the function of youth to supply this dynamic element in society; to be the standard-bearers of revolt against all that is evil and to prevent older people from suppressing all social progress and movement by the mere weight of their inertia.

...What do we find in this world of ours today? Utter misery is the lot of vast numbers of people and while a few live in luxury, the many lack even bread and clothing and have no opportunity for development. Wars and conflicts ravage the world and the energy that should go to build up a better order of society is spent largely in mutual competition and destruction...

...The immediate purpose of every human being should be to reduce this misery and to help in building up a better society, and a better society must necessarily aim at the elimination of all domination of one nation over another or of man over man. It must replace competition by cooperation...

...The freedom of India is dear to all of us... Our desire for freedom is a thing more of the mind than of the body, although even our bodies often suffer for the lack of freedom. There may be many who have the ordinary conveniences of life and are not hard put to it to find their daily bread. ...To the vast masses of our fellow countrymen present conditions spell hunger and deepest poverty, an empty stomach and a bare back... The most amazing and terrible thing about India is here poverty. It is not a dispensation from Providence or an inevitable condition of society. India has enough or can have enough for all her children if some of her own sons did not corner the good things and so deprive the masses of their dues. "Poverty", said Ruskin, "is not due to natural inferiority of the poor or the inscrutable laws of God. or drink, but because others have picked their pockets."... The control of wealth by the few not only means the unhappiness of many, but it exercises a power over men's minds... It is this mental outlook which paralyses the poor and the oppressed.

...In the past we have seen the curious phenomenon in India of the political extremist sometimes being a reactionary in social matters, and not unoften the political moderate has been socially more advanced. It is impossible to separate the political life of the country from its social and economic life and you cannot cure the social organism by treating one part of it only. The infections from one affected part continually spreads to other parts and the disease takes firmer root. Your political and social philosophy must, therefore, be a complete whole and your programme must comprise every department of national activity.

Social Welfare and Social Service

Social Welfare

What exactly is social welfare? The well-being of society, I take it. If so, it includes almost everything that one can think of, spiritual, cultural, political, economic and social. It covers thus the entire field of human activity and relationships. And yet, this wide and all-embracing sense is seldom applied to it, and we use the words in a far more restricted sense. The social worker, often enough, considers himself or herself as working in a field which is strictly separated from political action or economic theory. He or she will try to bring relief to suffering humanity, will fight disease and slum conditions, deal with unemployment, prostitution and the like. He may also seek to bring about some changes in the law in order to remedy present-day injustice. But he will seldom go down to the roots of the problem, for he accepts the general structure of society as it is and seeks only to tone down its glaring injustices.

The lady who visits the slums occasionally to relieve her conscience by the performance of good and charitable deeds is a type we need not consider. The less we have of this patronizing and condescending approach to the problem the better. But there are large numbers of earnest men and women who devote themselves to the service of their fellow creatures in the somewhat narrow way conceived above. They do good work, and to whatever extent they may benefit others, they certainly benefit themselves by the discipline and training that this service gives them.

Yet, it seems to me, that all this good work is largely wasted, because it deals with the surface of the problem only. Social evils have a history and a background, roots in our past, and intimate connections with the economic structure under which we live. Many of them are indeed the direct products of that economic system, just as many others are of religious superstition and harmful custom. Any scientific consideration of the problem of social welfare must, therefore, inevitably go down to these roots and seek out the causes. It must have the courage to look deep down into the well of truth and to proclaim fearlessly what it finds there. If it avoids politics and economics, and all that goes by the name of religion, for fear of treading on dangerous ground, then it moves on the surface only and can neither command much respect, nor achieve results.[9]

Social Service

...I am glad to learn that you have opened a camp for training in social service and rural life. Who trains these people? Social service is a highly organised and technical science now and it is desirable to take advantage of modern technique. The only people I know in India who know something about this are the Tata School of Social Studies. It might be worthwhile for your Government to keep in touch with them and get help from them.[10]

REFERENCES

1. Letter to Krishna Hutheesing, October 28, 1941.
2. Letter to Dhanvanthi Rama Rau, October 18, 1959.
3. Central Council of Local Self-Government, Delhi, September 6, 1963.
4. Speech in the Constituent Assembly, April 3, 1948.
5. Speech in the Constituent Assembly, April 3, 1948.
6. Address at the Scheduled Tribes and Scheduled Areas Conference, New Delhi, June 7, 1952.
7. Speech at a Seminar on Social Welfare in a Developing Economy, New Delhi September 22, 1965
8. Speech in the Lok Sabha, February 3. 1950.
9. The Hindustan Times 20 Oct. 1920.
10. Letter to Govind Ballabh Pant, New Delhi, March 18, 1948.

COMMUNICATION AND COMMUNICATIONS

TWELVE

COMMUNICATION AND COMMUNICATIONS

Language and Words

...I fear my views on the language question do not represent what might be called the majority opinion in India and are not very popular. But it has been a matter of sorrow to me that in such a vital question as language we should forget all artistry and all beauty and become the slaves of some pedagogues and grammarians who have no conception of art or beauty or the music of words. Each word is a thing of power with a history behind it, calling up images in one's mind. No word can ultimately be translated with accuracy into any other language. One can only find some synonym for it which does not round about us, a strait-jacket will deaden a language. The courtly languages of previous ages had much to commend them. But they are totally unsuited to a democratic age, where we aim at mass education. A language, therefore, must fulfil two functions: it must base itself on its ancient roots and, at the same time, vary and expand with growing needs and be essentially the language of the mass of people and not of a select coterie. This is all the more necessary in this age of science and technology and world communication. In so far as possible, that language should have common or similar words with other languages in regard to scientific or technical terms. It must, therefore, be a receptive language, accepting every word from outside that fits into its general structure. Sometimes that word may be slightly varied to suit the genius of the language.

Speech at the International Union of Official Travel Organizations, New Delhi, October 19, 1955.

...We may go on listing any number of approaches; and it is interesting to argue and to clarify our minds, because thinking is helped by the sharp exchange of ideas. But, unfortunately, all these words which at one time had some precise meaning have gradually tended to become debased and to lose their meaning by association with hosts of new ideas, new conflicts, new passions.[1]

Words are tricky things always. In the final analysis the word is the biggest thing in the world. All the knowledge we have, everything we possess, is a collection of words which represent ideas of course. A simple word like table or chair, if it is simply that, the matter ends there; but as soon as we get out of that category of tables and chairs and get to concepts which have emotional significance attached to them, they become very tricky. When we think of such words we get roused up; a certain emotion fills us. An emotion may fill us with enthusiasm but we cease to think straight. And when two persons meet whose emotions have been roused up in different ways by the same word, then it becomes quite impossible for them to have any reasonable discussion. In the international sphere today, there is so much emotion, passion and anger roused by words, and what the words are supposed to connote, that it is becoming very difficult to have consistent or reasonable discussion. Words are thrown at each other just as a bomb might be thrown at a person. Therefore I say: Beware of words, great as they are. What do we want? Not words, even though words may signify much.[2]

...A language is something infinitely greater than grammar and philology. It is the poetic testament of the genius of a race and a culture, and the living embodiment of the thoughts and fancies that have moulded them. Words change their meanings from age to age and old ideas transform themselves into new, often keeping their old attire. It is difficult to capture the meaning, much less the spirit, of an old word or phrase. Some kind of a romantic and poetical approach is necessary if we are to have a glimpse into that old meaning and into the minds of those who used the language in former days. The richer and more abundant the language, the greater the difficulty. Sanskrit, like other classical languages, is full of words which have not only poetic beauty but a deep significance, a host of associated ideas, which cannot be translated into a language foreign in spirit and outlook. Even its grammar, its philosophy, have a strong poetic content; one of its old dictionaries is in poetic form.

Discovery of India

I often wonder which is the most important of the many things that have distinguished India in the past in its history of thousands of years. I have no doubt in my mind that it is the Sanskrit language. I think it is that which has embodied the genius of our race, the wisdom of our race and almost everything that has come out in later years can somehow be found to have sprung from that magnificent language. What is language, Sanskrit or any other language? Thought represented in words. The most powerful thing in the world is thought. But thought remaining in the region of thought is inaccessible. It leads to nothing. It may almost be called an abortion, if I may use the phrase, although thought by itself is sometimes action also. The mere thinking is action. Thought has been and will be the greatest thing in the world, and everything else comes out of thought. But thought has to take shape in words, words of power, and in this language of our race, the most magnificent thoughts are clothed in words of power. And so, this language was probably the strongest cultural manifestation of the Indian people.

I am convinced that real mass progress in India can only be made through our own languages and not through a foreign language. I am anxious to prevent a new caste system being perpetuated in India - English-knowing caste separated from the mass of our people. That will be most unfortunate. This in fact happened during the British period. It could happen then because education was very limited. It cannot happen now, when education is becoming widespread.[3]

I cannot conceive of English being the principal medium of education in India in the future. That medium has to be Hindi or some other regional language. Only then can we remain in touch with our masses and help in a uniform growth.

But there are other aspects. One, I have mentioned above, about the necessity of knowing English or any other foreign language for scientific and technological purposes. Also, if I may say so with all respect, we are a narrow-minded people and are apt to live in our own shells. There is the danger of our getting cut off from the world of thought in all its aspects and becoming complacent in our own little world of India. For this reason also contacts with foreign languages are essential.

Thus I think that Hindi must be given every encouragement to grow and to be used for educational and administrative purposes, provided always that it grows on sound lines and not on superficial, journalistic lines. Secondly, Hindi (or some other regional language) has to be the medium of education.

Thirdly, English should be a compulsory second or third language. It is of course not necessary or possible for everybody in India to know English. But a very large number should know it for the reasons I have stated above. They can know it in two ways. One is a fully adequate knowledge of the language. The other is to know it as a language of comprehension, that is, to be able to read books and periodicals in it without perhaps being able to speak it easily. On the whole I am inclined to think that English as a compulsory subject in our schools (the medium being Hindi) is desirable. The schools will give some basic knowledge, enough perhaps for comprehension. After that, a relatively small number will proceed to a more thorough knowledge of English. It is obvious that English cannot be taken at the university stage. Universities are meant for specialized subjects, not for elementary teaching.

So far as teaching science and technology is concerned, I think that even there the medium should be Hindi in our schools. At a later stage English would be necessary for some years to come. Even when English is not necessary for the advanced teaching of science, it will nevertheless remain necessary for that wider contact with scientific literature.[4]

The Cerebral Process, Reading & Rumination

Why does one read books? To instruct oneself, amuse oneself, train one's mind, etc., etc.–Certainly all this and much more. Ultimately it is to understand life with its thousand facets and to learn how to live life. Our individual experiences are so narrow and limited, if we were to rely on them alone we would also remain narrow and limited. But books give us the experiences and thoughts of innumerable others, often the wisest of their generation, and lift us out of our narrow ruts. Gradually as we go up the mountain sides fresh vistas come into view, our vision extends further and further, and a sense of proportion comes to us. We are not overwhelmed by our petty and often transient loves and hates and we see them for what they are–petty and hardly noticeable ripples on the immense ocean of life. For all of us it is worthwhile to develop this larger vision for it enables us to see life whole and to live it well. But for those who cherish the thought of rising above the common herd of unthinking humanity and playing a brave part in life's journey, this vision and sense of proportion are essential to keep us on the right path and steady us when storms and heavy winds bear down on us.[5]

...What I would like you to do first of all is to think. Thinking is something which does not come automatically to a person. Gossiping with a neighbour is not thought. If you repeat something which somebody else has said, it is not thought. I do not expect all of you to become mighty thinkers, though some of you may. But I would like all of you to think and to develop the art of thinking. Nothing is more helpful to thinking than reading, that is, reading intelligently, because thereby you get other people's thoughts, and by weighing them you can think yourself. I have often said that it is very unfortunate that people think and read so little nowadays, especially in India. I do not call newspaper-reading reading. But any reading which makes you think is useful reading, even if it is a very good novel. Great novels always make one think, because they are pictures of life painted by great minds.

...The newspapers can perform a very valuable service, although newspapers too inevitably have become more like pocket digests than something that will enable people to think. I do not know how far it is possible to get out of the difficulty but it is dangerous for people to think less and less, and to be flooded by pocket magazines or newspapers instead of really worthwhile books. Newspapers have their place but newspapers do not often help one to think. How many of you would remember what you had read in the newspapers a week ago? You will find that you have almost entirely forgotten it, because it has left no impress on you although it might have excited you for a day or two. Probably the man who wrote it has forgotten it too. All of us, of course, cannot be creative artists or original thinkers, but we should accept other people's thoughts only after thinking for ourselves, and not blindly.[6]

Influence of Cinema

The cinema, let us remember, is one of the biggest influences in the modern world. There are many other things which influence people–books, newspapers and so on. But I think it is perfectly correct to say that the influence of the films in India is greater than the influence of newspapers and books combined...[7]

...Anything that has widespread influence is of the utmost importance to society and to Government. It cannot be treated as a joke or treated as something that can be classified as bad or as good and left at that. It has to be treated realistically as something of the highest importance for the life of the country. And because it is of the highest importance, a Government must be intimately concerned about it. As I have made clear, I do not want too much Governmental interference in artistic activities. But Government must inevitably be concerned with something which has such a wide influence. Suppose our producers produced a war film which encourages the war mentality. The Government of India would come down upon it with a big thump and stop it. There is no use telling me that we are interfering with the liberty of the individual. I just do not want war propaganda in India to pervert young people's minds. So I say there are limits. There is no reason why we should quarrel about it. There must be broad agreement on the main principles of such restraint among government, society and the industry itself. There may be difference of opinion as to where the line is to be drawn.

The cinema is a big industry. I must pay tribute to those who built it up in the last twenty or thirty years, for they have built something big starting from scratch and without much assistance and produced from time to time some very notable films. The mere quantity and the fact that this development has been practically unaided are creditable to them. Many people criticize the quality of many of our films from their rather highbrow point of view... But we have to meet a problem here which is not an Indian problem alone. It is melodrama that interests large numbers of people, whether in India, England or America or elsewhere. Public taste, to some extent, moulds what is presented to it. At the same time, what is presented should mould public taste.

Going Places

Tourism is intimately connected with the growth of communications. One view of world history would be to look at this growth of communications, particularly in the last two hundred years or so. Before that, one might say, communications had been static for thousands of years. The fastest means of transport or communication was probably a swift horse. Then, suddenly, came various changes as a consequence of the Industrial Revolution, and the pace of change became faster and faster. This growth of communications has brought the whole world much closer. Almost every country now sits at the doorstep of other countries, however far they may be. That is the physical change brought about by science. How far we have kept pace mentally with that physical change I do not know. Probably we have not kept pace with it, and hence some of our difficulties in international affairs. Politically, economically and otherwise, we function as national entities and independent governments, even coming into occasional conflict with one another. How far this fits in with the new world, with its highly-developed communications, is for you to think over. We have not advanced as far in the political and economic field as in the field of communications, and if this hiatus is not bridged, wrong consequences will flow from it.

One way to bridge that gulf is through people getting to know other countries and other peoples. Despite the great differences, there are certain basic factors common to all humanity, and common problems facing all people. Apart from their other advantages and pleasures, travel and tourism, I think, serve a much wider human purpose which is becoming increasingly important as the world becomes more and more closely knit together by communications. People talk of one world. While it is still a distant ideal from the political point of view, it is a reality from the point of view of communications...

What does a tourist come to see in India? It is entirely for the individual tourist to determine, because there are many aspects of India. India is so vast and so ancient a country that the tourist has to pick and choose. He can, of course, look at a cross-section of something at once very old and very new. We are, in a sense, more interested in the new than in the old, but we are ourselves the products of the old. The old is in us and around us, but our faces are turned towards building the new India. If you want to have some idea of what is passing through our minds, you will have to see the new India even more than the old.

You may go, for example, to Banaras, which is, I believe, one of the oldest cities not only in India but possibly in the world, sharing that honour with a few others like Damascus. It has been a continuing city. Delhi is not a continuing city in that sense, though it has been the site of great cities for a great many centuries. This New Delhi, where you are now meeting, is the eighth city. The present Old Delhi is the seventh city, and around these two are the remains of six Delhis. Banaras, on the other hand, has been important continuously throughout our history. We hear reports of its importance as a city of culture even 3,000 years ago. The Buddha, 2,500 years ago, chose Banaras to deliver his First Sermon, because Banaras was a city of learning and culture. If you now went to Banaras, you would see a somewhat picturesque city on the river banks but you would see many other things which are very unattractive. You would react in either of two ways. I do not of course like the unattractive side of Banaras, but when I go to Banaras, I see a series of pictures which arise in my mind and depict the past history of Banaras. The city becomes to me a picture gallery of historical things. It is natural for a visitor to like certain places and certain people and dislike others. But it is essential to know the background before forming judgements. It is difficult for a casual tourist to get all this background. I myself want to get this background right whenever I go to a foreign country. I am chiefly interested in two things, first, the background of that country, and secondly the people. I am less interested in buildings, old or new, and the normal sights of a place. The great architectural or cultural accomplishment a of people interest me as part of the background that has thrown up the nation. These considerations might at best apply to a limited number of visitors and tourists, but probably those limited numbers profit more by their travels than those who rush here and there and have a rather mixed and hazy memory of the various things they see. Even then, travel is good. Travel is better still if the traveller goes out with a receptive and friendly mind, and travel is best of all if he is not only an ambassador of his own country but comes back from that other country as an ambassador of that country to his own. Then travel has fulfilled its function.[8]

REFERENCES

1. Letter to G.V. Mavlankar, March 1, 1950)
2. At the meetingt of Coordination Board of Ministers for River Valley Projects October 13, 1954.
3. Speech at Pune August 1, 1956.
4. Letter to Ramdhari Sanha 'Dinkar', September 10, 1956.
5. Letter to Indira Gandhi, February 22, 1935.
6. At the India Editors' Conference' New Delhi August 13, 1954.
7. Inaugural speech at a Film Seminar, New Delhi February 27, 1955.
8. A Speech at the International Union of Official Travel Organisation, New Delhi, 19 October, 1955.

PEACE ON THE EARTH GOODWILL TO MEN

1. Gandhi Showed the Way
2. World Politics
3. Non-Aligned Nations
4. Co-Existence
5. So that All Can Prosper

THIRTEEN

PEACE ON THE EARTH GOODWILL TO MEN

Gandhiji Showed the Way

I was, of course, much younger then but still I have the most vivid memories of that change, because if affected me as it affected millions of our people. We were at that time a very frustrated people, hankering and yearning for freedom and not knowing what to do about it. We were helpless, unarmed, unorganized in any proper way and totally incapable, as it seemed, of facing a great Imperial Power which had been entrenched in our country for over a hundred and fifty years. Further, this was a power which was not superficially there, merely by force of arms but which had dug down deep into the roots of India. It seemed an extraordinary difficult task to remove it.

Some of our young men, in the depths of their frustration, took to violent courses that were completely futile. Individual acts of terrorism took place, which meant nothing at all in the wider context of things. On the other hand, the politics of some of our leaders then was so feeble that it could produce no result. So between the two, we did not know what we could do. It seemed degrading to follow the rather humiliating line which some of the leaders of Indian public life in those days recommended; and, on the other hand, it seemed completely wrong and futile to adopt the terrorist method which, apart from being bad in itself, could not possibly gain any results.

At the time, Gandhi came on the scene and he offered a way of political action to us. It was an odd way–a new way. What he said was not new in its essence. Great men had said it previously but there was a difference in that he applied that teaching to mass political action. Something which the individual had been taught to do in his individual life was suddenly sought to be adopted for mass action – and mass action in a vast country of people who, from the educational point of view, were illiterate, untrained and thoroughly frightened; people who were obsessed with fear and who (if I may refer to the peasantry of our country which formed about 80 per cent of our population) were kicked and cuffed by everybody who came in contact with them, whether it was a governmental agency or the moneylender whoever it was, they were treated badly. They never had any relief from the tremendous burden they endured.

Well, Gandhi came and he told them that there was a way out – a way of achieving freedom. 'First of all' he said, 'shed your fear. Do not be afraid, and then act in a united way but always peacefully. Do not bear any ill will in your hearts against your opponent. You are fighting a system, not an individual, not a race, not the people of another country. You are fighting the imperialist systems or the colonial system'.

Now, it was not very easy for us to understand all this; and much more difficult it must have been for others, our peasantry, for instance. But the fact remains that there was some power in his voice, something in him which seemed to infuse other people with courage and make them feel that this man was not an empty talker, that he meant what he said and that he would be able to 'deliver the goods', if I may put it so.

Almost magically, his influence spread. He was well known before also but not in this particular way. And within a few months we saw a change come over our countryside. The peasantry began to behave differently. It straightened its back. It could look you in the face. It had self-confidence and self-reliance. Now, this did not happen automatically, of course, for Gandhi's message was carried to these peasants in the countryside by tens of thousands of young men and young women. First of all they went to the people who became enthusiastic about it and accepted it. Within a few months, the whole aspect of India changed.

Now, it is simple enough to say, 'Do not be afraid.' There is nothing magical about that. Of what were we afraid? What is a person normally afraid of? Many things. We were afraid of being put in prison. We were afraid of our property being confiscated for sedition. We were afraid, if you like, of being shot at and killed as rebels. Well, Gandhi argued with us, 'After all, if you are so frightfully keen on freedom, what does it matter if you go to prison, if your property is confiscated or even if you are killed? It does not matter much, because you will get something infinitely more. Apart from serving for a great cause and apart from possibly achieving results, the mere act of doing this will fill you with a certain satisfaction and joy'.

Somehow or other that voice seemed to convince masses of people; and there came about a tremendous change.

Thus started in India what might be called the 'Gandhi era' in our politics, which lasted until his death and which, in some form or other, will always continue. I mention this so that you may have some kind of a picture of how we behaved. Large numbers of us gave up our normal professions and avocations and went to the villages preaching this gospel. We also preached other things which our political organization demanded and we forgot almost everything else that we used to do. Our lives changed, not very deliberately – they simply changed, automatically and completely, so much so that it was a little difficult for us even to interest ourselves in those activities with which we had been previously associated. We were absorbed in the new activity of the moment–and not just for a moment but for years.

Obviously, we could not have done so if we did not find a great deal of satisfaction in it. We did find satisfaction; and when people imagine that I have gone through a great deal of pain and suffering because I went to prison for a number of years, they are perhaps partly right. They are, however, fundamentally wrong in another sense, because most of us who endured privations felt that period to be the most significant in our lives. It was not a period which might be measured in terms of normal happiness but it was something deeper than that – a period in which we felt a certain satisfaction. Why? Because, for the moment, our ideals were in conformity with our actions or, to put it in the other way, we acted in accordance with our ideals. And there can be no greater satisfaction to an individual than when there is such a synthesis of thought and action in him. Then he becomes, for the moment, an integrated individual and he functions with power and strength and without doubt. The real difficulties seldom come from an external source. Real difficulties are those which arise in our own minds when we are in doubt; they can also arise when we are not able to act in accordance with our conviction for some reason. Then there is difficulty and obstruction within ourselves and complexes arise. We had the feeling of tremendous satisfaction in what we were doing, because during that period we became integrated human beings in whom thought and action more or less went together.

We wanted results, of course. We were working for results but for the moment we were satisfied with the act of doing, results apart. We had ups and downs, apparent failures for the moment. But such was the nature of the technique of action which Gandhi had taught us that even in a moment of apparent failure there really was no going back.

You may have heard that a large number of us, a hundred thousand of us, were in prison and apparently nothing was happening in India. The movement for freedom was suppressed. It was so, in a superficial sense. Six months later or a year later, suddenly one would find that the movement was very alive. Repeatedly, the British Government was amazed. It would think that it had put an end to this business; and then it would find that it had started off at a higher pitch than ever. A movement, which was a peculiar mixture of mass activity and individual action (that is, each individual doing something regardless of whether others did it or not), is a type very difficult to crush. It may be suppressed for a while; but because there is the individual incentive and because the individual wants to act regardless of whether others act or not, and when thousands and tens of thousands of individuals feel that way, it is very difficult to suppress them.

How do governments function? A democratic government in the ultimate analysis functions largely with the goodwill of the people and with their co-operation. It cannot go very much against them. Even an autocratic government has to have a measure of goodwill. It cannot function without it. In the ultimate analysis, a government functions because of certain sanctions which it has and which are represented by its army or police force. If the government is in line with the thought of a majority of the people, it is a democratic government and only a very small minority of the people will feel its pressure. Now, if an individual refuses to be afraid of these sanctions, what is the government to do about it? It may put him in prison. He is not afraid; he welcomes it. He may be, if you like, shot down. He is not afraid of facing death. Well, then a government has to face a crisis; that is, a government, in spite of its great power, cannot really conquer an individual. It may kill him but it does not overcome him. That is failure on the part of the government. A government, which is essentially based – apart from the other factors which I have mentioned – upon the sanctions it has, comes up against something–the spirit of man which refuses to be afraid of those sanctions.

Now, that is a thing which normal governments do not understand. They are upset by it. They do not know how to deal with it. They can, of course, deal with the individual in the normal way by treating him as a criminal. But that, too, does not work, because that man does not feel like a criminal: nor do others regard him as a criminal. So, it does not work.

So that, this process, this technique of action, was not one of overwhelming a government so much by mass action–although there was that phase of it–but rather one of undermining the prestige of a government before which an individual would not bow. Many of you, no doubt, have read something very like it in Thoreau's writings. This was developed on a mass scale by Gandhi. Naturally, the people of India were not very well trained; nor did they understand too well the philosophy of this technique of action. They were weak and frail human beings. Nevertheless, on the whole, they did function according to that technique; and ultimately they triumphed.

The coming of independence was peaceful in the sense that there was peace between India and the United Kingdom. It was done by agreement; and the whole process was completed in an admirably peaceful way, which does great credit both to India and England.

There is one factor I should like you to remember in this particular connection. Gandhi's technique of action was not only peaceful but also effective. It showed results. It showed its effectiveness most in the way it brought about freedom and the fact that it led to no ill will between the two countries. And after achieving that freedom, though we were not completely devoid of ill feeling–I cannot say that–yet it was extraordinary how suspicion, ill will and bitterness against England faded away from our country. And, as you know, we decided of our own free will to co-operate with her in many things and we have continued to co-operate with her.

World Politics[1]

I have come to you not so much in my capacity as Prime Minister of a great country or a politician but rather as a humble seeker after truth and as one who has continuously struggled to find the way, not always with success, to fit action to the objectives and ideals that he has held. The process is always difficult but it becomes increasingly so in this world of conflict and passion. Politicians have to deal with day-to-day problems and they seek immediate remedies. Philosophers think of ultimate objectives and are apt to lose touch with the day-to-day world and its problems. Neither approach appears to be adequate by itself. Is it possible to combine those two approaches and function after the manner of Plato's philosopher-kings?

In this world of incessant and feverish activity, men have little time to think, much less to consider ideals and objectives. Yet, how are we to act, even in the present, unless we know which way we are going and what our objectives are? It is only in the peaceful atmosphere of a university that these basic problems can be adequately considered. It is only when the young men and women, who are in the university today and on whom the burden of life's problems will fall tomorrow, learn to have clear objectives and standards of values that there is hope for the next generation. The past generation produced some great men but as a generation it led the world repeatedly to disaster. Two world wars are the price that has been paid for the lack of wisdom on man's part in this generation. It is a terrible price and the tragedy of it is that, even after the price has been paid, we have not purchased real peace or a cessation of conflict and an even deeper tragedy is that mankind does not profit by its experience and continues to go the same way that led previously to disaster.

We have had wars and we have had victory and we have celebrated that victory; yet, what is victory and how do we measure it? A war is fought presumably to gain certain objectives. The defeat of the enemy is not by itself an objective but rather the removal of an obstruction towards the attainment of the objective. If that objective is not attained, then that victory over the enemy brings only negative relief and indeed is not a real victory. We have seen, however, that the aim in wars is almost entirely to defeat the enemy and the other and real objective is often forgotten. The result has been that the victory attained by defeating the enemy has only been a very partial one and has not solved the real problem; if it has solved the immediate problem, it has, at the same time, given rise to many other and sometimes worse problems. Therefore, it becomes necessary to have the real-objective clear in our minds at all times whether in war or in peace and always to aim at achieving the objective.

I think also that there is always a close and intimate relationship between the end we aim at and the means adopted to attain it. Even if the end is right but the means are wrong it will vitiate the end or divert us in a wrong direction. Means and ends are thus intimately and inextricably connected and cannot be separated. That, indeed, has been the lesson of old taught us by many great men in the past but unfortunately it is seldom remembered.

I am venturing to place some of these ideas before you, not because they are novel but because they have impressed themselves upon me in the course of my life which has been spent in alternating periods of incessant activity and conflict and enforced leisure. The great leader of my country, Mahatma Gandhi, under whose inspiration and sheltering care I grew up, always laid stress on moral values and warned us never to subordinate means to ends. We were not worthy of him and yet, to the best of our ability, we tried to follow his teaching. Even the limited extent to which we could follow his teaching yielded rich results. After a generation of intense struggle with a great and powerful nation, we achieved success and, perhaps, the most significant part of it, for which credit is due to both parties, was the manner of its achievement. History hardly affords a parallel to the solution of such a conflict in a peaceful way, followed by friendly and co-operative relations. It is astonishing how rapidly bitterness and ill will between the two nations have faded away, giving place to co-operation. And we in India have decided of our own free will to continue this co-operation as an independent nation.

I would not presume to offer advice to other and more experienced nations in any way. But may I suggest for your consideration that there is some lesson in India's peaceful revolution which might be applied to the larger problems before the world today? That revolution demonstrated to us that physical force need not necessarily be the arbiter of man's destiny and that the method of waging a struggle and the way of its termination are of paramount importance. Past history shows us the important part that physical force has played. But it also shows us that no such force can ultimately ignore the moral forces of the world; and if it attempts to do so, it does so at its peril. Today, this problem faces us in all its intensity, because the weapons that physical force has at its disposal are terrible to contemplate. Must the twentieth century differ from primitive barbarism only in the destructive efficacy of the weapons that man's ingenuity has invented for man's destruction? I do believe, in accordance with my master's teaching, that there is another way to meet this situation and solve the problem that faces us.

...India is a very old country with a great past. But she is a new country also with new urges and desires. Since August 1947, she has been in a position to pursue a foreign policy of her own. She was limited by the realities of the situation which we could not ignore or overcome. But even so, she could not forget the lesson of her great leader. She has tried to adapt, however imperfectly, theory to reality in so far as she could. In the family of nations she was a newcomer and could not influence them greatly to begin with. But she had a certain advantage. She had great potential resources that could, no doubt, increase her power and influence. A greater advantage lay in the fact that she was not fettered by the past, by old enmities or old ties, by historic claims or traditional rivalries. Even against her former rulers there was no bitterness left. Thus, India came into the family of nations with no prejudices or enmities, ready to welcome and be welcomed. Inevitably, she had to consider her foreign policy in terms of enlightened self-interest but at the same time she brought to it a touch of her idealism. Thus, she has tried to combine idealism with national interest. The main objectives of that policy are: the pursuit of peace, not through alignment with any major power or group of powers but through an independent approach to each controversial or disputed issues, the liberation of subject peoples, the maintenance of freedom, both national and individual, the elimination of racial discrimination and the elimination of want, disease and ignorance which affect the greater part of the world's population. I am asked frequently why India does not align herself with a particular nation or a group of nations and told that because we have refrained from doing so we are sitting on the fence. The question and the comment are easily understood, because in times of crisis it is not unnatural for those who are involved in it deeply to regard calm objectivity in others as irrational, short-sighted, negative, unreal or even unmanly. But I should like to make it clear that the policy India has sought to pursue is not a negative and neutral policy. It is a positive and a vital policy that flows from our struggle for freedom and from the teaching of Mahatma Gandhi. Peace is not only an absolute necessity for us in India in order to progress and develop but is also of paramount importance to the world. How can that peace be preserved? Not by surrendering to aggression, not by compromising with evil or injustice but also not by talking and preparing for war! Aggression has to be met, for it endangers peace. At the same time, the lesson of the last two wars has to be remembered and it seems to me astonishing that, in spite of that lesson, we go the same way. The very process of marshalling the world into two hostile camps precipitates the conflict which it has sought to avoid. It produces a sense of terrible fear, and that fear darkens men's minds and leads them into wrong courses. There is perhaps nothing so bad and so dangerous in life as fear. As a great President of the United States said, there is nothing really to fear except fear itself.

Our problem, therefore, becomes one of lessening and ultimately putting an end to this fear. That will not happen if all the world takes sides and talks of war. War becomes almost certain then.

We are a member of the family of nations and we have no wish to shirk any of the obligations and burdens of that membership. We have accepted fully the obligations of membership in the United Nations and intend to abide by them. We wish to make our full contribution to the common store and to render our full measure of service. But that can only be done effectively in our own way and of our own choice. We believe passionately in the democratic method and we seek to enlarge the bounds of democracy both on the political and the economic plane, for no democracy can exist for long in the midst of want and poverty and inequality. Our immediate needs are economic betterment and raising the standards of our people. The more we succeed in this, the more we can serve the cause of peace in the world. We are fully aware of our weaknesses and failings and claim no superior virtue; but we do not wish to forfeit the advantage that our present detachment gives us. We believe that the maintenance of that detachment is not only in our interest but also in the interest of world peace and freedom. That detachment is neither isolationism nor indifference nor neutrality when peace or freedom is threatened. When man's liberty or peace is in danger we cannot and shall not be neutral; neutrality then would be a betrayal of what we have fought for and stand for.

If we seek to ensure peace we must attack the root causes of war and not merely the symptoms. What are the underlying causes of war in the modern world?

One of the basic causes is the domination of one country by another or an attempt to dominate. Large parts of Asia were ruled till recently by foreign and chiefly European Powers. We ourselves were part of the British Empire, as were also Pakistan, Ceylon and Burma. France, Holland and Portugal still have territories over which they rule. But the rising tide of nationalism and the love of independence have submerged most of the Western Empires in Asia. In Indonesia; I hope that there will soon be an independent Sovereign State. We hope also that French Indo-China will achieve freedom and peace before long under a government of its own choice. Much of Africa, however, is subject to foreign Powers, some of whom still attempt to enlarge their dominions. It is clear that all remaining vestiges of imperialism and colonialism will have to disappear.

Secondly, there is the problem of racial relations. The progress of some races in knowledge or in invention, their success in war and conquest, has tempted them to believe that they are racially superior and has led them to treat other nations with contempt. A recent example of this was the horrible attempt, so largely successful, to exterminate the Jews. In Asia and Africa, racial superiority has been most widely and most insolently exhibited. It is forgotten that nearly all the great religions of mankind arose in the East and that wonderful civilizations grew up there when Europe and America were still unknown to history. The West has too often despised the Asian and the African and still, in many places, denies them not only equality of rights but even common humanity and kindliness. This is one of the great danger points of our modern world; and now that Asia and Africa are shaking off their torpor and arousing themselves, out of this evil may come a conflagration of which no man can see the range of consequences. One of your greatest men said that this country cannot exist half slave and half free. The world cannot long maintain peace if half of it is enslaved and despised. The problem is not always simple nor can it be solved by a resolution or a decree. Unless there is a firm and sincere determination to solve it, there will be no peace.

The third reason for war and revolution is the misery and want of millions of people in many countries and, in particular, in Asia and Africa. In the West, though the war has brought much misery and many difficulties, the common man generally lives in some measure of comfort - he has food, clothing and shelter to some extent. The basic problem of the East, therefore, is to obtain these necessaries of life. If they are lacking, then there is the apathy of despair or the destructive rage of the revolutionary. Political subjection, racial inequality, economic inequality and misery - these are the evils that we have to remove if we would ensure peace. If we can offer no remedy, then other cries and slogans will make an appeal to the minds of the people.

Many of the countries of Asia have entered the family of nations; others we hope will soon find a place in this circle. We have the same hopes for the countries of Africa. This process should proceed rapidly and America and Europe should use their great influence and power to facilitate it. We see before us vast changes taking place, not only in the political and economic spheres but even more so in the minds of men. Asia is becoming dynamic again and is passionately eager to progress and raise the economic standards of her vast masses. This awakening of a giant continent is of the greatest importance to the future of mankind and requires imaginative statesmanship of a high order. The problems of this awakening will not be solved by looking at it with fear or in a spirit of isolationism by any of us. It requires a friendly and understanding approach, clear objectives and a common effort to realize them. The colossal expenditure of energy and resources on armaments is an outstanding feature of many national budgets today but that does not solve the problem of world peace. Perhaps, even a fraction of that outlay, utilized in other ways and for other purposes, will provide a more enduring basis for peace and happiness.

Non-Aligned Nations[2]

We call ourselves non-aligned countries. The word "non-aligned" may be differently interpreted, but basically it was coined and used with the meaning of being non-aligned with the great power blocs of the world. "Non-aligned" has a negative meaning. But if we give it a positive connotation it means nations which object to lining up for war purposes, to military blocs, to military alliances and the like. We keep away from such an approach and we want to throw our weight in favour of peace. In effect, therefore, when there is a crisis involving the possibility of war, the very fact that we are unaligned should stir us to feel that more than ever it is up to us to do whatever we can to prevent such a calamity coming down upon us.

If in this crisis some action of ours helps to remove the fear of war, then we have justified and strengthened ourselves. I know that the key to the situation does not lie in the hands of this conference. It lies essentially in the hands of the two great powers, the United States of America and the Soviet Union. Nevertheless, this conference or rather the countrieson which are represented in this conference are not so helpless that they look on while war is declared and the world is destroyed. The time, the place and the occasion are now and here to take up the question of war and peace and make it our own and show to the world that we stand for peace and that, so far as we can, we shall fight for it in the ways open to us. The power of nations assembled here is not military power or economic power;

nevertheless it is power. Call it moral force. It does make a difference obviously what we in our combined wisdom feel and think about this issue of war and peace.

Some six, seven or eight years ago, non-alignment was a rare phenomenon. A few countries here and there asked about it and other countries rather made fun of it or at any rate did not take it seriously. "Non-alignment? What is this? You must be on this side or that," - that was the argument. That argument is dead today. The whole course of history of the last few years has shown a growing opinion spread in favour of the concept of non-alignment. Why? Because it was in tune with the course of events; it was in tune with the thinking of the vast numbers of people, whether the country concerned was non-aligned or not, because they hungered passionately for peace and did not like this massing up of vast armies and nuclear bombs on either side. Therefore, their minds turned to those countries who refused to line up.

We have arrived at a position today where there is no choice left between an attempt between negotiations for peace or war. If people refuseXto negotiate, they must inevitably go to war. I am amazed that rigid and proud attitudes are taken up by the great countries as being too high and mighty to negotiate for peace. I submit that it is not their prestige which is involved in such attitudes but the future of the human rare. It is our duty and function to say that they must negotiate.

I believe firmly that the only possible way to solve many of these problems ultimately is complete disarmament. I consider disarmament an absolute necessity for the peace of the world. I think that without disarmament the present difficulties, fears and conflicts will continue. We cannot expect to achieve disarmament suddenly even if this conference wants it. For the present moment the only thing which we can do is to lay stress on the need to negotiate with a view to getting over these fears and dangers. If that is done, the next and other steps follow.

The most important thing for the world today is for the great powers directly concerned to meet together and negotiate with a will to peace. And if this conference throws its weight in favour of such an approach, it will be a positive step which we take in order to help.

The most fundamental fact of the world today is the development of new and mighty forces. We have to think in terms of the new world. There is no doubt that imperialism and the old-style colonialism will vanish. Yet the new forces may help others to dominate in other ways over us, and certainly the under-developed and the backward. Therefore, we cannot afford to be backward.

We have to build in our own countries societies where freedom is real. Freedom is essential, because freedom will give us strength and enable us to build prosperous societies. These are for us basic problems. When we think in terms of these basic problems, war becomes an even greater folly than ever. If we cannot prevent war, all our problems suffer and we cannot deal with them. But if we can prevent war, we can go ahead in solving our other problems. We can help to liberate the parts of the world under colonial and imperial rule and we can build up our own free, prosperous societies in our respective countries. That is positive work for us to do. Therefore, I venture to submit to this assembly that we must lay the greatest stress on the removal of this major danger of war today. Not only is this incumbent on us but if we do this we shall be in line with the thinking of millions and millions of people. Non-alignment has received strength from the fact that millions of people are not aligned and that they do not want war.

Let us use this strength rightly, with courtesy and with a friendly approach so that we may influence those who have the power of war and peace in their hands. Let us try, if not to prevent war for all time, to push it away so that in the meantime the world may learn the ways of mutual co-operation.

Co-existence

Truth is much too big a thing for a single human mind to encompass or understand. Therefore Indian philosophy has always said that you can see only a bit of the truth. Let others see the other parts of the truth. Out of this synthesis may come an understanding which may help a wider appreciation of the truth. One has to accept this doctrine of peaceful co-existence, trying to argue, trying to understand, trying to impress, trying to convince but not trying to interfere and upset the other.

We accepted religions coming there from outside. Christianity came to India in the first century of the Christian era long before it went to Europe and it established itself peacefully, without conflict. The Zoroastrians came to India from Iran when they were pushed out by the Muslims. The Jews came about the first century. They established themselves quietly and there was no trouble. And so various people have come to India from outside and been established. India has stood for this kind of peaceful co-existence between different sets of ideas and different faiths. It is a continuation of that idea that makes us put forward the ideal of peaceful co-existence in the world today. It does not mean surrendering anything which we hold dear. It does not mean trying to impose our will on others either. Such an approach will help to develop a world free of conflicts, except, maybe, friendly conflicts in the realm of the mind. Therefore, I do not see any difficulty in the Soviet Union and the United States, as other countries, arriving at the stage of peaceful co-existence, each country no doubt influencing the other not by fierce arguments and denunciations but by actually living its own life.

So that all can prosper

In the present-day world, people talk of the atom bomb and are afraid of all the possible consequences which even the present generation might have to face. It is a very extraordinary situation, because one may say that science and the application of science have developed so much that it should be easily possible for the whole world to satisfy not only the primary needs of humanity but other needs also and to have full opportunities of individual or group development without the necessity of any conflict. I think that it can be mathematically shown that it is possible for the whole world to prosper if the resources of the world were turned in the direction of the betterment of humanity instead of so much of them being used for and wasted for purposes of war and the preparation for war. For the first time in history, mankind has the key to its happiness in its own hands. If this problem had arisen two or three hundred years ago, it would, perhaps, have been difficult to solve, because all mankind could not prosper together at that time.

I should like to refer briefly to some of our other problems. Many of the countries represented here have only recently become independent. They have tremendous problems and have, above all, the problem of making good economically and socially, because most of these countries are under-developed. It is right and proper that the affluent countries should help in this process. They have to some extent done so. I think they should do more in this respect, but ultimately the burden will lie on the people of the countries themselves. This problem has to be faced by each one of our countries.[3]

REFERENCES

1. Address on the occasion of the conferment of the degree of Doctor of Laws at Columbia University, New York, October 17, 1949.
2. From speech at the Conference of non-aligned Nations, Belgrade, September 2, 1961
3. At Belgrade 2, September 1961.

APPENDICES

1. The Dawn of Freedom and the Tasks Ahead
2. Work Projects New Faith
3. Tha Last Wish
4. Biographical Chronology
5. Books by Nehru
6. Books and Articles on Nehru

APPENDIX -I

The Dawn of Freedom And The Tasks Ahead

Long years ago we made a tryst with destiny, and now the time comes when we shall rideem our pledge, not wholly or in full measure, but very substantially. At the stroke of the midnight hour, when the world sleeps, India will awake to life and freedom. A moment comes, which comes but rarely in history, when we step out from the old to the new, when an age ends, and when the soul of a nation, long suppressed, finds utterance. It is fitting that at this solemn moment we take the pledge of dedication to the service of India and her people and to the still larger cause of humanity.

At the dawn of history India started on her unending quest, and trackless centuries are filled with her striving and the grandeur of her success and her failures. Through good and ill fortune alike she has never lost sight of that quest or forgotten the ideals which gave her strength. We end today a period of ill fortune and India discovers herself again. The achievement we celebrate today is but a step, an opening of opportunity, to the greater triumphs and achievements that await us. Are we brave enough and wise enough to grasp this opportunity and accept the challenge of the future?

Freedom and power bring responsibility. The responsibility rests upon this assembly, a sovereign body representing the sovereign people of India. Before the birth of freedom we have endured all the pains of labour and our hearts are heavy with the memory of this sorrow. Some of those pains continue even now. Nevertheless, the past is over and it is the future that backons to us now.

That future is not one of ease or resting but of incessant striving so that we may fulfil the pledges we have so often taken and the one we shall take today. The service of India means the service of the millions who suffer. It means the ending of poverty and ignorance and disease and inequality of opportunity. The ambition of the greatest man of our generation has been to wipe every tear from every eye. That may be beyond us, but as long as there are tears and suffering, so long our work will not be over.

And so we have to labour and to work, and work hard, to give reality to our dreams. Those dreams are for India, but they are also for the world, for all the nation and people are too closely knit together today for any one of them to imagine that it can live apart. Peace has been said to be indivisible; so is freedom, so is prosperity now, and so also is disaster in this one world that can no longer be split into isolated fragments.

To the people of India, whose representatives we are, we make an appeal to join us with faith and confidence in this great adventure. This is no time for petty and destructive criticism, no time for ill will or blaming others. We have to build the noble mansion of free India where all her children may dwell.

The appointed day has come-the day appointed by destiny-and India stands forth again, after long slumber and struggle, awake, vital, free and independent. The past clings on to us still in some measure and we have to do much before we redeem the pledges we have so often taken. Yet the turning point is past, and history begins anew for us, the history which we shall live and act and others will write about.

It is a fateful moment for us in India, for all Asia and for the world. A new star rises, the star of freedom in the East a new hope comes into being, a vision long cherished materializes. May the star never set and that hope never be betrayed!

We rejoice in that freedom, even though clouds surround us, and many of our people are sorrow- striken and difficult problems encompass us. But freedom brings responsibilities and burdens and we have to face them in the spirit of a free and disciplined people.

On this day our first thoughts go to the architect of this freedom, the Father of our Nation, who, embodying the old spirit of India, held aloft the torch of freedom and lighted up the darkness that surrounded us. We have often been unworthy followers of his and have strayed from his message, but not only we but succeeding generations will remember this message and bear the imprint in their hearts of this great son of India, magnificient in his faith and strength and courage and humility. We shall never allow that torch of freedom to be blown out, however high the wind or stormy the tempest.

Our next thoughts must be of the unknown volunteers and soldiers of freedom who, without praise or reward, have served India even unto death.

We think also of our brothers and sisters who have been cut off from us by political boundaries and who unhappily cannot share at present in the freedom that has come. They are of us and will remain of us whatever may happen, and we shall be sharers in their good and ill fortune alike.

The future beckons to us. Whither do we go and what shall be our endeavour? To bring freedom and opportunity to the common man, to the peasants and workers of India; to fight and end poverty and ignorance and disease; to build up a prosperous, democratic and progressive nation, and to create social, economic and political institutions which will ensure justice and fullness of life to every man and woman.

We have hard work ahead. There is no resting for any one of us till we redeem our pledge in full, till we make all the people of India what destiny intended them to be. We are citizens of a great country, on the verge of bold advance, and we have to live up to that high standard. All of us, to whatever religion we may belong, are equally the children of India with equal rights, privileges and obligations. We cannot encourage communalism or narrow-mindedness, for no nation can be great whose people are narrow in thought or in action.

To the nations and people of the world we send greetings and pledge ourselves to co-operate with them in furthering peace, freedom and democracy.

And to India, our much-loved motherland, the ancient, the eternal and the ever-new, we pay our reverent homage and we bind ourselves afresh to her service.

A Message to the Press, *The Statesman*, 15 August, 1917.

APPENDIX-II

Work Projects New Faith[1]

Our engineers tell us that probably nowhere else ın the world is there a dam as high as this. The work bristles with difficulties and complications. As I walked round the site I thought that these days the biggest temple and mosque and gurdwara is the place where man works for the good of mankind. Which place can be greater than this, this Bhakra Nangal, Where thousands and lakhs of men have worked, have shed their blood and sweat and laid down their lives as well? Where can be a greater and holier place than this, which we can regard as higher?

Then again it struck me that Bhakra Nangal was like a big university where we can work and while working learn, so that we may do bigger Things.

REFERENCE

1. At Nangal Canal Opening, 8 July 1954.

APPENDIX-III

The Last Wish

I have received so much love and affection from the Indian people that nothing that I can do can repay even a small fraction of it, and indeed there can be no repayment of so precious a thing as affection. Many have been admired, some have been revered, but the affection of all classes of the Indian people has come to me in such abundant measure that I have been overwhelmed by it. I can only express the hope that in the remaining years I may live, I shall not be unworthy of my people and their affection.

To my innumerable comrades and colleagues, I owe an even deeper debt of gratitude. We have been joint partners in great undertakings and have shared the triumphs and sorrows which inevitably accompany them.

I wish to declare with all earnestness that I do not want any religious ceremonies performed for me after my death. I do not believe in any such ceremonies and to submit to them, even as a matter of form, would be hypocrisy and an attempt to delude ourselves and others.

When I die. I should like my body to be cremated. If I die in a foreign country, my body should be cremated there and my ashes sent to Allahabad. A small handful of these ashes should be thrown into the Ganga and the major portion of them disposed of in the manner indicated below. No part of these ashes should be retained or preserved.

My desire to have a handful of my ashes thrown into the Ganga at Allahabad has no religious significance, so far as I am concerned. I have no religious sentiment in the matter. I have been attached to the Ganga and the Jamuna rivers in Allahabad ever since my childhood and, as I have grown older, this attachment has also grown. I have watched their varying moods as the seasons changed, and have often thought of the history and myth and tradition and song and story that have become attached to them through the long ages and become part of their flowing waters. The Ganga, especially, is the river of India, beloved of her people, round which are intertwined her racial memories, her hopes and fears, her songs of triumph, her victories and her defeats. She has been a symbol of India's age-long culture and civilization, ever-changing, ever-flowing, and yet ever the same Ganga. She reminds me of the snow-covered peaks and the deep valleys of the Himalaya, which I have loved so much,and of the rich and vast plains below, where my life and work have been cast. Smiling and dancing in the morning sunlight, and dark and gloomy and full of mystery as the evening shadows fall, a narrow, slow and graceful stream in winter, and a vast roaring thing during the monsoon, broad-bosomed almost as the sea, and with something of the sea's power to destroy, the Ganga has been to me a symbol and a memory of the past of India, running into the present and flowing on to the great ocean of the future. And though I have discarded much of past tradition and custom, and am anxious that India should rid herself of all shackles that bind and constrain her and divide her people, and suppress vast numbers of them and prevent the free development of the body and the spirit; though I seek all this, yet I do not wish to cut myself off from that past completely. I am proud of that great inheritance that has been, and is, ours, and I am conscious that I too, like all of us, am a link in that unbroken chain which goes back to the dawn of history in the immemorial past of India. That chain I would not break, for I treasure it and seek inspiration from it. And as witness of this desire of mine and as my last homage to india's cultural inheritance, I am making this request that a handful of my ashes by thrown into the Ganga at Allahabad to be carried to the great ocean that washes India's shore.

The major portion of my ashes should, however, be disposed of otherwise. I want these to be carried high up into the air in an aeroplane and scattered from that height over the fields where the peasants of India toil, so that they might mingle with the dust and soil of India and become an indistinguishable part of India.

(21 June 1954)

APPENDIX-IV

Biographical Chronology

(14th November 1889 to 27th May 1964)

1889	Was born in Allahabad on November 14, the son of Motilal and Swaruprani Nehru.
1905-7	Received School education at Harrow, Middlesex.
1907-10	Received higher education at Trinity College, Cambridge
1910-12	Practised at Inner Temple, London.
1912	Returned to India and started practice at Allahabad High Court.
1913	Became Joint Secretary, Allahabad branch of St. John Ambulance Brigade.
1916	Married Kamala Kaul on February 8.
1917	Daughter, Indira was born on November 19.
1918	Became the Secretary of the Home Rule League.
1919	Started the newspaper, Independent, with Motilal Nehru.

1920	Joined the Non-co-operation Movement.
1921	Arrested on December 6 for participating in the Volunteer Movement, urged the boycott of the visit of the Prince of Wales to India.
1922	Released on March 3; Again arrested on May 11 for picketing cloth shops.
1923	Released on January 26; Elected Chairman Allahabad Municipal Board in April;
1925	Resigned January, Arrested September 19 for defying an order banning entry into Nabha State; Released October 6.
	Presided in October over the United Provinces Political Conference, Benaras,
	Founded in December, the Hindustani Seva Dal.
	General Secretary, Indian National Congress, 1923-5.
1926-7	Visited Europe and Britain. Attended on February 10, 1927 the congress of Oppressed Nationalities, Brussels.
	Visited the Soviet Union in November.
	Moved in December the 'Independence Resolution' at the Madras Session of the Indian National Congress. General Secretary, Indian National Congress. 1927-9.
1928	Founded the Independence for Indian League in August
	Presided in September over the all Bengal Students Conference. Participated in the boycott of the Simon Commission,
	Lathi-charged in November in Lucknow.

1929 Presided over the Nagpur session of the All India Trade Union Congress on November 30. Presided over the Lahore session of the Indian National Congress on December 29.

1930 Participated in the Salt Satyagraha Movement and arrested on 14 April. (Released 11 October). Arrested on October 19 for a speech made in favour of the no-tax campaign.

1931 Released on January 26. Arrested December 26 for breach of an internment order prohibited him from leaving the municipal limits of Allahabad. Released September 4, 1935.

1936 Kamla Nehru died on February 28 in Lausanne, Switzerland.

Presided on April 23 over the Lucknow session of the Indian National Congress on April 23. Presided over the Faizpur session of the Indian National Congress on December 27.

1938 Visited Spain, France, Britain and some other European countries.

Chairman, National Planning Committee

1939 Visited Sri Lanka and China.

Drafted the Congress resolution on the war.

1940 Chosen to be the second satyagrahi in the Individual Satyagraha Movement.

Arrested on 31 October for speeches made in Gorakhpur. Released on 4 December 1941.

1942 Negotiated with Sir Stafford Cripps March-April.

Moved the 'Quit India' resolution at the All-India Congress Committee meeting on August 7. Arrested on August 9.

1945 Released on 15 June.

Represented the Congress at the Simla Conference from June 25 to July 14. Appeared in November as a lawyer for the defence at the trial of the Indian National Army Officers. Elected President of the All-India State People's Conference in December.

1946 Visited South-east Asia in March.

Held discussions with members of the British Cabinet Mission in April. June Elected President of the Indian National Congress in May. (Resigned in September) Arrest and release. Vice-President of the Viceroy's Executive Council in the Interim Government and member for External Affairs and Commonwealth Relations. Moved on 13 December the 'Objectives Resolution' in the Constituent Assembly.

1947 Inaugurated the Asian Relations Conference, on 23 March, New Delhi. Broadcasted to the nation on 3 June accepting the partition proposals.

Became The First Prime Minister of Free India on August 15.

1948 Attended in October the Commonwealth Prime Ministers' Conference, London.

Addressed the special Session of the United Nations General Assembly, Paris.

1949 Inaugurated on 20 January the conference of Eighteen Nations to condemn Dutch aggression on Indonesia. Visited the U.S.A. and Canada in October-November.

1950	Became Chairman, Planning Commission in March; held this office till his death.
1951	Elected President Indian National Congress.
1952	Formed new government in May after the first general elections.
1953	Convened Chief Ministers' Conference in November, New Delhi.
1954	Issued joint statement with Chou-Een-lai the Prime Minister of China when he visited India in June, the statement listed the five principles (Panchsheel).
1955	Moved the resolution on a 'Socialistic Pattern of Society' at the Avadi session of the Indian National Congress in January.
1956	Attended Conference at Brioni on 17-18 July with President Nasser of Egypt and President Tito of Yugoslavia. Attended the Conference of the Prime Ministers of Indonesia, Burma, Ceylon and India held in New Delhi in November.
1957	Formed new government in after the second General elections.
1959	Sponsored resolution on co-operative farming and state trading of food grains at the Nagpur session of the Indian National Congress held in January.
1960	Addressed the United Nations General Assembly, New York on October. 3.
1961	Participated in the Conference of Non-aligned Nations, Belgrade in september.
1962	Formed new government in April after the Third General elections.

	Presided over the National Integration Council meeting in June.
1963	Reorganised the Cabinet and the Congress under the 'Kamaraj Plan'.
1964	Died on 27 May in New Delhi. Cremated at what is now called Shanti Vana on the banks of the Yamuna.

APPENDIX-V

Books by Nehru

Autobiography with musings on recent events in India. London, Bodley Head, 1958. (1436)

The basic approach. New Delhi, All India Congress Committee, 1973.

Chinese aggression in war and peace. Delhi, Publication Division, 1962.

Collection of speeches . Delhi, Publication Division.
Vol. I 1946-49
Vol. II 1949-52
Vol. III 1953-1957.

Congressmen's primer for socialism 2nd edn. New Delhi, All India Congress Committee, 1976.

The Discovery of India. 3rd edn. London, Meridian, 1951.

Eighteen months in India, 1936-37; being further essays and writings. Allahabad, Kitabistan, 1938.

Freedom from fear; reflections on the personality and teachings of Gandhiji. New Delhi, Gandhi Samarak Nidhi, 1960.

Glimpses of world history; being further letters to his daughter, written in prison and containing a rambling account of history for young people with 50 maps ed. by J.B. Hornabin 2nd edn. Bombay, Asia 1962. (1936)

Glorious thoughts of Nehru; being a treasury of over twelve thousand invaluablë and inspiring thoughts, views and observations of Jawaharlal Nehru. New Delhi, New Book Society of India, 1968.

Great Nehru's 2nd edn. New Delhi, Tagore Memorial Publications, 1950.

Independence and after. Delhi, Ministry of Information and Broadcasting, 1949.

India and the World. New Delhi, Lakshmi, 1967 (1962)

India-China relations. Delhi, Publication Division, 1959.

India today and tomorrow. New Delhi. ICCR, 1959.

India's foreign policy : Selected speeches, September 1946 - April 1961. Delhi, The Publication Division, Ministry of Information and Broadcasting 1961.

India's freedom. London, Unwin, 1962.

India's independence and social revolution, Delhi, Vikas, 1984.

India's quests, being letters on Indian history from Glimpses of world history. Bombay, Asia,1963.

India's spokesman; from speeches and addresses. Madras, Macmillan, 1960.

Inside America. New Delhi, National Book Stall, New Delhi.

Jawaharlal Nehru : Excerpts from his writings and speeches. Delhi, Ministry of Information and Broadcasting Publications Division, 1964.

Jawaharlal Nehru's letters to P.N. Rajabhoj. Poona, Bharat Dalit Sewak Sangh, 1969.

Letters from a father to his daughter. Allahabad, Kitabistan, 1938.

Mahatma Gandhi. Bombay, Asia, 1966.

Nehru and Africa; a retracts from Jawaharlal Nehru's Speeches on Africa (1945-63). New Delhi, Indian Council for Africa, 1964.

Nehru in his own worlds : His replies to various questions. Edited by Ram Narayan Chaudhary. Ahmedabad, Narjivan. 1964.

Nehru on Gandhi. New York, The John Day, 1948.

Nehru on world history. London, Bodley Head, 1970.

Nehru talks....an exclusive interview. New York, Cowles Magazines, 1954.

Nehru's letter to Cheu-En-Lai (November 14, 1962). ,New Delhi, Publications Division, 1962.

Nehru's letter to his sister. London, Faber and Faber, 1963.

On co-operation. Rev. edn. Delhi, Publications Division, 1962.

On community development and Panchayati Raj. Delhi, Publications Division, 1963.

On socialism : Selected speeches and writings. New Delhi, Perspective Publications, 1964.

One's nations, one heart, selected speeches, 1957-63. Delhi, Publications Division, 1963.

Pakistan seeks to profit from Chinese aggression. Delhi, Publications Division, 1963.

Panchsheel. New Delhi, Lok Sabha Secretariat, 1958.

Planning and develoment. New Delhi, Publications Division, 1956.

Prime Minister on Goa. New Delhi, Ministry of External Affairs, 1962.

Question of language. Allahabad, AICC, 1937.

Recent essays and writing on the future of India, Communalism and other subjects. Allahabad, Kitabistan, 1934.

A rose never withers it lives in rememberance. New Delhi, External Publicity Division, 1966.

Selected works of Jawaharlal Nehru. New Delhi, Orient Longman, 1972.

Socialism by consent. Calcutta, Publicity Department, 1957.

Socialism of Jawaharlal Nehru. New Delhi, Abhinav, 1981.

Soviet Russia. Bombay, Chetna, 1929.

Sri Ramakrishna and Swami Vivekananda. (3rd ed.) Madras, Ramkrishna Math, 1960.

Statement given by Pt. Jawaharlal Nehru to a Court in Nabha, at the time of his trial in 1923: A leaf from our national diary. Chandigarh, Director of Public Relations, 1973.

Thought on women. Delhi, Nehru Memorial and Museum library 1975.

Unity of India : Collected writings 1937-1940. New York, John Day, 1942.

University of Delhi. Thirty sixth convocation addressed by Shri Jawaharlal Nehru. Delhi, 1958.

We accept China's challenge. Delhi, Publication Division, 1962.

Where we are? Allahabad, Kitabistan, 1939.

Window in prison and prison land. Allahabad, M.N. Pandey, 1953.

Wit and wisdom of Gandhi, Nehru, Tagore. New Delhi, New Books Society of India, 1968.

APPENDIX-VI

Books and Articles on Nehru

Akhileshwan Singh
Political leadership of Jawahar Lal Nehru. New Delhi, Deep & Deep, 1985. 299p.

Athar Husain, S.
Nehru's concept of nationalisation and productivity. *Indian Worker* 30 (39) 28 June 1982. p15-17.

Audichya, Janardan
Had Nehru any economic ideology. *Modern Review* 143 (4) April 1979. p238-40.

Balasubrahmanian, M.
Nehru : Study in secularism. New Delhi, Uppal, 1980. 120p.

Chakravarty, S.
Nehru's concept of planning. *Lok Rajya* 29(16) 16 December 1973. p18-20.

Chaudhuri, Ram Narayan, ed.
Nehru in his own words (his replies to various questions). Ahmedabad, Navajivan, 1964. xxii, 218p.

Crisis of the spirit; address. *Cultural Forum* 6(4) November 1964 p86-90.

Crocker, Walter
Nehru: A contemporaty estimate. London, George Allen and Unwin, 1966. 186p.

Damodaram, A.K.
Jawaharlal Nehru and world order. *Mainstream* 25(9) 15 November 1986. p13-17.

Das, A.M.
Nehru's vision of parliamentary democracy. *Journal of Parliamentary Information* 32(2) June 1986. p219-32.

Das, M.N.
Political Philosophy of Jawaharlal Nehru . London Allen & Unwin, 1961. 256p.

Dasgupta, R.K.
Nehru on socialism. *Mainstream* 15(39) 28 May 1977. p7-10+.

Dutt, R.C.
Socialism of Jawaharlal Nehru. New Delhi, Abhinav, 1981. xxiv, 248p.

Dwivedi, R.N.
Nehru on culture. *Cultural Forum* 6(4) November 1964. p125-59.

Ganesh Prasad
Nehru's approach to communalism. *Mainstream* 7(42) 21 June 1969 p13-15+.

Nehru and nationalism. *Mainstream* 9(39) 29 May 1971. p22-25.

Shaping of Nehru's world-view. *Mainstream* 20 (39) 29 May 1982. p17-21.

Gayan, Naba K.
Jawaharlal Nehru: Nationalisation and social change. *Secular Democracy* 13(6) June 1980 p23-28.

Ghose, Sankar
Nehru's approach to socialism. *Secular Democacy* 9(21-22) November 1976. p154-58.

Girija Shankar
Evolution of socialist ideas of Jawaharlal Nehru, 1932-64. *Quarterly Review of Historical Studies* 18(4) 1978-79. p218-29.

Gopal, S.
Mind of Jawaharlal Nehru. Madras, Sangam, 1980. 49p.

How Nehru saw the tribals. *Vanyajati* 12(3) July 1964 p122-25.

Jacob, Alice
Nehru and the judiciary. *Journal of the Indian Law Institute* 19(2) April-June 1977 p169-81.

Jag Mohan
Jawaharlal Nehru and his socialism. *Mainstream* 24 (38) 24 May 1986. p83-86.

Jain, K.P.
Nehru as an economist. *United Asia* 16(5) September-October 1964. p292-98.

Jawaharlal Nehru on community development. *Kurukshetra* 20(1) 1 October 1971 p33-35.

Jawaharlal Nehru on nation buildings. *Yojana* 24(14-15) 15 August 1980. p7-10.

Jayaswal, Sitaram, (comp.)
Nehru on society education and culture. Agra, Vinod Pustak Mandir, 1965. xciii, 149p.

Karunakaran, K.P.
Phenomenon of Nehru. New Delhi, Gitanjali, 1979. 219p.

Khanna, G.L
Nehru in brief. Patiyala, Chandan Lal Khanna, 1971. 136p.

Khanna, R.M., ed.
Nehru's message to youth. Delhi, Allied, 1944.

Kohli, Manorama
Nehru's world view and China policy. *China Report* 21(6) November-December 1985. p497-502.

Krasa, Miloslav
Nehru on India, Czechoslovakia and world event. *Indo Asian Culture* 18(2) April 1969. p3-23.

Krishna Iyer, V.R.
Nehru and constitution. *Mainstream* 15(13) 27 November 1976. p7-8+.

Krishna Menon, V.K.
Nehru and internationalism. *Mainstream* 15(11) 13 November 1976. p7-9.

Man Mohan Singh, H.K.
Jawaharlal Nehru and economic change. *Economic and Political Weekly* (Special Number) 10(33-35) August 1975. p1325-38.

Mathur, B.S.
Nehru on cooperation. *AICC Economic Review* 18(10) 1 December 1966 p26-28.

Misra, O.P.
Economic philosophy of Pandit Jawahar Lal Nehru. Allahabad, Chugh, 1978. 218p.

Mitrokhin, L. and Feelin, Nikolai, ed.
India's great Soviet people's about Nehru. Bombay, Allied, 1975. 103p.

Mohale, B.V.
Nehru and Gandhi on education : A comparative study. *Education Quarterly* 17(66) June 1965. p92-97.

Mohammad Ghouse

Nehru and securalism. *Journal of the Indian Law Institute* 20(1) January-March 1978 p103-16.

Momin, A.R.

Nehru as a humanist. *Lok Rajya* 28(14) 16 November 1972. p3-5

Mukerjee, Bimala Prasad

Nehru's sense of social history. *Perspective* 2(4) November 1978. p29-32.

Mullick, B.H,

Nehru on police. Dehradun, Palit and Dutt, 1970. 80p.

Nanda, B.R.

Nehru's : Motilal and Jawaharlal. London, Allen and Unwin, 1962. 357p.

Narasimhaiah, C.D.

Jawaharlal Nehru. Mysore, Rao and Raghavan, 1959. 60p.

Narasimhaiah, L.D.

Jawaharlal Nehru: A study of his writings and speeches. Mysore, Rao and Raghavan, 1960. 174p.

Narayana, K.R.

Nehru's non-alignments: Origin and early phase. *Mainstream* 18(46) 12 July 1980. p9-12+.

Nasenko, Yuri

Jawaharlal Nehru and India's foreign policy. New Delhi, Sterling, 1977. p351p.

Neeraj

Nehru and democracy in India. New Delhi, Metropolitan, 1971 xii, 290p.

Nehru and the working class. *Haryana Labour Journal* 6(2) April-June 1975 p5-11

Nehru on non-alignment. *Secular Democracy* 9(14-15) 31 July-15 August 1976. p55-57.

Nehru on public sector. *Yojana* (Annual Number) 25(1-2) 26 January 1981. p16-17.

Nehru on socialism. *Link* 10(14) October 1966. p170-75.

Nehru on the constitution. *Link* 7(24) 26 January 1965. p18-21.

Nehru's contribution to democracy, socialism and peace. *Journal of Parliamentary Information* 29(4) December 1983. p428-39.

Nehru's contribution to socialism. *Link* 6(43) 7 June 1964. p18-19.

Nurul Hasan, S

Nehru and non-alignment. *Mainstream* 18(12) 17 November 1979. p7.

Parthasarthi, G.

Nehru on democracy, socialism and peace. *Mainstream* 23(12) 1984. p9-10+.

Patel, Rajni

Nehru and socialism. *Swarajya* 23(4) 23 July 1978. p5-8.

Patil, V.S.

Jawaharlal Nehru's concept of socialism. *Journal of Karnataka University*, Vol. 13, 1977. p107-15.

Patil, V.T.

Nehru and democratic socialism. *Journal of Political Studies* 13(2) September 1980 p1-5.

Nehru and the meaning of freedom. *Journal of Karntaka University* (Hindi) Vol. 20 1976 p143-45.

Nehru's early socialism and the Indian national movement. *Modern Review* 140(5) November 1977 p 303-07.

Studies on Nehru. Delhi. Sterling, 1988. 412p.

Pillai, R.C.
Jawaharlal Nehru and his critics, 1923-47. New Delhi, Gitanjali, 1986. 279p.

Pradhan, Benudhar
Socialist thought of Jawaharlal Nehru. Gurgaon. The Academic Press, 1974. 342p.

Raghuveer Singh
Prolegomena to a conceptual treatment of Nehru's view of democracy. *Political Science Review* 11(2-3) April-September 1972 p166-77.

Rajan, M.S.
Jawaharlal Nehru and non-alignment. *Indian and Foreign Review* 18(8) 1 February 1981. p 10-12.

Rana, A.P.
Nehru and international political modernization : A view from the seventies. *India Quarterly* 35(1) January-March 1979. p67-82.

Rathore, L.S.
Political ideas of Jawaharlal Nehru : some reflection. *Indian Journal of Political Science* 46(4) October-December 1985. p451-73.

****
NEWLY KEYED IN PORTION
7*****************************

Roy, Ranjit
Nehru and democracy. Mainstream (Republic Day Number) 17(22-23) 1979. p55-57.

Saiyidain, K. G.
Nehru and integration. Mainstream 9(39) 29 May 1971. p19-20+.

Shah, A. D. ed.
Jawaharlal Nehru: A critical tribute. Bombay, P.C. Manaklala & Sons. 1965. 125p.

Sheean, Vincent
Nehru: The years of power. London, Victor Collancz, 1960.

Singh, Bishwanath
Nehru's philosophy of socialism. *AICC Economic Review* 16(24) 27 May 1965. p21-22+.

Singh, R. P.
Nehru on education: New Delhi, Sterling, 1966.

Singh, V. B.
Nehru on socialism. New Delhi, Publication Division, 1977. 139p.

Singh, B.K.
Nehru's concept of cooperation. *Kurukshetra* 14(3) December 1965. p15-17.

Some intimate glimpses and authentic voice of Nehru. *Organiser* 33(47) April 1982. p25-26.

Subrahmanyam, K.
Nehru's concept of Indian defence. *Institute of Defence Studies and Analysis Journal* 5(2) October 1972. p196-211.

Tariq Ali
Nehru and the Gandhi's Indian dynasty. London, Pan Books, 1985. 301p.

This beautiful world of ours. *Kurukshetra* 13(2) November 1964. p103-07.

Vidyarthi, L.P.
Nehru's approach to tribal culture. *Vanyajati* 14(4) October 1966. p170-75.

Viswanathaiah, K. V.

Jawaharlal Nehru's concept of democratic socialism. *Indian Journal of Political Science* 26(4) October-December 1965. p91-99.

What is culture? address. *Cultural Forum* 6(4) November 1964. p81-85.

What Nehru told Chau-en-Lai. Link 28(52) 3 August 1986. p11-16.

Index